BLACK TIE & Boots

TIMELESS TRADITIONS FROM THE NEW WEST

A Wyoming Cookbook

The UNIVERSITY OF WYOMING is the state's nationally recognized research university focused on students who seek personalized learning opportunities in a unique Rocky Mountain environment. UW is the perfect size: big enough for great opportunities and small enough for students to become involved and to make a difference. All proceeds from the sale of *Black Tie & Boots* will benefit University Libraries.

Wyoming is one of the nation's highest states, with an average elevation of 6,700 feet. Preparation of food at high altitude may require changes in time, temperature, or ingredients. The recipes in this cookbook, unless otherwise noted, are written for cooking at sea level—the convention for most cookbooks. If you live at elevations higher than 3,000 feet and you have tried a baked product recipe that does not turn out as expected, here are some helpful tips on how to alter the recipe:
• Reduce any of the ingredients that provide leavening, such as baking powder, baking soda, or yeast.
• Beat egg whites to the soft peak stage.
• Do not overbeat mixtures that contain eggs, such as cheesecakes.

For further information about high-altitude baking, you can order *Altitude Adjusters* (1998, B734) or *Baking at High Altitude* (2003, B427) from the College of Agriculture's Cooperative Extension Service. Visit their Web site at: www.uwyo.edu/uwces/pubs_orange_sub.asp or call (307) 766-2115.

BLACK TIE & Boots
Timeless Traditions from the New West

Introduction

Food is, of course, one of the essentials of life. But to spirited and hardy folk it can be a celebration of life itself. It seems that's the way it's always been in Wyoming, whether a robust chuck wagon meal after a day on a dusty cattle trail; a patriotic Fourth of July barbecue in any of this state's wonderful small towns; a happy post-game celebration after another great win at War Memorial Stadium; or a commencement dinner for proud family and friends.

Throughout Wyoming, food has also been a source of pride for the many ethnic groups that have made Wyoming home: Native Americans in Fremont County; Basques in Johnson County; Greeks, Italians, Slavs, and the descendents of Chinese miners and rail workers in Sweetwater County; and the sons and daughters of Scandinavia, Mexico, Central America, Africa, England, France, Ireland, Scotland, Germany, and so many other countries who live throughout the state, all who use food to honor their past and preserve their culture for the future.

This book is a tribute to the role of food in our grand state of Wyoming and a collection of some of the best darn recipes our residents and alumni from all over the country have to offer. From beef and lamb to fish and game, from appetizers to desserts, from vegetables to breads, we are so pleased and delighted to offer you 10 mouth-watering chapters bursting with some 300 truly delicious recipes, all tested for ease of preparation, exceptional taste, and eye-pleasing presentation. No matter what the occasion—black tie or boots—you will find the best of Wyoming within these pages.

We surely hope you will share these recipes with your family and friends, and then make *Black Tie & Boots, Timeless Traditions from the New West* a tasteful (pun intended!!) gift for holidays, birthdays, anniversaries, and all of the special events in your life. And enjoy!!!

With affection and warm regards,

Al and Ann Simpson

Commencement Dinner Celebration

There is nothing grander to celebrate on a university campus than student graduation. Each May, thousands of family members and friends gather on the UW campus to celebrate commencement. The President's Picnic provides a box lunch for everyone at noon while dinner may be a family affair at home.

The Menu

SPINACH CITRUS SALAD WITH
FRESH BERRIES AND KIWI*

MEDITERRANEAN GRILLED LEG OF LAMB*

PORTOBELLO TOWERS* WITH
MASHED POTATOES, PROSCIUTTO,
AND GRUYÈRE

FRESH GREEN BEANS IN HERB BUTTER*

DILL BREAD*

GRAND MARNIER CHOCOLATE TORTE

Pictured recipes on page 6

Contents

Wine and Hors d'Oeuvres before the Theatre

The UW Theatre and Dance students are some of the best in the nation. They dazzled Kennedy Center audiences at the prestigious 2004 American College Theatre Festival with the award-winning play Good Morning Athens: A Rock Musical, an original work by a UW senior.

The Menu

EGGPLANT "CAVIAR" WITH
CLOSE-TO-YOUR-VEST CRACKERS*

GOAT CHEESE WITH LEMON AND CAPERS*

SIX-SPICE FRIED SHRIMP*

THE ULTIMATE COSMOPOLITAN*

PORCUPINE SCALLOPS WITH
ORANGE MINT DIPPING SAUCE*

TURKEY MEATBALLS IN
ORANGE CRANBERRY SAUCE*

*pictured recipes

Appetizers & Beverages

WYOMING
BEEF WELLINGTONS

1/2 pound beef tenderloin, sliced
1 tablespoon butter
1/2 cup finely chopped onion
4 ounces mushrooms, chopped
1/4 pound chicken livers
2 tablespoons brandy
1/2 teaspoon brown sugar
1/4 teaspoon garlic powder
1/4 teaspoon ground nutmeg
1/8 teaspoon cayenne pepper
Salt and pepper to taste
Pastry for 2 (9-inch) pies

Sear the tenderloin quickly in the butter in a skillet until brown. Place in a food processor and pulse to coarsely chop. Sauté the onion and mushrooms in the skillet until almost tender. Add the chicken livers, brandy, brown sugar, garlic powder, nutmeg, cayenne pepper, salt, and pepper. Cook until the chicken livers are cooked through. Remove from the heat and let stand until cool. Add the chicken liver mixture to the tenderloin in the food processor and pulse to combine. Do not purée. Chill thoroughly.

Roll out the pastry on a lightly floured surface. Cut out circles with a 2-inch round cutter. You may prepare the pastries to this point and chill, covered, until ready to use. Preheat the oven to 375 degrees. Spoon 1/2 teaspoon of the beef mixture onto each pastry round. Moisten the edge of the pastry with water; fold over and crimp with a fork. Repeat with the remaining pastry rounds and beef mixture. Place on a baking sheet. Bake for 8 to 10 minutes.

STEAK DIJON ROLL-UPS

MAKES 16 APPETIZERS

1 (2-pound) sirloin steak, cut into 1/4-inch-thick slices
1/2 cup Dijon mustard
4 large dill pickles, quartered lengthwise
1 large onion, cut into 16 slices
3 tablespoons vegetable oil
1/2 teaspoon garlic powder
1/2 teaspoon paprika
1/4 teaspoon salt
1/4 teaspoon pepper
2 tablespoons cornstarch
5 cups water

Pound the sirloin slices with a meat mallet until thin. Spread 1 tablespoon Dijon mustard on each sirloin slice. Top with 2 pickle quarters and 2 onion slices. Roll up and secure with wooden picks. Repeat the procedure with the remaining sirloin slices, Dijon mustard, pickles, and onion slices. Heat the oil in a deep skillet over medium-high heat. Add the roll-ups and cook for 2 to 3 minutes on each side or until brown. Sprinkle with the garlic powder, paprika, salt, pepper and cornstarch. Cook the roll-ups for 10 to 12 minutes or until almost blackened. Add the water and simmer, covered, for 1 hour. Remove the roll-ups from the skillet and cut into 1/2-inch slices to serve.

APPETIZER MEATBALLS IN CABERNET SAUCE

MAKES 30 TO 45 MEATBALLS

1¹/2 pounds ground beef
2 eggs
1 onion, chopped
³/4 cup dry bread crumbs
1 teaspoon seasoned salt
¹/4 teaspoon rubbed sage
¹/4 teaspoon pepper
¹/2 cup milk
1¹/2 teaspoons Worcestershire sauce
Cabernet Sauce

Combine the ground beef, eggs, onion, bread crumbs, seasoned salt, sage, pepper, milk, and Worcestershire sauce in a bowl and mix well. Shape the mixture into 1¹/2-inch balls. Cook in a large nonstick skillet over medium heat for 20 minutes or until brown, turning occasionally. Combine the meatballs with the Cabernet Sauce in a slow cooker and heat on High for 2 hours.

NOTE: *This recipe also makes a great meatball sandwich.*

CABERNET SAUCE

1 (26-ounce) jar pasta sauce
¹/2 (750-ml) bottle cabernet (about 1¹/2 cups)
¹/4 cup vinegar
¹/4 cup hot red pepper sauce, or to taste
1 cup packed brown sugar
1 teaspoon garlic powder
¹/2 teaspoon cayenne pepper

Combine the pasta sauce, cabernet, vinegar, hot pepper sauce, brown sugar, garlic powder, and cayenne pepper in a slow cooker.

TEX-MEX AVOCADO EGG ROLLS

MAKES 24 APPETIZERS

1 (5-ounce) package Spanish rice mix
1 pound hot bulk pork sausage
1 (15-ounce) can black beans, drained
  and rinsed
1 cup chopped green onions
1 1/2 cups salsa
2 cups (8 ounces) shredded Monterey
  Jack cheese
1/2 cup chopped canned jalapeño chiles
24 egg roll wrappers
2 or 3 avocados, sliced
Vegetable oil for deep-frying

Prepare the rice mix using the package
directions and let cool. Brown the sausage
in a large skillet, stirring until crumbly; drain.
Remove from the heat and let stand until
cool. Stir in the rice, beans, green onions,
salsa, cheese, and jalapeño chiles. Spoon
about 1/3 cup of the sausage mixture onto the
center of each egg roll wrapper. Top with an
avocado slice. Fold 1 corner of the wrapper
over the filling and tuck in the edges. Dip
fingers in water and rub across the remaining
corner of the wrapper and press to seal.
Repeat until all the wrappers are filled. Heat
the oil to 375 degrees in a deep heavy
saucepan. Fry the egg rolls, a few at a time,
for 3 minutes or until golden brown, turning
if needed. Serve warm.

CHICKEN AND SPINACH DUMPLINGS WITH ROASTED TOMATO DIPPING SAUCE

MAKES 42 DUMPLINGS

1 (10-ounce) package frozen
    chopped spinach, thawed
5 to 6 garlic cloves, minced
1/2 onion, minced
10 to 15 mushrooms, minced
1 pound ground chicken
1 tablespoon ground cumin

1/2 teaspoon salt
1/4 teaspoon pepper
42 won ton wrappers
1/4 cup (about) vegetable oil
    (to coat the steamer)
Roasted Tomato Dipping
    Sauce

Squeeze the excess water from the spinach and finely chop. Combine the spinach, garlic, onion, mushrooms, chicken, cumin, salt, and pepper in a large bowl and mix well using your hands. Place a small spoonful of the chicken mixture on the center of a won ton wrapper, being careful not to overfill. Dip fingers in water and rub across the won ton wrapper edges. Gather the edges of the won ton wrapper around the filling and pinch together to seal. Brush a steamer with oil. Place the dumplings, a few at a time, in the steamer and steam for 7 to 8 minutes or until the dumplings separate from the steamer. Repeat for the remaining dumplings, brushing the steamer with oil each time. Serve with Roasted Tomato Dipping Sauce.

NOTE: *Dumplings may be reheated in the microwave. Sprinkle with a few drops of water and cover with plastic wrap.*

ROASTED TOMATO DIPPING SAUCE

MAKES 2 CUPS

5 tomatoes
2 to 3 chile peppers
1/2 onion, diced
2 to 3 fresh cilantro stems,
    chopped

2 garlic cloves, chopped
1/4 teaspoon chili powder
    (optional)
Salt and pepper to taste

Preheat the oven to 400 degrees. Arrange the tomatoes on a baking sheet lined with parchment paper. Roast for 25 minutes. Use immediately or refrigerate for up to 2 days. Roast the chiles on a baking sheet lined with foil in a preheated 500-degree oven, under a broiler, or on the grate of a grill for 15 to 30 minutes or until blackened and blistered, turning frequently. Seed and dice the roasted tomatoes and chiles. Combine the tomatoes, chiles, onion, cilantro, garlic, chili powder, salt, and pepper in a blender and purée.

HOT CHICKEN WINGS

Be sure to have lots of napkins and water on hand!

MAKES 18 TO 24 APPETIZERS

2 pounds chicken wings,
   tips removed
1/2 cup (1 stick) butter

1 to 2 (4 1/2-ounce) bottles red
   hot cayenne pepper sauce

Preheat the oven to 400 degrees. Arrange the wings on a rack in a shallow baking pan or in a broiler pan. Bake for 30 minutes. Turn the wings and bake for 30 minutes longer or until crispy. Melt the butter in a saucepan over low heat. Add the hot pepper sauce and heat. Dip the wings into the sauce to coat completely. Just before serving, place the wings in a broiler pan and broil for 30 seconds to crisp the coating.

THAI TURKEY NACHOS

MAKES 8 SERVINGS

1/2 pound cooked turkey,
   shredded
1 1/2 tablespoons lime juice
Salt and pepper to taste
2 tablespoons vegetable oil
2 red bell peppers, minced
2 garlic cloves, minced
1 teaspoon ground cumin
1 teaspoon crushed oregano
1 (15-ounce) can black beans,
   drained and rinsed

1 cup (4 ounces) shredded
   Monterey Jack cheese
1 cup (4 ounces) crumbled
   queso fresco
Tortilla chips
1 bunch green onions,
   chopped
1/2 cup sliced black olives
1/2 cup chopped cilantro
Sour cream and salsa

Preheat the oven to 450 degrees. Combine the turkey, lime juice, salt, and pepper in a bowl and mix well. Heat the oil in a large skillet over medium-high heat. Add the bell peppers, garlic, cumin, and oregano and sauté for 3 minutes or until tender. Add the beans and cook for 1 minute, stirring constantly. Combine the cheeses in a bowl. Arrange a layer of tortilla chips in a 9×13-inch baking dish. Layer the bell pepper mixture, turkey, cheese mixure, green onions, olives, and cilantro 1/2 at a time over the tortilla chips. Bake for 10 minutes or until the cheeses melt. Serve with sour cream and salsa.

NOTE: *Mexican cheeses are fabulous! "Queso fresco" is a Mexican-style cheese found in most supermarkets. It comes in a 12-ounce round that crumbles easily. If you cannot find it, just double the amount of Monterey Jack.*

ORANGE CRANBERRY SAUCE

MAKES ABOUT 4 CUPS

1 (16-ounce) can whole
    cranberry sauce
1 cup fresh or frozen
    cranberries
1 cup orange juice
2 tablespoons cider
    vinegar
1 teaspoon minced fresh
    ginger
$1/2$ teaspoon ground
    allspice

Combine the cranberry
sauce, cranberries, orange
juice, vinegar, ginger, and
allspice in a saucepan. Bring
to a boil. Reduce the heat
and simmer for 5 minutes.

TURKEY MEATBALLS IN ORANGE CRANBERRY SAUCE

MAKES 16 MEATBALLS

1 pound ground turkey
1 shallot, finely chopped
1 cup bread crumbs
1 egg, lightly beaten
1 teaspoon salt, or to taste
Orange-Cranberry Sauce
1 (15-ounce) can mandarin oranges, drained

Preheat the oven to 375 degrees. Combine the turkey, shallot, bread
crumbs, egg, and salt in a bowl and mix well. Shape into 16 meatballs.
Arrange the meatballs in a shallow baking pan and bake for 25 minutes.
Place the meatballs in a serving dish. Pour the Orange-Cranberry
Sauce over the meatballs. Garnish with the mandarin oranges.

GOLDEN MINIATURE CRAB CAKES WITH CURRIED RÉMOULADE SAUCE

MAKES 8 CRAB CAKES

1 pound crab meat
1 egg
1 teaspoon salt
1/2 cup diced green onions
2 tablespoons butter
2 tablespoons all-purpose
  flour
1/4 cup milk
1/2 teaspoon curry powder
1/4 teaspoon ground nutmeg
1/8 teaspoon cayenne pepper
Bread crumbs
1 tablespoon butter
Curried Rémoulade Sauce

Combine the crab meat, egg, and salt in a medium bowl and mix well. Sauté the green onions in 2 tablespoons butter in a skillet over medium heat until translucent. Stir in the flour and cook for 1 to 2 minutes or until bubbly, stirring constantly. Stir in the milk, curry powder, nutmeg, and cayenne pepper and heat through. Add to the crab mixture and mix lightly until combined. Shape into 8 cakes. Chill, covered, for 1 to 2 hours or until firm. Coat the crab cakes with the bread crumbs. Melt 1 tablespoon butter in a large skillet. Add the crab cakes and cook for 3 to 4 minutes on each side until golden brown. Serve with the Curried Rémoulade Sauce.

CURRIED RÉMOULADE SAUCE

MAKES ABOUT 2 CUPS

1 cup mayonnaise
1/2 cup sour cream
1 shallot, minced
2 tablespoons capers,
  rinsed
2 tablespoons lemon juice
1 teaspoon curry powder
1 teaspoon minced garlic
1 teaspoon salt

Combine the mayonnaise, sour cream, shallot, capers, lemon juice, curry powder, garlic, and salt in a small bowl and mix well. Chill until ready to serve.

GARLIC MUSSELS

Easy to make and delicious, these mussels are a favorite dish in the tapa bars of Madrid.

MAKES 12 MUSSELS

12 medium to large mussels, scrubbed
Extra-virgin olive oil (preferably Spanish)
3 garlic cloves, crushed
3 tablespoons chopped fresh parsley

The paper-thin skin from garlic cloves can easily be removed by blanching the individual cloves in boiling water for 30 seconds and then rinsing them immediately in cold water.

Open the mussels but leave them on the half shells. Cut the muscle anchoring the mussel to the shell. Preheat the broiler to 375 to 400 degrees. Place the mussels in a shallow baking pan and drizzle generously with olive oil. Top each mussel with a pinch of garlic. Sprinkle with the parsley. Broil for 5 minutes.

NOTE: *Mussels may be added to boiling water for a few minutes to make opening the shells easier, but be careful not to overcook. A flat wooden pick is an easy way to add the garlic.*

CURRIED COCONUT MUSSELS

MAKES 6 SERVINGS

2 tablespoons olive oil
1 onion, finely chopped
1 tablespoon curry powder
1 teaspoon turmeric
1 (14-ounce) can coconut milk
1/4 cup white wine
1 (2-pound) box cooked green-lipped mussels

Heat the olive oil in a skillet. Add the onion and cook until translucent, stirring frequently. Stir in the curry powder and turmeric. Add the coconut milk and mix well. Pour the wine into the coconut milk can. Pour into the skillet and mix well. Cook for 15 minutes, stirring occasionally. Preheat the oven to 350 degrees. Arrange the mussels in a shallow baking pan. Pour the sauce over the mussels. Bake for 20 to 30 minutes. Serve hot.

OYSTER-STUFFED MUSHROOMS

MAKES 16 APPETIZERS

1 (8-ounce) can oysters, drained
2 teaspoons lemon juice
16 mushroom caps
Lemon pepper
16 slices bacon (about 1 pound)

Sprinkle the oysters with the lemon juice. Sprinkle the mushroom caps with lemon pepper and stuff with the oysters. Partially cook the bacon in the microwave until hot but still limp. Wrap 1 bacon slice around each stuffed mushroom cap and secure with a wooden pick. Place the mushrooms on a grill pan and grill over medium coals until the bacon is crisp, turning frequently.

PORCUPINE SCALLOPS WITH ORANGE-MINT DIPPING SAUCE

MAKES 24 SCALLOPS

8 to 10 phyllo pastry sheets, thawed if frozen
1 cup all-purpose flour
1 tablespoon curry powder
1 teaspoon salt
2 eggs
24 sea scallops
Vegetable oil for frying
Orange-Mint Dipping Sauce

Cut the phyllo sheets into 2-inch-wide strips. Stack the strips and cut into very thin julienne strips. Toss in a bowl to separate; cover. Stir together the flour, curry powder, and salt in a small bowl. Whisk the eggs in a small bowl. Dry the scallops on paper towels. Dip the scallops into the flour mixture, then the eggs, and then the phyllo strips. Press the phyllo onto the scallops, covering completely. Place the scallops in a shallow baking pan until ready to fry. Preheat the oven to 350 degrees. Heat the oil (at least 3 inches deep) to 350 degrees in a large heavy saucepan. Fry the scallops, a few at a time, for 30 seconds or until golden brown. Remove to the baking pan. Bake for 5 to 10 minutes. Serve warm with Orange-Mint Dipping Sauce.

ORANGE-MINT DIPPING SAUCE

MAKES ABOUT 1 1/2 CUPS

1 cup orange marmalade
1/4 cup chopped fresh
  mint leaves
1 tablespoon lime juice
1 tablespoon cider
  vinegar
1 tablespoon red pepper
  flakes, or to taste

Combine the marmalade, mint, lime juice, vinegar, and red pepper flakes in a small bowl and mix well.

SIX-SPICE FRIED SHRIMP

MAKES 32 TO 48 SHRIMP

2 pounds large shrimp, peeled and deveined
2 teaspoons paprika
1 teaspoon chili powder
1 teaspoon garlic powder
1 teaspoon salt
1/2 teaspoon ground cumin
1/2 teaspoon white pepper
Extra-virgin olive oil for frying
Romaine lettuce leaves, torn into large pieces

Pat the shrimp dry on paper towels. Combine the paprika, chili powder, garlic powder, salt, cumin, and white pepper and mix well. Place the shrimp in a large paper or sealable plastic bag. Add the spice mixture and shake well to coat thoroughly. Heat the olive oil in a large skillet over medium-high heat. Add the shrimp in a single layer and cook for 3 minutes. Turn the shrimp and cook for 2 to 3 minutes longer. Remove to a serving platter. To serve, place a shrimp on a piece of lettuce and wrap the lettuce around the shrimp.

NOTE: *For a quick and easy version, use cooked shrimp and flash-fry in the heated olive oil.*

SHRIMP CEVICHE

MAKES ABOUT 2 CUPS

1 pound large shrimp, peeled and deveined
1/2 red bell pepper, finely chopped
1/2 red onion, finely chopped
1/4 cup finely chopped celery
1/4 cup coarsely chopped cilantro
1 jalapeño chile, seeded and finely chopped, or to taste
Juice of 2 limes
Salt and pepper to taste

Add the shrimp to a large pot of boiling water. Return to a boil and remove the shrimp immediately. The shrimp will have just begun to turn pink. Rinse with cold water; drain. Coarsely chop the shrimp. Combine the shrimp, bell pepper, onion, celery, cilantro, and jalapeño chile in a bowl and mix well. Stir in the lime juice and mix well. Season with salt and pepper. Chill, covered, for several hours. Serve with tortilla chips.

SARDINE DEVILED EGGS

MAKES 12 DEVILED EGGS

6 hard-cooked eggs
1 (4-ounce) can oil-packed sardines
2 tablespoons mayonnaise
Salt and pepper to taste
Parsley and anchovies (optional)

Cut the hard-cooked eggs in half lengthwise. Remove the yolks and press through a fine sieve into a large bowl. Mash the undrained sardines in a small bowl. Add the sardines and mayonnaise to the egg yolks and mix well. Season with salt and pepper. Place the egg yolk mixture in a pastry bag with a rose tip and pipe into the egg whites. Arrange the eggs on a serving platter and garnish with sprigs of parsley or anchovies if desired. Chill, covered, until ready to serve. Serve cold.

SALMON APPLE PATTIES

MAKES 24 PATTIES

2 eggs
1 (15-ounce) can salmon, drained and flaked,
   skin and bones removed
3/4 cup crushed saltines
1/2 cup diced apple
2 tablespoons chopped celery
2 tablespoons chopped onion
1/4 teaspoon pepper
1/4 teaspoon garlic powder
1/4 teaspoon parsley flakes
1 1/2 cups cornmeal
Vegetable oil for frying

Whisk the eggs in a bowl. Add the salmon, saltines, apple, celery, onion, pepper, garlic powder, and parsley and mix well. Shape into 24 patties. Place the cornmeal in a shallow dish. Coat the salmon patties with the cornmeal. Chill, covered, for 30 to 60 minutes or until firm. Heat the oil in a large heavy skillet over medium-low heat. Add the patties, a few at a time, and cook for 3 minutes per side, turning once.

A UW student from the Hadeland region of Norway, later to become a UW Distinguished Alumnus, arrived at the University of Wyoming in 1958, bringing this recipe for Norwegian gravlax with him. His professor altered the ingredients and process slightly over the years, but his many students of Scandinavian descent still enjoyed a "taste of home" when he served it.

DILLED MUSTARD SAUCE

MAKES ABOUT 2 1/2 CUPS

1/4 cup sugar
1/4 cup Dijon mustard
6 tablespoons red wine vinegar
1 1/2 cups vegetable oil
2 tablespoons chopped dill weed
1 teaspoon lemon juice
1/2 teaspoon salt

Combine the sugar, Dijon mustard, and vinegar in a food processor and process for 3 seconds to blend. Slowly add the oil, with the processor running, until blended. Stop the processor and stir in the dill weed, lemon juice, and salt. Pour into a serving bowl.

MAKES 192 APPETIZERS

1/2 cup plain, kosher, or pickling salt (not iodized)
1/2 cup sugar
1/4 cup white pepper
1/4 teaspoon saltpeter (sodium or potassium nitrate, for curing meat or fish)
2 (3- to 3 1/2-pound) salmon fillets, boned (farm-raised preferred)
1/4 cup brandy
2 cups fresh or frozen dill weed
Club crackers
Dilled Mustard Sauce

Combine the salt, sugar, white pepper, and saltpeter in a small bowl and mix well. Trim the tail ends of the salmon fillets so that they will fit into a large shallow dish. Place the fillets skin side down on a cutting board and brush with the brandy. Sprinkle the salt mixture evenly over the fillets to cover completely. Cover 1 fillet completely with the dill weed to about 1/8-inch thickness. Carefully place the second fillet on top of the dilled fillet. Place the fillets carefully in a 4-gallon plastic bag. Squeeze as much air as possible from the bag; seal with a twist tie. Place the plastic bag in the shallow dish and refrigerate. Carefully turn over the bag every 8 hours for 72 hours. After the first day, liquid will begin to form in the bag. The brining action draws the water out of the fish and cures it.

Remove the fish from the plastic bag. Brush off the dill and brining mixture and rinse thoroughly under cold running water. Place the fillets skin side down on paper towels. Dry the fillets with paper towels, pressing firmly. Wrap the fillets with waxed paper and seal with masking tape. Place in a clean shallow dish and refrigerate for 24 hours to firm the fish. To serve, place the fillets on a large cutting board. Cut each fillet in half lengthwise. Slice diagonally across, just to the skin, into 1/8-inch slices. Serve each salmon strip on a club cracker with a dollop of Dilled Mustard Sauce.

NOTE: *The cured fillets will keep up to a week refrigerated. To freeze, wrap tightly in plastic wrap, then foil. Seal with masking tape. Label and date. Gravlax can be frozen for up to 2 months without losing flavor or texture. Do not refreeze.*

CAVIAR QUESADILLAS

MAKES 20 TO 21 APPETIZERS

1 cup sour cream
1 teaspoon fresh lemon juice
2 teaspoons finely chopped
   red onion
1 (4-ounce) jar black lumpfish
   caviar

3 large flour tortillas
Additional sour cream
3 scallions, minced

Combine 1 cup sour cream, the lemon juice, and onion in a small bowl and mix well. Rinse the caviar gently with cold water in a fine mesh strainer; drain in the strainer. Spoon the caviar onto paper towels to further drain. Fold the caviar gently into the sour cream mixture, reserving about 1 teaspoon caviar for garnish. Cut each tortilla into 3-inch circles with a round cutter or small glass. Spoon a generous teaspoonful of the caviar mixture onto each tortilla round. Fold the tortilla rounds in half. Garnish each quesadilla with a small dollop of sour cream, a tiny amount of caviar, and a sprinkle of scallions.

BRUSCHETTA WITH FRESH HERBS AND FETA

MAKES 24 APPETIZERS

6 Roma tomatoes, finely
   chopped
4 garlic cloves, finely chopped
1/4 cup finely chopped green
   bell pepper
10 to 14 fresh basil leaves,
   finely chopped
1/4 cup (about) fresh oregano
   leaves, finely chopped
1/2 cup (about) fresh cilantro,
   finely chopped

1/4 cup (1 ounce) shredded
   mozzarella cheese
1/4 cup crumbled feta cheese
2 tablespoons habanero
   pepper sauce, or to taste
Salt and pepper to taste
1 (8-ounce) loaf French bread
   baguette
2 tablespoons olive oil

Combine the tomatoes, garlic, bell pepper, basil, oregano, cilantro, mozzarella and feta cheeses, habanero sauce, salt, and pepper in a large bowl and mix well. Chill, covered, for 1 hour for flavors to blend. Preheat the oven to 425 degrees. Cut the baguette into 1/2-inch slices. Brush both sides of each slice lightly with the olive oil and place on an ungreased baking sheet. Bake for 5 minutes or until crisp and light brown, turning once. Top each baguette slice with the tomato mixture and serve.

COCKTAIL CORN CAKES

MAKES 24 CAKES

3 tablespoons cornmeal
1/2 cup all-purpose flour
1/4 teaspoon baking powder
1/4 teaspoon salt
1 egg
1/4 cup milk

1 tablespoon melted butter
2/3 cup corn
2 green onions, sliced
1/4 teaspoon cayenne pepper,
    or to taste
Sour cream

Combine the cornmeal, flour, baking powder, and salt in a large bowl. Whisk the egg in a small bowl. Whisk in the milk and butter. Stir into the flour mixture. Add the corn, green onions, and cayenne pepper and mix well. The batter can be made to this point and chilled, covered, for up to 1 day. Heat a lightly oiled griddle or skillet. Test 1 teaspoon of the batter and add additional flour if cake is too thin or additional milk if the batter is too thick. Spoon 1 tablespoon of the batter onto the griddle for each cake. Cook for 1 to 2 minutes per side or until golden. Top each corn cake with a dollop of sour cream. Serve warm or at room temperature.

CURRIED EDAMAME AND MACADAMIA NUTS

MAKES 4 SERVINGS

Edamame, which is a young green-shelled soybean, has become extremely popular in the United States. It usually can be found in the fresh or frozen vegetable section of most supermarkets.

1 teaspoon sugar
1 teaspoon salt
1/2 teaspoon curry powder, or
    to taste
1/8 teaspoon turmeric

1/2 pound macadamia nuts
1/2 pound fresh edamame,
    shelled, or frozen
    edamame, thawed

Preheat the oven to 350 degrees. Combine the sugar, salt, curry powder, and turmeric in a large bowl and mix well. Arrange the macadamia nuts on a baking sheet. Toast for 8 to 10 minutes or until the oil rises to the surface and the nuts are shiny. Add the nuts to the curry mixture and toss to coat well. Cool completely. Pat the edamame dry with paper towels and place in a bowl. Sift the nuts from the seasonings, reserving the seasonings. Add the nuts to the edamame. Sprinkle with the reserved seasonings if more spiciness is desired.

JAPANESE EGGPLANT CRISPS WITH TOMATO RELISH

MAKES 24 APPETIZERS

2 eggs
1 cup all-purpose flour
1 teaspoon salt
2 cups panko (Japanese bread crumbs)
1 Japanese eggplant, cut into 24 slices
Vegetable oil for frying
1 cup shredded Parmesan cheese
Sun-dried tomatoes and chopped chives
Tomato Relish

Whisk the eggs in a small bowl. Stir together the flour and salt in a bowl. Place the panko in a shallow dish. Dip the eggplant slices, 1 at a time, in the seasoned flour, then in the eggs, and then in the panko, pressing the panko firmly onto the eggplant to coat completely. Place on a baking sheet. Heat oil to 350 degrees in a heavy saucepan. Fry the eggplant slices, a few at a time, in the hot oil until golden brown. Drain on paper towels. Preheat the broiler. Arrange the fried eggplant slices on a baking sheet. Top each with a small amount of the Parmesan cheese. Broil until the cheese melts. Garnish with sun-dried tomatoes and chives. Serve warm with Tomato Relish.

TOMATO RELISH

MAKES ABOUT 1 3/4 CUPS

1 cup cherry tomatoes, sliced
1/2 cup sun-dried tomatoes, chopped
1 tablespoon cider vinegar
1 tablespoon minced dried onion
1 teaspoon chopped garlic
1 teaspoon salt

Combine the cherry tomatoes, sun-dried tomatoes, vinegar, minced onion, garlic, and salt in a small saucepan and heat through.

Many cultures around the globe have invented distinct types of bread crumbs for cooking. Panko is the preferred type in Japan. Panko bread crumbs have a coarser texture than most others, making for a much lighter and crunchier casserole topping and coating for deep-fried foods. Panko is especially good for breading seafood. Look for panko in the Asian foods section of most supermarkets or specialty groceries.

NUT-CRUSTED BRIE BITES
WITH MELBA SAUCE

MAKES 16 APPETIZERS

1/2 cup finely chopped
    walnuts
1/2 cup finely chopped pecans
1/2 cup finely chopped
    almonds
1/4 cup sesame seeds

3 eggs
8 ounces Brie cheese, cut into
    1-inch pieces and chilled
Vegetable oil for frying
Prepared melba sauce

Combine the walnuts, pecans, almonds, and sesame seeds in a large bowl. Whisk the eggs in a bowl. Dip the cheese pieces, a few at a time, in the eggs, coating well. Coat with the nut mixture. Heat the oil (about 2 inches deep) to 350 degrees in a heavy saucepan. Fry the coated cheese pieces, a few at a time, until golden brown. Do not overcook or the cheese will melt out. Drain on paper towels. Serve warm with prepared melba sauce, pears, and French baguette slices.

BLUE CHEESE AND WALNUT
SHORTBREAD

MAKES 36 APPETIZERS

1 cup crumbled blue cheese
6 tablespoons butter, softened
1 cup all-purpose flour
1/2 cup cornstarch
1/2 teaspoon pepper
1/2 teaspoon salt

2/3 cup chopped walnuts
6 ounces cream cheese,
    softened
1 cup walnut halves
1/2 cup apricot preserves

Combine the blue cheese and butter in a mixing bowl and beat until smooth and creamy. Stir together the flour, cornstarch, pepper, and salt. Add to the blue cheese mixture and mix well. Add the chopped walnuts and mix well. Shape the dough into a ball and wrap in plastic wrap. Chill in the refrigerator for 1 hour. Preheat the oven to 325 degrees. Roll the dough to 1/2-inch thickness on a floured surface. Cut into 1-inch circles or squares. Place on a parchment-lined baking sheet. Bake for 25 minutes and let cool. To serve, place a dollop of the cream cheese on each shortbread and top with a walnut half and a small amount of apricot preserves.

CLOSE-TO-YOUR-VEST CRACKERS

Quick & Easy

This recipe is so delicious but so easy that it should be kept "close to your vest."

MAKES 6 SERVINGS

1/4 pound saltines
1/4 cup (1/2 stick) butter, melted

Favorite seasoning (such as Cajun or Mrs. Dash)

Preheat the oven to 300 degrees. Dip both sides of each cracker in the butter. Sprinkle with seasoning. Place on a foil-lined baking sheet. Bake for 8 minutes. Remove to a wire rack to cool completely.

RUSTIC COUNTRY PÂTÉ

MAKES 1 LARGE LOAF OR 2 SMALL LOAVES

2 pounds pork shoulder roast
1 1/2 pounds veal or beef roast
1 tablespoon salt
1 teaspoon ground cinnamon
1/2 teaspoon ground allspice

1/2 teaspoon ground cloves
1/2 teaspoon pepper
1/4 teaspoon ground nutmeg
Fresh thyme (optional)

Place the roasts in a large pan and add water to cover. Bring to a boil. Reduce the heat and simmer, covered, for 2 to 3 hours or until the meat falls off the bone. Remove the roasts from the pan, reserving the liquid and discarding the bones. Cut or shred the meat into small pieces. Line a 5×9-inch loaf pan or 2 smaller loaf pans with cheesecloth, extending the cloth several inches over all sides of the pan. Place about 1/3 of the meat in the pan. Spoon 2 to 3 tablespoons of the reserved liquid over the meat. Press the meat with a wooden spoon. Combine the next 6 ingredients in a bowl and mix well.

Sprinkle 1/3 of the spice mixture over the meat. Repeat the layers, adding reserved liquid before pressing firmly after each layer. Fold the cheesecloth over the loaf and tie. Cover with foil and place a heavy weight, such as a large juice can or bottle, on the top. Chill in the refrigerator for 8 to 10 hours. Remove the loaf from the pan and discard the cheesecloth. Trim the edges of the pâté if desired. Slice the pâté. Cut each slice into quarters. Cut each quarter in half diagonally to make triangles. Garnish with sprigs of fresh thyme if desired. Serve with cornichons, French baguette slices, and grainy mustard.

HOT CRAB MEAT DIP

Quick & Easy

MAKES 2 CUPS

8 ounces cream cheese,
  softened
3 tablespoons mayonnaise
1 teaspoon Dijon mustard
1/4 teaspoon salt

2 tablespoons dry white wine
1 (7-ounce) can crab meat,
  drained and flaked
Salt and pepper to taste

Combine the cream cheese, mayonnaise, Dijon mustard, and salt in the top of a double boiler over simmering water. Heat until smooth and blended, stirring constantly. Stir in the wine. Add the crab meat and mix well. Adjust the seasonings to taste. Pour into a serving dish. Serve with melba rounds or toast triangles.

HORSESHOE OYSTER LOG

Quick & Easy

MAKES 10 TO 12 SERVINGS

2 (4-ounce) cans smoked
  oysters
16 ounces cream cheese,
  softened
1 garlic clove, crushed
1 tablespoon finely chopped
  green onions
1 tablespoon mayonnaise

1 tablespoon milk
2 teaspoons Worcestershire
  sauce
Dash of hot red pepper sauce
1/4 teaspoon white pepper
1/2 cup chopped parsley
Chopped pimentos (optional)

Mash the oysters in a bowl. Combine the cream cheese, garlic, green onions, mayonnaise, milk, Worcestershire sauce, hot pepper sauce, and white pepper in a mixing bowl and mix well. Spread half the cream cheese mixture into a rectangle on a foil-lined baking sheet or tray. Spread the oysters along the center of the rectangle. Top with the remaining cream cheese mixture, spreading to cover the oysters. Chill, covered with plastic wrap, for 2 to 8 hours or until firm. Remove the cream cheese rectangle from the foil with a long spatula, rolling as for a jelly roll into a log. Roll the log in the parsley and pimentos. Arrange on a serving platter and shape into a horseshoe. Serve with crackers.

BLACK MAGIC CAVIAR MOLDS

MAKES 8 TO 10 SERVINGS

4 hard-cooked eggs, grated
2 tablespoons chopped parsley
2 tablespoons chopped red onion
1 cup sour cream
1 tablespoon prepared horseradish
2 teaspoons grated lemon zest
2 teaspoons chopped fresh chives
2 large tomatoes, seeded and diced
1 (2-ounce) jar black caviar

Combine the eggs, parsley, and onion in a small bowl. Combine the sour cream, horseradish, lemon zest, and chives in a mixing bowl and beat until stiff. Line eight to ten 5-ounce plastic cups or other small molds with plastic wrap, extending the plastic over the edges. Spoon about 1/4 cup of the sour cream mixture into each cup. Place the tomatoes on top. Top with the egg mixture and press down. Cover the cups with the plastic wrap. Chill for 1 to 2 hours. Remove the molds from the cups and invert onto a serving plate. Remove the plastic wrap. Top each mold with the caviar.

NOTE: *For an even more elegant hors d'oeuvre, smoked salmon may be substituted for the tomatoes.*

SMOKED SALMON AND CRAB PÂTÉ

MAKES 2 CUPS

6 ounces smoked salmon
6 ounces crab meat or cocktail
    shrimp
6 ounces cream cheese,
    softened
1/3 cup chopped chives or
    green onion tops

1 1/2 tablespoons capers,
    drained and chopped
1 1/2 tablespoons grated
    lemon zest
Toasted rye bread
Additional lemon zest,
    capers, and smoked salmon

Finely chop the salmon and crab meat in a food processor. Add the cream cheese and process until combined. Spoon into a bowl and add the chives, capers, and lemon zest. Chill, covered, in the refrigerator. Spread the pâté on toasted rye bread. Garnish each serving with lemon zest, capers, and smoked salmon.

SMOKED TROUT LOG

MAKES 10 TO 12 SERVINGS

16 ounces cream cheese,
    softened
1 garlic clove, crushed
1 tablespoon minced onion
1 tablespoon minced chives
1 teaspoon minced jalapeño
    chile
1 tablespoon mayonnaise
1 tablespoon milk
1/4 teaspoon salt

2 teaspoons Worcestershire
    sauce
1/8 teaspoon white pepper
Dash of Tabasco sauce
1 cup flaked smoked trout
1/2 cup finely chopped
    pistachio nuts, pecans,
    or walnuts
Parsley and pimento
    (optional)

Combine the cream cheese, garlic, onion, chives, jalapeño chile, mayonnaise, milk, salt, Worcestershire sauce, white pepper, and Tabasco sauce in a food processor and process until well mixed. Spoon the cream cheese mixture onto a foil-lined baking sheet and shape into an 8×10-inch rectangle. Spread the trout evenly over the rectangle. Cover loosely with plastic wrap. Chill for several hours or overnight until firm. Remove the cream cheese rectangle from the foil with a long narrow spatula and roll as for a jelly roll. Shape into a log. Roll in the nuts, covering completely. Serve immediately or chill, tightly wrapped in plastic wrap, for up to 3 days. Arrange the log on a serving platter. Garnish with parsley and pimento if desired. Serve with crackers.

GOAT CHEESE WITH LEMON AND CAPERS

*This appetizer is deceptively easy to prepare
but very tasty and pretty.*

MAKES 6 TO 8 SERVINGS

1 (4-ounce) log goat cheese
Grated zest of 1 lemon
Minced fresh garlic
Capers
Fresh rosemary (minced leaves and whole sprigs)
Extra-virgin olive oil (organic preferred)
1 lemon, thinly sliced

Place the goat cheese on a small serving platter. Sprinkle with the lemon zest, garlic, capers, and minced rosemary. Drizzle with the olive oil. Garnish with the lemon slices and rosemary sprigs. Serve with water crackers or thin slices of sourdough baguette.

CHEDDAR AND OLIVE
CHEESE BALL

*Flavor will be enhanced if the cheese balls are made
two to three days before serving.*

MAKES 2 LARGE OR 3 SMALL CHEESE BALLS

8 ounces cream cheese,
  softened
16 ounces (4 cups) shredded
  sharp Cheddar cheese, at
  room temperature
1/2 cup chopped pimento-
  stuffed green olives
1 tablespoon parsley flakes

1 tablespoon grated onion
1 tablespoon Worcestershire
  sauce
1 teaspoon lemon juice
1/2 teaspoon minced garlic
1/2 teaspoon Tabasco sauce
1 to 2 cups chopped walnuts

Beat the cream cheese in a large mixing bowl until smooth. Add
the Cheddar cheese, olives, parsley, onion, Worcestershire sauce, lemon
juice, garlic, and Tabasco sauce and mix well. Divide the mixture into
2 or 3 portions and shape each portion into a ball. Spread the walnuts
on a large sheet of waxed paper. Roll the cheese balls in the walnuts,
coating completely. Wrap tightly in plastic wrap, then in foil. Chill for
several hours or overnight until firm. Serve with crackers.

NOTE: *Cheese balls may be frozen for up to 1 year. Allow to thaw for several
hours before serving.*

GREEN OLIVE PECAN SPREAD

Quick & Easy

MAKES 2 CUPS

8 ounces cream cheese,
  softened
1 cup chopped green olives

1/2 cup mayonnaise
1/2 cup chopped pecans
White pepper to taste

Combine the cream cheese, olives, mayonnaise, pecans, and white
pepper in a blender and process until blended. Spoon into a serving
dish. Chill, covered, until ready to serve. Serve with baked pita chips
or bagel crisps.

TROPICAL MANGO CHUTNEY SPREAD

MAKES 2 CUPS

8 ounces cream cheese, softened
1 (8- to 9-ounce) jar mango chutney, such as Major Grey's
1/2 cup salted peanuts
2 bunches green onions (white part only), thinly sliced
1 teaspoon crushed coconut powder

Spread the cream cheese into a 1/2-inch-thick round on a small serving plate. Pour the chutney onto the cheese round, spreading to cover the top completely. Top with the peanuts and green onions. Sprinkle with the coconut powder. Serve with crackers.

COWBOY KICKIN' CHICKEN DIP

Quick & Easy

This dip has just the right amount of spice and always gets rave reviews at parties!

MAKES 4 TO 5 CUPS

16 ounces regular or low-fat cream cheese
1 (10-ounce) can white chicken, drained
2 (10-ounce) cans cream of chicken soup
1 (4-ounce) can diced jalapeño chiles

Combine the cream cheese, chicken, soup, and undrained jalapeño chiles in a slow cooker. Heat on Low until warm, stirring occasionally. You may combine the ingredients in a microwave-safe bowl and microwave on Low until heated through, if desired. Serve warm with corn chips or ruffled potato chips.

BREAD BOWL FONDUE

MAKES 4 TO 6 SERVINGS

1 round loaf Italian bread
1 tablespoon butter, melted
1 cup sour cream
1 cup (4 ounces) shredded
   Gruyère cheese

4 ounces cream cheese,
   softened
2 tablespoons grated onion
1 teaspoon Worcestershire
   sauce

Preheat the oven to 350 degrees. Slice off the top crust of the bread loaf and set aside. Cut through the center of the bread to 1/2 inch from the edge, continuing around the edge of the loaf. Pull the bread from the center of the loaf with a fork. Cut into 1-inch cubes. Place the bread cubes on an oiled baking sheet and drizzle with the butter. Bake for 10 to 15 minutes or until golden brown. Combine the sour cream, Gruyère cheese, cream cheese, onion, and Worcestershire sauce in a mixing bowl and mix well. Spoon the cheese mixture into the bread bowl and cover with the top crust. Place the bread bowl in a pie plate. Bake, covered with foil, for about 1 hour or until hot and bubbly. Serve with the toasted bread cubes and assorted fresh vegetables.

HOT ARTICHOKE DIP WITH CRUMBLED BACON

MAKES 2 CUPS

2 (14-ounce) cans artichoke
   hearts (not marinated),
   drained and coarsely
   chopped
1/2 cup mayonnaise
1 to 2 teaspoons crushed
   tarragon
1 to 3 garlic cloves, crushed

1/2 to 1 cup shredded asiago
   cheese
1 small onion, chopped
Pepper to taste
Olive oil
4 slices bacon, crisp-cooked
   and crumbled

Preheat the oven to 350 degrees. Combine the artichokes, mayonnaise, tarragon, garlic, cheese, onion, and pepper in a large bowl and mix well. Spoon the mixture into a small baking dish coated with olive oil. Sprinkle with the bacon. Bake for 30 minutes or until golden brown. This may be baked ahead of time and reheated in the microwave just before serving. Serve warm with slices of sourdough baguette, lavash, or rye crisp bread.

Eggplant "Caviar"

Makes 2 to 3 cups

1 large eggplant
1 large onion, chopped
1 large green bell pepper, chopped
1 large garlic clove, crushed
1/2 cup olive oil
2 large tomatoes, peeled and chopped
2 tablespoons white wine
Salt and pepper to taste

Preheat the oven to 400 degrees. Place the eggplant on a baking sheet and bake for 20 minutes. Let cool slightly. Peel and chop the eggplant. Sauté the onion, bell pepper, and garlic in the olive oil in a large skillet. Add the eggplant, tomatoes, wine, salt, and pepper. Simmer for 30 minutes to 1 hour or until thickened, stirring occasionally. Chill, covered, in the refrigerator. Serve with toast or crackers.

SPICY BLACK OLIVE SALSA

2 tomatoes, chopped
1 (6-ounce) can pitted black olives, drained and chopped
1 (4-ounce) can diced jalapeño chiles
3 green onions, chopped
1 1/2 tablespoons olive oil
1 1/2 teaspoons garlic salt
1 1/2 teaspoons red wine vinegar
Dash of hot red pepper sauce

Combine the tomatoes, olives, undrained jalapeño chiles, green onions, olive oil, garlic salt, vinegar, and hot pepper sauce in a large bowl and mix well. Chill, covered, for 1 hour. Serve with corn chips or crackers.

BLENDER SALSA

Quick & Easy

MAKES 3 CUPS

1 small onion, quartered
1 (14-ounce) can Italian stewed tomatoes
1 (14-ounce) can diced tomatoes with green chiles
3 tablespoons chopped jalapeño chiles, or to taste
2 tablespoons cider vinegar
1 teaspoon oregano
Dash of ground cumin
Dash of garlic salt
Salt and pepper to taste
2 to 3 teaspoons sugar

Place the onion, stewed tomatoes, tomatoes with green chiles, jalapeño chiles, vinegar, oregano, cumin, garlic salt, salt, pepper, and sugar in a blender and process to the desired consistency. Chill, covered, for 1 to 8 hours.

FRESH GARDEN SALSA

MAKES 4 CUPS

3 cups chopped tomatoes
8 ounces green chiles, chopped or diced
2 bunches green onions, chopped
2 garlic cloves, crushed
1/4 cup white vinegar
1/4 cup vegetable oil
1/2 teaspoon salt
1/2 teaspoon pepper
1/4 cup coarsely chopped cilantro
1/3 to 1/2 cup medium picante sauce

Combine the tomatoes, green chiles, green onions, garlic, vinegar, oil, salt, and pepper in a large bowl and mix well. Stir in the cilantro and picante sauce. Chill, covered, for 1 hour or longer to allow the flavors to blend. Serve with chips or use on tacos. The salsa may be stored in the refrigerator for up to 8 days.

———◆◆◆———

TANGY GERMAN SALSA

MAKES 10 SERVINGS

1 (15-ounce) can diced tomatoes
1 (8-ounce) can tomato sauce
1/2 to 2/3 cup canned sauerkraut
1/3 pound baby carrots
1/4 small onion
1 to 2 jalapeño chiles, or to taste
1/2 teaspoon minced garlic, or to taste
1 teaspoon salt, or to taste

Combine the tomatoes, tomato sauce, undrained sauerkraut, carrots, onion, jalapeño chiles, garlic, and salt in a blender or food processor and process to the desired consistency. Serve immediately or chill, covered, for up to 1 week. Serve with tortilla chips, fresh vegetables, or as a condiment with eggs or meats.

ROASTED RED PEPPER AND SUN-DRIED TOMATO DIP

*This dip also makes an excellent spread for meat,
cheese, and veggie sandwiches.*

MAKES 1 CUP

2 large garlic cloves
1/2 cup diced roasted red
   bell peppers
1/2 cup sun-dried tomatoes
   in oil

1/2 teaspoon red wine vinegar
1/4 teaspoon cayenne pepper
1/2 cup mayonnaise
2 to 4 ounces mascarpone or
   cream cheese, softened

Mince the garlic in a food processor. Add the bell peppers, sun-dried tomatoes, vinegar, and cayenne pepper and process to blend. Add the mayonnaise and mascarpone cheese and pulse to blend until smooth. Spoon into a bowl. Chill, covered, for 8 to 10 hours. Serve with assorted fresh vegetables.

HOLIDAY CRANBERRY CHUTNEY

MAKES 4 CUPS

2 cups fresh cranberries
2 cups sugar
1 cup water
2 medium apples, chopped
1 1/2 tablespoons grated
   orange zest

1 1/2 cups chopped celery
1 1/4 cups orange juice
1 cup golden or dark seedless
   raisins
1 cup chopped walnuts
1 teaspoon ground ginger

Combine the cranberries, sugar, and water in a large saucepan over medium heat. Bring to a boil, stirring frequently. Reduce the heat to low and simmer for 15 minutes. Remove from the heat. Stir in the apples, orange zest, celery, orange juice, raisins, walnuts, and ginger. Pour into a jar or bowl. Cover and refrigerate until chilled. Serve with crackers or as a topping with baked Brie. The chutney may be stored in the refrigerator for 2 weeks or frozen.

SAN ANTONIO GUACAMOLE

MAKES 1 1/2 TO 2 CUPS

2 large avocados, chopped
Juice of 1 large lime
Juice of 1/2 orange
1 tablespoon finely chopped onion
1/8 teaspoon sea salt, or to taste
1/4 cup chunky salsa
2 tablespoons coarsely chopped cilantro

Coarsely mash the avocados with a fork in a small bowl. Add the lime juice, orange juice, onion, salt, and salsa and mix well. Stir in the cilantro. Chill, covered, until ready to serve. Serve with tortilla chips.

IRISH CREAM LIQUEUR

MAKES 4 CUPS

1 1/3 cups liquor (such as rum, brandy, or whiskey)
1 (14-ounce) can sweetened condensed milk
1 cup heavy cream
4 eggs
2 tablespoons chocolate syrup
2 teaspoons instant coffee granules
1 teaspoon vanilla extract
1/2 teaspoon almond extract

Combine the liquor, condensed milk, heavy cream, eggs, chocolate syrup, coffee granules, and flavorings in a blender and blend on low until well mixed. Chill, covered, in the refrigerator. Serve over ice if desired. May be stored, tightly covered, in the refrigerator for up to 3 weeks.

NOTE: *If you are concerned about using raw eggs, use eggs pasteurized in their shells, which are sold at some specialty food stores, or use an equivalent amount of pasteurized egg substitute.*

Gallery walks have become a popular way to spend an evening in many communities throughout the country. Laramie is no exception. On the first Friday of every month, residents of this small High Plains town can visit numerous art galleries in the historic downtown, enjoying refreshments provided by the gallery owners while browsing the latest collections of sculpture, paintings, and other fine art.

JAMAICAN BUCKAROO

MAKES 1 SERVING

Crushed ice
Fresh mint leaves
1 1/2 ounces rum (Jamaican preferred)
Ruby red grapefruit juice
Mint leaf

Fill a tall glass half full with ice. Crush 1 or 2 mint leaves and add to the glass. Add the rum. Fill with grapefruit juice and stir. Garnish with a mint leaf if desired. Enjoy!

———◆◆◆———

THE ULTIMATE COSMOPOLITAN

MAKES 8 SERVINGS

16 ounces (2 cups) vodka
8 ounces (1 cup) orange-flavored liqueur (Cointreau preferred)
8 ounces (1 cup) cranberry juice
4 ounces (1/2 cup) fresh lime juice, strained
Maraschino cherries

Combine the vodka, orange liqueur, cranberry juice, and lime juice in a plastic pitcher and mix well. Freeze, covered, for 2 hours or until ice-cold. Pour into chilled martini glasses and garnish each with a cherry.

NOTE: *The drink mixture will keep indefinitely in the freezer without freezing solid.*

BEST-EVER BLOODY MARY
FOR ONE

MAKES 1 SERVING

3 tablespoons vodka
3/4 cup vegetable juice
   cocktail
2 tablespoons beef bouillon
1 1/4 teaspoons Worcestershire
   sauce
1 1/2 teaspoons lemon juice
1 teaspoon Pickapeppa Sauce

1/2 teaspoon coarsely ground
   horseradish
Dash of hot red pepper sauce
Celery salt to taste
Ice
Lemon pepper
Lime wedge
Celery stick (optional)

Combine the vodka, vegetable juice cocktail, bouillon, Worcestershire sauce, lemon juice, Pickapeppa Sauce, horseradish, hot pepper sauce, and celery salt in a tall glass and stir well. Fill with ice. Sprinkle with lemon pepper. Garnish with lime. Serve with a celery stick stirrer, if desired.

BEST-EVER BLOODY MARY
FOR A CROWD

MAKES 20 SERVINGS

3 3/4 cups vodka
7 1/2 cups vegetable juice
   cocktail
1/4 cup plus 1 tablespoon
   Worcestershire sauce
2 1/2 cups beef bouillon
1/2 cup plus 2 tablespoons
   lemon juice
1/2 cup Pickapeppa Sauce
1 teaspoon hot red pepper
   sauce, or to taste

3 tablespoons plus 1 teaspoon
   coarsely ground
   horseradish
1 to 2 teaspoons celery salt,
   or to taste
Ice
Lemon pepper
Lime wedges
Celery sticks (optional)

Combine the vodka, vegetable juice cocktail, Worcestershire sauce, bouillon, lemon juice, Pickapeppa Sauce, hot pepper sauce, horseradish, and celery salt in a gallon container and mix well. Fill tall glasses with ice and add the Bloody Mary mixture. Sprinkle with lemon pepper. Garnish with lime. Serve with celery stick stirrers, if desired.

GLÖGG

This is a popular Norwegian holiday drink.
It can be served at room temperature but is best if heated—
a wonderful sipping drink for those cold Wyoming winter evenings.

MAKES 32 SERVINGS

1 pound golden raisins
1²/₃ cups sugar
60 cardamom pods, broken
8 cinnamon sticks
12 whole cloves
2 (750-ml) bottles brandy
4 (750-ml) bottles port (domestic preferred)
1/2 cup plus 1 tablespoon sugar
2 teaspoons almond extract

Place the raisins, 1²/₃ cups sugar, cardamom, cinnamon sticks, and cloves on a large piece of cheesecloth. Bring the corners of the cheesecloth together to form a bag and tie or sew the bag securely. Place the spice bag in a large kettle and add just enough water to cover the bag. Bring to a boil. Reduce the heat and simmer, covered, for 1 hour.

Remove the spice bag from the kettle and discard. Combine the brandy and port in the kettle. Cover and bring to a boil. Place 1/2 cup plus 1 tablespoon sugar in a small nonstick skillet and cook until the sugar melts and turns dark brown, stirring constantly with a wooden spoon. Add the burnt sugar to the kettle and mix well. Remove from the heat. Ignite the glögg carefully with a lighted match and allow to burn for 6 to 8 seconds; cover with the pan lid until the flame subsides. Stir in the extract. Let stand until cool. Pour into bottles or jars and store in the refrigerator. Serve warm or at room temperature.

EASY MARGARITAS

1 (12-ounce) can frozen lemonade concentrate,
  partially thawed
1 (12-ounce) can frozen limeade concentrate,
  partially thawed
Water
Juice of 3 large lemons
Juice of 3 large limes
24 ounces (3 cups) tequila
4 ounces (1/2 cup) Triple Sec or other
  orange-flavored liqueur
Cracked ice

Combine the lemonade and limeade concentrates in a 1-gallon plastic pitcher or other large container. Add 4 or 5 concentrate cans of cold water, the lemon and lime juices, 2 concentrate cans of tequila, and 2/3 concentrate can of Triple Sec and mix well. Serve over cracked ice in salted margarita glasses.

NOTE: *For frozen margaritas, place equal amounts of the margarita mixture and cracked ice in a blender and blend until smooth.*

SOUR APPLE MARTINIS

MAKES 8 SERVINGS

16 ounces (2 cups) vodka
8 ounces (1 cup) Sour Apple Pucker
8 ounces (1 cup) Triple Sec
4 ounces (1/2 cup) fresh lemon juice, strained
Thin slices Granny Smith apple

Combine the vodka, Sour Apple Pucker, Triple Sec, and lemon juice in a plastic pitcher or other large freezer-proof container and mix well. Freeze, covered, for 2 hours or until ice-cold. Pour into chilled martini glasses. Garnish each with an apple slice.

NOTE: *The drink mixture will keep indefinitely in the freezer without freezing solid.*

TOM AND JERRY'S BATTER

*A traditional Christmas drink, children can drink this
with extra batter and no liquor.*

MAKES 6 CUPS BATTER, 16 DRINKS

12 egg whites, at room temperature
1 cup superfine sugar
1/2 teaspoon vanilla extract
12 egg yolks
1 cup superfine sugar
1 pint (2 cups) rum (Jamaican preferred)
1 pint (2 cups) brandy
Hot water
Grated nutmeg

Beat the egg whites in a large mixing bowl until very stiff. Stir in
1 cup sugar and the vanilla. Beat the egg yolks in a mixing bowl until
thoroughly blended. Beat in 1 cup sugar until smooth. Fold in the egg
white mixture. Pour 1 ounce (2 tablespoons) each rum and brandy
into a large mug. Add a large spoonful of the batter. Fill the mug with
hot water and stir gently. Sprinkle with nutmeg. Drink 2 slowly and
go to bed!

NOTE: *If you are concerned about using raw eggs, use eggs pasteurized in their
shells, which are sold at some specialty food stores, or use equivalent amounts of
pasteurized egg substitute and meringue powder.*

ORANGE CANTALOUPE JUICE

MAKES 2 TO 4 SERVINGS

1/2 ripe cantaloupe, seeded
2 to 3 oranges, peeled and quartered

Cut the rind from the cantaloupe. Cut the cantaloupe into
1-inch strips. Process the cantaloupe and oranges in a juicer until
liquefied. Pour into a pitcher and chill until ready to serve. You may
make this with other fruit combinations, such as pineapple, pear,
grapefruit, and orange; carrot and orange; watermelon and pineapple;
pineapple, nectarine, and orange; or apple, grapefruit, and orange.

COWBOY COFFEE

MAKES 16 (8-OUNCE) CUPS

1 gallon very cold fresh water
1½ cups regular-grind coffee

Pour 12 to 14 cups of the water into a clean gallon-size campfire coffeepot. Bring the water to a rolling boil. Reduce the heat to low. Add the coffee slowly, watching closely to be sure it doesn't boil over (the coffee will foam up as it starts to boil). Boil the coffee gently for no more than 1 minute. Remove from the heat. Add 1½ to 2 cups water to the coffeepot to help the grounds settle. Pour through a strainer or directly into mugs.

CRANBERRY MINT TEA

MAKES 2 SERVINGS

1¾ cups cranberry juice
¼ cup water
1 mint tea bag
Fresh mint leaves (optional)

Pour the juice and water into a small saucepan. Add the tea bag and heat until just below boiling. Pour into a teapot and steep for 1 minute. Pour into cups and garnish with mint leaves, if desired. May also be served over ice.

Guests on cowboy adventure rides always remark on how great the campfire coffee is. This method of "Cowboy Coffee" originated with a guide who led pack trips into the Teton Wilderness area during the 1970s. The secret, she says, "is using very cold, fresh, good-tasting water; nearly any brand of coffee will do. And, you *do not* keep adding coffee and water to your leftover grounds, like the old cowboy tales tell you; always start with a clean pot and fresh water!" She adds, "Don't put eggshells in there like they did in the old cowboy stories, or you'll end up with eggshells in your cup!"

Vedauwoo Picnic after the Vertical Dance

The majestic rock formations of Vedauwoo, just east of Laramie, form the backdrop for the annual Vertical Dance at Vedauwoo. Every summer UW dance students perform for picnickers at this magical spot.

The Menu

GAZPACHO ANDALUZ*

CURRIED EDAMAME AND MACADAMIA NUTS*

RUSTIC COUNTRY PÂTÉ WITH BAGUETTE SLICES AND CORNICHON GARNISH*

GRILLED ROMAINE WITH APPLES, BLUE CHEESE, AND BACON*

SPINACH AND MUSHROOM CHEESECAKE WITH SALSA*

FRUIT PIZZA*

HAWAIIAN BARS*

pictured recipes

Breads & Brunches

BASQUE BREAD

This delicious bread is great with soup or beans.

MAKES 1 ROUND LOAF

2 tablespoons butter
2 tablespoons sugar
$^1/_2$ teaspoon salt
$^3/_4$ cup boiling water

$^1/_2$ envelope dry yeast
   ($1^1/_2$ teaspoons)
$2^1/_2$ cups (about) all-purpose
   flour

Stir the butter, sugar, and salt into the boiling water in a large bowl. Cool until lukewarm. Add the yeast and stir until dissolved. Let stand for 15 minutes. Add the flour gradually, mixing to form a stiff dough. Knead on a lightly floured surface for 10 minutes or until the dough is smooth and elastic. Shape into a ball and place in a lightly greased bowl, turning to coat the surface. Cover and let rise in a warm place until doubled in bulk. Punch down the dough. Place the dough in a greased 8- or 9-inch round baking dish and cover with the greased lid. Let rise in a warm place until the dough touches the lid. Preheat the oven to 375 degrees. Bake, covered, for 12 minutes. Reduce the oven temperature to 325 degrees and bake, uncovered, for 30 to 35 minutes or until the bread tests done.

DILL BREAD

This round loaf is moist and dense with a pleasing aroma and texture.

MAKES 1 ROUND LOAF

1 envelope dry yeast
$^1/_4$ cup warm water
1 cup creamed cottage cheese,
   at room temperature
2 tablespoons sugar
1 tablespoon melted butter or
   vegetable oil

$3^1/_2$ tablespoons dill weed
1 teaspoon salt
$^1/_4$ teaspoon baking soda
1 egg, beaten
$2^1/_4$ to $2^1/_2$ cups (about)
   all-purpose flour

Dissolve the yeast in the warm water. Combine with the next 7 ingredients in a large bowl and mix well. Add the flour gradually, mixing to form a stiff dough. Knead on a lightly floured surface until the dough is no longer sticky, adding 1 to 3 tablespoons flour if needed. Shape into a ball and place in a greased bowl, turning to coat the surface. Cover and let rise in a warm place for 1 hour or until doubled in bulk. Punch down the dough. Place the dough in a greased 8- or 9-inch round baking dish and let rise until doubled in bulk. Preheat the oven to 350 degrees. Bake for 40 to 50 minutes or until the bread tests done.

MULTIGRAIN FRENCH BREAD

MAKES 2 LOAVES

1 envelope dry yeast
2 teaspoons honey
2 cups warm water (110 to 115 degrees)
5 cups (about) unbleached flour
1 cup whole wheat flour
1/2 cup wheat germ
2 teaspoons salt

Dissolve the yeast and honey in the warm water in a large mixing bowl and let stand for 5 minutes. Stir together 3 cups of the unbleached flour, the whole wheat flour, wheat germ, and salt. Stir into the yeast mixture and mix well. Turn the dough onto a lightly floured surface. Knead for about 5 minutes, adding more flour as needed until the dough is smooth and elastic and no longer sticky. Shape into a ball and place in a greased heat-resistant bowl, turning to coat the surface. Cover and let rise on the back burner of the stove with the oven set to 350 degrees or in other warm place for 45 to 60 minutes or until doubled in bulk.

Turn the dough onto a lightly floured surface and punch down. Divide into 2 portions and shape into loaves. Cut 4 shallow slits diagonally across the top of each loaf with a sharp bread knife. Place the loaves in 2 greased 4×8-inch loaf pans. Cover and let rise in a warm place for about 30 minutes. Preheat the oven to 400 degrees. Bake for 10 minutes. Reduce the oven temperature to 350 degrees and bake for 30 to 35 minutes longer or until the loaves sound hollow when lightly tapped.

AWESOME OATMEAL
RAISIN BREAD

MAKES 2 LOAVES

2 cups rolled oats
1 1/2 cups boiling water
1/2 cup milk, scalded
1/2 cup molasses
3 tablespoons sugar
1 tablespoon butter
1/2 teaspoon salt

1 envelope dry yeast
1/2 cup lukewarm water
1 egg, beaten
1 to 2 cups raisins
5 cups (about) all-purpose
   flour
Butter, melted

Place the oats in a large mixing bowl and add the boiling water
and scalded milk. Stir in the molasses, sugar, 1 tablespoon butter, and
salt and mix well. Let stand until lukewarm. Dissolve the yeast in the
lukewarm water. Add the yeast, egg, and raisins to the oat mixture
and mix well. Beat in the flour gradually until no longer sticky. Turn
the dough onto a lightly floured surface and knead until smooth and
elastic. Shape into a ball and place in a greased bowl, turning to coat
the surface. Cover and let rise in a 100-degree oven or other warm
place for about 1 hour or until doubled in bulk. Punch down the
dough and let rise again in the warm oven for about 45 minutes or
until not quite doubled in bulk. Preheat the oven to 350 degrees.
Divide the dough into 2 portions and shape into loaves. Place in
2 well-greased 5×9-inch loaf pans. Brush the tops of the loaves with
melted butter. Bake for 40 to 45 minutes or until the loaves test done.

SOURDOUGH CORN BREAD

MAKES 8 TO 9 SERVINGS

2 eggs
1 cup Sourdough Starter
1 1/2 cups yellow cornmeal
1 (12-ounce) can evaporated milk (1 1/2 cups)
2 tablespoons sugar
1/4 cup (1/2 stick) butter, melted
3/4 teaspoon baking soda
1/2 teaspoon salt

Preheat the oven to 450 degrees. Beat the eggs in a large bowl. Stir in the Sourdough Starter, cornmeal, evaporated milk, and sugar and mix well. Stir in the butter, baking soda, and salt. Spoon into a greased 9×9-inch baking pan. Bake for 25 to 30 minutes.

SOURDOUGH YEAST BREAD

MAKES 2 LOAVES

1 teaspoon dry yeast (optional)
1 cup warm water (optional)
2 egg yolks
1 cup Sourdough Starter
1/4 cup vegetable oil
2 tablespoons sugar or honey
2 teaspoons salt
1/2 teaspoon baking soda
5 to 5 1/2 cups all-purpose flour

For faster-rising bread, dissolve the yeast in the warm water and let stand for 5 minutes. Beat the egg yolks in a large mixing bowl. Stir in the yeast mixture, Sourdough Starter, oil, sugar, salt, baking soda, and 3 cups of the flour and mix well. Add the remaining flour gradually, beating until the dough forms a ball. Place in a greased bowl, turning to coat the surface. Cover and let rise in a warm place for about 1 hour or until doubled in bulk. Turn onto a lightly floured surface and knead until smooth and elastic. Divide into 2 portions and shape into loaves. Place in 2 greased 5×9-inch loaf pans; let rise again until doubled in bulk. Preheat the oven to 400 degrees. Bake for 10 minutes. Reduce the oven temperature to 350 degrees and bake for 40 minutes longer or until the loaves test done.

Sourdough was an important staple for many Wyoming families, such as one UW graduate from the class of 1928. She married in 1930 and spent the first few summers of her married life on horseback, riding the trails in the Wind River Range north of Pinedale with her husband, who worked for the U.S. Forest Service. They carried all their necessities, which included the sourdough jug, on pack horses, cooking and baking their meals in Dutch ovens in the coals of the campfire.

SOURDOUGH STARTER

1 cup all-purpose flour
2 cups warm water
1/2 envelope dry yeast (1 1/2 teaspoons)

Combine the flour, water, and yeast in a bowl and mix well. Let stand in a warm place, uncovered, for 2 days. Store the Starter, covered, in the refrigerator between uses. Remove it from the refrigerator several hours in advance of using to allow it to come to room temperature. Replenish the Starter by adding flour and water to restore it to its original consistency. Let stand for 24 hours or longer before returning it to the refrigerator.

CHRISTMAS GUMDROP BREAD

Quick & Easy

MAKES 5 MINIATURE LOAVES

3 eggs
1 cup baking mix
1/2 cup sugar
1 1/2 teaspoons vanilla extract
1 (10-ounce) jar maraschino cherries, drained
1 cup dried apricots, chopped
1 cup pitted dates, chopped
1 cup small gumdrops
1 cup chopped walnuts or other nuts

Preheat the oven to 300 degrees. Beat the eggs in a large bowl. Add the baking mix, sugar, and vanilla and mix well. Stir in the cherries, apricots, dates, gumdrops, and walnuts and mix well. Divide the batter among 5 greased miniature loaf pans. Bake for 1 hour and 20 minutes or until a wooden pick inserted in the center comes out clean. Cool in the pans for 5 minutes. Remove to wire racks to cool completely. Batter may also be used to make muffins.

NOTE: *For high altitudes, add 1 tablespoon all-purpose flour.*

COWBOY JOE'S HOOFPRINTS

Quick & Easy

This is a fun bread to serve at tailgates or informal gatherings.

MAKES 12

1 (12-count) package refrigerator breadsticks
2 tablespoons melted butter
Poppy seeds and/or black sesame seeds
Additional melted butter

Preheat the oven to 375 degrees. Unroll the breadsticks and separate on a parchment-lined baking sheet. Shape into "horseshoes." Brush with 2 tablespoons butter. Sprinkle with poppy seeds. Bake for 10 to 11 minutes or until golden brown. Brush with additional butter before serving.

DILL BREAD RING

Quick & Easy

Although it may take all day to rise, this bread is truly "quick and easy" to make, and beautifully rounds out almost any meal.

MAKES 10 SERVINGS

1/4 cup olive oil
1 tablespoon dill weed
1 (36-count) package frozen dinner rolls
1/4 cup olive oil
1 tablespoon dill weed
1/2 teaspoon garlic powder

Coat a bundt pan with butter-flavored nonstick cooking spray. Pour 1/4 cup olive oil into the pan. Sprinkle 1 tablespoon dill weed evenly over the olive oil. Roll each frozen dough ball in the oil mixture. Arrange the dough balls in 2 layers in the pan. Pour 1/4 cup olive oil over the rolls. Sprinkle with 1 tablespoon dill weed and the garlic powder. Cover and let rise for 8 to 10 hours. Preheat the oven to 350 degrees. Bake for 15 to 20 minutes. Cool in the pan for 5 minutes. Invert onto a serving platter. Place a bowl of olive oil in the center of the ring for dipping the rolls.

NOTE: *The flavor of this bread may be varied by using other seasonings, both savory and sweet. Instead of dill, try chopped sun-dried tomatoes, garlic, chopped onions, or poppy seeds. For a sweet bread, use melted butter instead of the olive oil, and a cinnamon-sugar mixture.*

"GRAY" BISCUITS

Excellent biscuits with great flavor, texture, and appearance

MAKES 9 SERVINGS

2 cups all-purpose flour
1 tablespoon baking powder
1/2 teaspoon salt
4 rounded tablespoons butter-flavored shortening
1 cup milk
Butter

Preheat the oven to 500 degrees. Sift the flour, baking powder, and salt into a large bowl. Cut the shortening into the flour mixture with a pastry blender until crumbly. Stir in the milk until combined. Turn the dough onto a lightly floured surface and pat out to 1 1/2-inch thickness. Cut with a round biscuit cutter and place in a greased 8×8-inch baking dish. Dot with the butter. Bake for 15 minutes or until golden brown.

Prepared by a cook for a logging camp in the 1930s, these "absolute best biscuits" were an instant favorite. Sixty-five years later, an undergraduate student majoring in animal science brought this family recipe with her to UW, where the biscuits were regularly requested at many student get-togethers. If your biscuits don't look "gray" like the original ones did, it's probably because you washed your hands before making them, which was not always the custom in logging camps.

HERBED BUTTERMILK BISCUITS

Quick & Easy

MAKES 6 TO 8 SERVINGS

6 tablespoons butter
3 tablespoons grated Parmesan cheese
1 tablespoon minced onion
1 tablespoon chopped fresh parsley
1 1/2 teaspoons dillseed
1 (10-count) can refrigerator buttermilk biscuits

Preheat the oven to 400 degrees. Melt the butter in a 9-inch round baking pan in the oven. Stir the Parmesan cheese, onion, parsley, and dillseed into the butter. Unroll the biscuits and cut each in half. Roll each into a ball. Roll the balls in the herb butter, coating completely and arranging in the pan. Bake for 12 to 15 minutes or until golden brown.

ZUCCHINI MUFFINS

MAKES 18 MUFFINS

4 cups all-purpose flour
2 cups sugar
1¹/₂ teaspoons baking powder
1¹/₂ teaspoons baking soda
1 teaspoon cinnamon
1 teaspoon ground nutmeg
1 teaspoon salt
3 eggs

1 cup vegetable oil
2 teaspoons vanilla extract
2 cups shredded zucchini
1 cup chopped dates
1 cup chopped walnuts
1 (8-ounce) can crushed
   pineapple, drained

Preheat the oven to 400 degrees. Combine the flour, sugar, baking powder, baking soda, cinnamon, nutmeg, and salt in a bowl. Whisk the eggs, oil, and vanilla in a large bowl until blended. Stir in the zucchini, dates, walnuts, and pineapple and mix well. Add the flour mixture, stirring just until combined. Do not overmix. Spoon 1/4 cup batter into each of 18 greased muffin cups. Bake for 20 minutes. Remove to a wire rack to cool.

NOTE: *For high altitudes, add ¹/₂ cup flour.*

RUM-RAISIN CINNAMON ROLLS

*These cinnamon rolls were written up in USA Today
many years ago as the "Best Buns in Town—Cinnamon that is!"
by a reporter who was in Meeteetse, Wyoming, doing a
story on the black-footed ferret.*

MAKES 16 ROLLS

2 envelopes dry yeast
1/2 cup warm water
1 (12-ounce) can evaporated
  milk
1/2 cup warm water
1/2 cup granulated sugar
2 teaspoons salt
1/2 cup (1 stick) butter, melted
5 cups (about) all-purpose
  flour

1/2 cup (1 stick) butter, melted
2 cups packed brown sugar
2 tablespoons maple syrup
1 tablespoon ground
  cinnamon
1/2 teaspoon cream of tartar
1 cup raisins
1/4 cup rum or amaretto
1 cup chopped pecans

Dissolve the yeast in 1/2 cup warm water in a large mixing bowl and let stand for 5 minutes or until bubbly. Add the evaporated milk, 1/2 cup water, granulated sugar, salt, and 1/2 cup melted butter and mix well. Stir in the flour, a few cups at a time, beating well until no longer sticky. Turn the dough onto a lightly floured surface and knead for 3 to 5 minutes or until smooth and elastic. Shape into a ball and place in a greased bowl, turning to coat the surface. Cover and let rise in an oven that has been preheated to the lowest setting, then turned off, for 1 hour or until doubled in bulk.

Combine 1/2 cup melted butter, the brown sugar, maple syrup, cinnamon, and cream of tartar in a bowl and mix well. Combine the raisins and rum in a microwave-safe glass measure and microwave on High for 2 minutes; stir. Punch down the dough and roll out on a lightly floured surface to an 8×13-inch rectangle. Spread the brown sugar mixture over the dough. Sprinkle evenly with the raisins and pecans. Roll up, starting from the long side. Seal the seam by pinching the dough. Cut into 2-inch slices by placing a piece of heavy thread under the roll, bringing it around the roll, then crossing the thread at the top and pulling quickly in opposite directions. Place the rolls in a greased 9×13-inch baking pan. Let rise in a warm place for 30 minutes.

Preheat the oven to 350 degrees. Pour a small amount of warm water slowly over the rolls, about halfway up to the top of the pan. The water keeps the rolls and filling soft and will evaporate during baking. Line the lower oven rack with foil in case the water bubbles over. Bake for 25 to 30 minutes or until the rolls test done. Invert the rolls onto a foil-lined baking sheet.

BUTTER-ALMOND COFFEE CAKE

Quick & Easy

MAKES 15 SERVINGS

1 cup sour cream
1 cup granulated sugar
2 eggs
1¼ cups all-purpose flour
2 teaspoons baking powder

½ cup (1 stick) butter
1 cup confectioners' sugar,
  sifted
¼ cup slivered almonds

Preheat the oven to 400 degrees. Combine the sour cream, granulated sugar, eggs, flour, and baking powder in a large bowl and mix well. Spread into a greased 9×13-inch baking pan. Bake on the top oven rack for 10 minutes. Melt the butter in a saucepan and remove from the heat. Add the confectioners' sugar all at once and mix well. Remove the coffee cake from the oven and immediately spread with the butter mixture. Sprinkle with the almonds. Bake for 15 minutes longer on the top oven rack. Cool for 5 minutes before slicing.

WELSH CURRANT CAKES

This is a traditional Welsh recipe, best eaten warm with lashings of butter.

MAKES 20 SERVINGS

½ cup (1 stick) cold butter,
  cut into pieces
1¾ cups all-purpose flour
½ cup superfine sugar
¼ teaspoon baking powder
¼ teaspoon ground
  cinnamon

⅛ teaspoon ground allspice
⅛ teaspoon ground nutmeg
Pinch of salt
⅓ cup dried currants
1 egg
⅓ cup milk

Cut the butter into the flour in a large bowl with your fingers or a pastry blender until crumbly. Add the sugar, baking powder, cinnamon, allspice, nutmeg, salt, and currants and mix well. Whisk the egg and milk together in a bowl until blended and add to the flour mixture. Mix until the dough forms a ball. Turn onto a lightly floured surface and roll out to ¼-inch thickness. Cut into 2-inch rounds. Cook on a lightly greased hot griddle for 3 minutes per side or until golden brown.

MULE CREEK JUNCTION PANCAKES

This make-ahead batter is ready in the refrigerator for light, fluffy pancakes any day. . .Yum!

MAKES 30 (4-INCH) PANCAKES

These pancakes, served to guests on Wyoming cowboy adventure rides, are the heartiest you'll ever eat. The recipe was handed down from the proprietor of a little café that was once open at Mule Creek Junction, part of the Cheyenne to Deadwood Stage Route on the Wyoming-South Dakota border.

2 tablespoons baking soda
2 tablespoons sugar
1 teaspoon salt
1 quart buttermilk
4 cups all-purpose flour
2 tablespoons baking powder
1 envelope dry yeast
1 cup vegetable oil
1 cup half-and-half
2 tablespoons light corn syrup
3 eggs, beaten

Combine the baking soda, sugar, and salt in a large bowl and mix well. Stir in the buttermilk until well blended. Sift the flour and baking powder into the buttermilk mixture and mix well. Add the yeast, oil, half-and-half, corn syrup, and eggs in the order listed and mix well. Chill, covered, overnight in the refrigerator. Ladle 1/4 to 1/3 cup batter for each pancake into a hot buttered skillet and cook until golden brown on both sides.

NOTE: *The batter will keep in the refrigerator for up to 2 weeks.*

PUMPKIN CHOCOLATE CHIP PANCAKES

Pumpkin and chocolate are a marriage made in heaven for children and adults alike!

MAKES 15 (5- TO 6-INCH) PANCAKES

2 cups all-purpose flour
2 tablespoons sugar
4 teaspoons baking powder
1 teaspoon salt
1 teaspoon ground cinnamon
4 egg yolks
1 1/2 cups 2% milk

1 cup canned pumpkin
1/4 cup (1/2 stick) butter, melted
4 egg whites, at room temperature
1/2 to 3/4 cup semisweet chocolate chips

Sift together the flour, sugar, baking powder, salt, and cinnamon in a large bowl. Whisk the egg yolks in a medium bowl. Whisk in the milk, pumpkin, and melted butter until blended. Add the pumpkin mixture to the dry ingredients, stirring just until blended. Beat the egg whites in a small mixing bowl until stiff. Fold into the pumpkin batter. Stir in the chocolate chips. Ladle the batter onto a hot buttered griddle and cook until golden brown on both sides.

HOT PEPPER JELLY TURNOVERS

MAKES 24 TO 36 TURNOVERS

1/2 cup (1 stick) butter or
   margarine
1 (5-ounce) jar Old English
   cheese spread

1 cup all-purpose flour
2 tablespoons water
Dash of cayenne pepper
1 (4-ounce) jar hot pepper jelly

Place the butter, cheese spread, flour, water, and cayenne pepper in a food processor and process until combined. Shape the dough into a ball. Chill, wrapped in plastic wrap, for 8 to 10 hours. Preheat the oven to 375 degrees. Roll out the dough on a lightly floured surface until very thin. Cut into rounds with a 2-inch biscuit cutter. Place 1/4 teaspoon jelly in the center of each round and fold over. Crimp the edge with a fork to seal. Repeat filling, folding, and crimping the rounds until all the dough is used. Place on a baking sheet and bake for 10 to 20 minutes.

NOTE: *Hot pepper jelly is important for a savory turnover. For a sweet variation, fill with marmalade and sprinkle with confectioners' sugar.*

APPLE, HAM, AND EGG BRUNCH BAKE

This recipe won a trophy from the Apple Commission at the Grant County Fair, Washington State, in 1978.

MAKES 8 TO 10 SERVINGS

2 cups baking mix
1/2 cup cold water
1/2 pound cooked ham, diced
2 apples, peeled and sliced
1 cup (4 ounces) shredded
   Cheddar cheese
3 eggs

1/4 cup milk
2 tablespoons sugar
1/4 teaspoon ground allspice
1/4 teaspoon ground nutmeg
Pinch of salt
Pinch of pepper
Additional nutmeg

Preheat the oven to 350 degrees. Combine the baking mix and water in a bowl, stirring to form a soft dough. Beat vigorously for 20 strokes. Press the dough onto the bottom and 1/2 inch up the sides of a lightly greased 9×13-inch baking pan. Top evenly with the ham, then the apple slices, then the cheese. Whisk the eggs in a bowl until frothy. Whisk in the milk, sugar, allspice, nutmeg, salt, and pepper. Pour the egg mixture evenly over the cheese. Sprinkle lightly with nutmeg. Bake for 30 to 35 minutes or until golden brown. Cut into squares.

BAKED EGGS BENEDICT

MAKES 4 SERVINGS

3 tablespoons butter
1 onion, chopped
3 tablespoons all-purpose
   flour
2 cups milk
4 English muffins, halved and
   toasted
8 thin slices cooked ham, cut
   to fit the English muffins

1/2 cup sliced mushrooms
5 hard-cooked eggs, sliced
11/2 cups (6 ounces) shredded
   sharp Cheddar cheese
Chopped parsley or parsley
   flakes
Paprika

Melt the butter in a large skillet. Add the onion and sauté over
medium heat until translucent. Stir in the flour and cook for 2 to
3 minutes or until bubbly, stirring constantly. Add the milk gradually
and cook until thickened, stirring frequently. Preheat the oven to
300 degrees. Arrange 2 muffin halves in each of 4 small shallow
baking dishes and top each with a ham slice. Reserve 8 mushroom
slices for garnish. Arrange the remaining mushrooms equally over
the ham-topped muffins. Reserve 8 center egg slices for garnish. Top
each muffin with an equal amount of the remaining egg slices. Spoon
the sauce over the muffins. Sprinkle with the cheese. Bake for about
30 minutes or until bubbly. Garnish with the reserved egg and
mushroom slices, parsley, and paprika.

To prepare the Eggs
Benedict ahead,
prepare the sauce and
cook the eggs the day
before serving. Chill,
covered, overnight in
the refrigerator. Reheat
the sauce and bring the
ingredients to room
temperature before
assembling.

MEXICAN EGGS

Quick & Easy

MAKES 4 GENEROUS SERVINGS

2 tablespoons vegetable oil
2 pounds bulk pork sausage
1 onion, chopped
1 (40-ounce) package frozen
   shredded hash brown
   potatoes, thawed

8 eggs
Salt and pepper to taste
1/2 cup sour cream
1/2 cup salsa

Heat the oil in a large skillet. Add the sausage and onion and cook
until the sausage is brown and the onion is translucent, stirring to break
up the sausage. Add the potatoes and mix well. Cook until the potatoes
are tender and brown, turning frequently. Make 8 indentations in the
sausage mixture with a large spoon. Break 1 egg into each indentation.
Season with salt and pepper. Cook, covered, over medium-low heat for
20 minutes or until the eggs are done. Top with sour cream and salsa.

MAPLE PECAN TOPPING

MAKES ABOUT
2 1/2 CUPS

1 cup packed brown
  sugar
1/2 cup (1 stick) butter or
  margarine, softened
2 tablespoons maple
  syrup
1 cup chopped pecans

Combine the brown sugar,
butter, syrup, and pecans in
a bowl and mix well.

SAUSAGE EGG CASSEROLE WITH MAPLE PECAN TOPPING

This is an easy, do-ahead recipe, just right for Christmas breakfast or any busy morning!

MAKES 10 TO 12 SERVINGS

1 (16-ounce) loaf raisin bread
1 (8-ounce) package smoked
  sausage links or patties
6 eggs
1 1/2 cups milk
1 1/2 cups half-and-half

1 teaspoon vanilla extract
1/4 teaspoon ground
  cinnamon
1/4 teaspoon ground nutmeg
Maple Pecan Topping

Cube the bread and layer in a greased 9×13-inch baking pan. Brown the sausage in a large skillet; drain. Cut the sausage into bite-size pieces and stir into the bread cubes. Beat the eggs in a large bowl. Add the milk, half-and-half, vanilla, cinnamon, and nutmeg and mix well. Pour over the bread and sausage. Chill, covered, for 8 hours to overnight in the refrigerator. Preheat the oven to 350 degrees. Spoon the Maple Pecan Topping over the casserole. Bake for 35 to 40 minutes.

RANCH HAND'S FAVORITE EGG SCRAMBLE

This egg dish is popular with guests and hired hands at a cattle ranch in northwest Platte County.

MAKES 6 SERVINGS

12 eggs, or 18 egg whites, or
  4 cups pasteurized
  egg substitute
1 1/2 cups milk
1 1/2 cups cooked wild rice

1 1/2 cups grilled plain or
  Southwest-seasoned
  chicken breast strips
1 1/2 cups (6 ounces) shredded
  Pepper Jack cheese

Preheat the oven to 350 degrees. Beat the eggs in a large bowl. Add the milk and mix well. Heat the wild rice and chicken in a large ovenproof nonstick skillet. Add the egg mixture. Cook just until the mixture begins to set, stirring and lifting the mixture from the bottom of the skillet. Stir in the cheese. Place the skillet in the oven and bake for 5 to 10 minutes or until a knife inserted in the center comes out clean. Serve with black beans.

CHILES RELLENOS

MAKES 5 SERVINGS OR 10 RELLENOS

12 Anaheim chiles, roasted
   and peeled
1 (15-ounce) can green chile
   sauce
12 egg yolks
1 heaping tablespoon
   all-purpose flour

1/8 teaspoon salt
2 to 4 tablespoons milk
12 egg whites, stiffly beaten
8 ounces (2 cups) shredded
   mozzarella cheese

Pat the chiles dry on paper towels. Chop 2 chiles and add to the green chile sauce in a small saucepan. Heat the sauce and keep warm. Whisk together the egg yolks, flour, and salt in a bowl until blended. Add the milk, 1 tablespoon at a time, whisking constantly just until blended. Fold the egg yolk mixture gently into the egg whites. Coat an 8x12-inch griddle with nonstick cooking spray and heat to medium-high. Spoon 10 portions (2 tablespoons each) of the batter onto the griddle, forming chile-shaped portions. Turn the pancakes over when just firm and immediately sprinkle each with 2 tablespoons cheese. Top each with 1 whole chile. Sprinkle each with additional cheese. Spoon additional batter over the cheese and along 1 side of each relleno and cook until the bottom is light brown. Turn onto the uncooked side and cook until brown. Remove to a warm serving plate. Spoon 2 tablespoons of the green chile sauce over each relleno.

SOUTHWESTERN BREAKFAST CASSEROLE

MAKES 8 SERVINGS

1/2 cup all-purpose flour
1/2 teaspoon salt
1/2 cup (1 stick) butter,
   melted
8 eggs, lightly beaten
2 cups ricotta cheese
1 or 2 (4-ounce) cans diced
   green chiles

4 cups (16 ounces) shredded
   mild Cheddar or Monterey
   Jack cheese, or combination
1/2 teaspoon pepper
1 green bell pepper, thinly
   sliced into rings
1 red bell pepper, thinly sliced
   into rings

The Southwestern Breakfast Casserole may be prepared the night before. Chill, covered, in the refrigerator. Increase the baking time to 1 hour.

Preheat the oven to 375 degrees. Combine the flour, salt, and butter in a large bowl and mix well. Stir in the eggs. Add the ricotta cheese, chiles, shredded cheese, and pepper and mix well. Pour into a lightly greased 9×13-inch baking dish. Arrange the bell pepper rings on top. Bake for 45 to 50 minutes or until the top is light brown.

More than three hundred species of wildflowers grow in Wyoming, from common yarrow to Indian paintbrush, the state wildflower. These wildflowers offer a full spectrum of color throughout spring, summer, and fall, and many native species make good choices for home gardens. If you have ever been frustrated at how quickly your beautiful cut flowers wilt in the vase, try this: Mix one can of lemon-lime soda (not diet) with one quart room-temperature water and one teaspoon bleach. Pour the mixture into a vase containing cut flowers, and watch in amazement at how long they stay fresh!

SPINACH AND MUSHROOM CHEESECAKE

MAKES 10 SERVINGS

1 1/2 cups bread crumbs
5 tablespoons butter, melted
24 ounces cream cheese, softened
1/2 cup heavy cream
1/2 teaspoon ground allspice
1/2 teaspoon cayenne pepper
White pepper to taste
Pinch of salt
4 eggs, at room temperature

1 cup (4 ounces) shredded Swiss cheese
1 (10-ounce) package frozen chopped spinach, thawed and squeezed dry
2 1/2 tablespoons sliced green onions
1 pound mushrooms, sliced
3 tablespoons butter
Additional mushrooms

Preheat the oven to 350 degrees. Combine the bread crumbs and 5 tablespoons melted butter and press onto the bottom of a 9-inch springform pan. Bake for 10 minutes; cool. Reduce the oven temperature to 325 degrees. Beat the cream cheese, cream, allspice, cayenne pepper, white pepper, and salt in a large mixing bowl until smooth. Beat in the eggs, 1 at a time. Remove half of the cream cheese mixture to a separate bowl and fold in the Swiss cheese. Fold the spinach and green onions into the cream cheese mixture in the first bowl. Spread the spinach mixture evenly over the crumb crust. Sauté the sliced mushrooms in 3 tablespoons butter in a skillet over medium-high heat until the moisture has evaporated. Spoon the mushrooms evenly over the spinach layer. Top with the Swiss cheese mixture and spread evenly. Bake for 1 1/2 hours. Turn off the oven and leave the cheesecake in the oven with the door ajar for 1 hour. Cool completely and remove the side of the pan. Serve at room temperature. Garnish with mushrooms. Serve with fresh tomato sauce or salsa.

SPINACH, BACON, AND MUSHROOM FRITTATA

*This Italian omelet makes a great brunch, lunch, or Sunday supper
with grilled tomatoes or salad, and focaccia.*

MAKES 6 SERVINGS

3 tablespoons butter
8 ounces baby portobello mushrooms, sliced
6 ounces baby spinach
8 eggs
1/4 cup water
1/2 cup grated Parmigiano-Reggiano or
    other Parmesan cheese
1/2 teaspoon thyme
1/4 teaspoon salt
6 to 8 slices bacon, crisp-cooked and crumbled
1/2 cup grated Parmigiano-Reggiano or
    other Parmesan cheese

Melt the butter in a large ovenproof nonstick skillet over medium
heat. Add the mushrooms and spinach and cook for 5 minutes or until
the mushrooms are tender and the spinach is wilted. Preheat
the broiler. Whisk the eggs in a medium bowl until light and frothy.
Whisk in the water, 1/2 cup Parmesan cheese, the thyme, and salt.
Pour over the mushrooms and spinach in the skillet. Sprinkle with the
bacon. Cook, covered, over medium heat for 8 to 10 minutes or just
until set. Sprinkle with 1/2 cup Parmesan cheese. Place the skillet in
the lowest oven position and broil for 1 minute or until the frittata is
puffy and the cheese is bubbly. Serve hot or at room temperature.

NOTE: *The possibilities are endless for ingredients to add to a frittata. Asparagus,
onions, prosciutto or ham, tomatoes, avocados, red and green bell peppers, and
zucchini are just a few ideas.*

COWBOY QUICHE

Cut into bite-size pieces, this quiche also makes a great appetizer.

MAKES 10 TO 12 SERVINGS

1 pound ground sirloin
1 cup finely chopped green onions
1/2 cup finely chopped red bell pepper
1/2 cup canned diced green chiles
2 garlic cloves, minced
1 tablespoon salt-free Mrs. Dash seasoning
1 teaspoon salt
1 teaspoon pepper
12 eggs, or 4 cups pasteurized egg substitute
1 1/2 cups milk or soy milk
2 cups (8 ounces) shredded sharp Cheddar cheese
Sour cream
Additional chopped green onions and
   shredded Cheddar cheese

Preheat the oven to 350 degrees. Sauté the ground sirloin, green onions, bell pepper, green chiles, garlic, Mrs. Dash seasoning, salt, and pepper in a large nonstick skillet, stirring until the beef is brown and crumbly. Whisk the eggs in a large bowl until frothy. Whisk in the milk. Add the beef mixture and 2 cups cheese and mix well. Pour into a greased 9×13-inch baking dish. Bake for 1 hour or until a wooden pick inserted in the center comes out clean. Let stand for 5 minutes before cutting into squares. Garnish with sour cream, green onions, and cheese. Serve with your favorite salsa.

CARAMELIZED ONION AND BACON TART

In Germany, this dish is served in the fall with a new wine called Federweiser.

MAKES 12 SERVINGS

1¼ cups (about) all-purpose flour
1 envelope dry yeast
½ cup scalded milk, cooled to lukewarm
½ cup (1 stick) plus 1 tablespoon butter, melted
1 teaspoon salt
¾ cup diced bacon (6 to 8 slices)
3 pounds onions, sliced and separated into rings
4 eggs
1 cup sour cream
1 tablespoon caraway seeds

Place 1 cup of the flour in a large bowl and make a well in the center. Sprinkle the yeast over the flour. Pour the warm milk over the flour and sprinkle with the remaining ¼ cup flour. Cover the bowl with a cloth and let stand for 15 minutes. Add the butter and salt to the flour mixture and beat until the dough is smooth and elastic. Shape into a ball and place in a lightly greased bowl, turning to coat the surface. Cover and let rise in a warm place for 30 minutes.

Cook the bacon in a large skillet until crisp; remove and drain on paper towels. Add the onions to the bacon drippings in the skillet and sauté until golden brown. Remove from the heat and let cool.

Turn the dough onto a lightly floured surface and roll into a 10×15-inch rectangle. Place the dough in a greased 10×15-inch baking pan with sides. Whisk the eggs in a large bowl until frothy. Whisk in the sour cream and caraway seeds. Fold the onions and bacon into the egg mixture and pour over the dough. Let stand for 15 minutes. Preheat the oven to 400 degrees. Bake for 20 to 30 minutes. Cut into squares and serve warm.

NOTE: *The tart may also be cut into smaller squares and served as an appetizer.*

SAVORY TOMATO GOAT CHEESE TART

MAKES 8 SERVINGS

1/4 cup pine nuts
11/2 cups all-purpose flour
1/2 teaspoon salt
1/2 cup (1 stick) cold butter, cut into small pieces
1/4 to 1/2 cup cold water
4 small Roma tomatoes, sliced
2 eggs
1/2 cup heavy whipping cream
1/2 cup (2 ounces) goat cheese, crumbled or chopped
1/4 cup prepared pesto or fresh pesto
Additional sliced tomatoes

Preheat the oven to 350 degrees. Spread the pine nuts on a baking sheet. Toast in the oven for about 5 minutes or until golden brown.

Combine the flour and salt in a bowl. Add the butter and cut in with a pastry blender until crumbly. Stir in the water to form a slightly sticky dough. Chill the dough for 30 minutes. Preheat the oven to 400 degrees. Turn the dough onto a lightly floured surface and roll into a 10-inch round about 1/4-inch thick. Place the dough in a 9-inch tart pan. Cover the crust with parchment paper and fill with pie weights. Bake for 30 minutes.

Remove the pie weights and parchment paper. Arrange the tomato slices over the crust, overlapping slightly. Bake for about 15 minutes or until the edges of the tomatoes look dry. Combine the eggs, cream, goat cheese, and pesto in a mixing bowl and beat well. Pour over the tomatoes. Bake for 25 minutes or until the filling is set. Cool for 10 minutes before serving. Garnish with sliced tomatoes and the pine nuts. Serve warm or cold.

GEM CITY GRANOLA

Quick & Easy

MAKES 14 CUPS

2 pounds quick-cooking oats
1/2 pound flaked coconut,
   toasted
2 cups Grape-Nuts cereal
1 1/2 cups packed brown sugar
1 cup sliced almonds, toasted
   if desired
1 cup chopped pecans

1 cup shelled unsalted
   sunflower seeds
1 cup wheat germ
1/2 cup sesame seeds
1 cup chopped dates
1 cup raisins
1/2 teaspoon salt

Combine the oats, coconut, cereal, brown sugar, almonds, pecans, sunflower seeds, wheat germ, sesame seeds, dates, raisins, and salt in a large bowl, stirring by hand until mixed. Store in an airtight container.

NOTE: *You may also add your favorite dried fruits, such as cranberries, blueberries, cherries, apples, strawberries, and so forth.*

Once described by the *San Francisco Examiner* as "the hippest little Cowboy town in the West," Laramie is home to the University of Wyoming, the only accredited four-year degree-granting institution in the state and at 7,220 feet, the highest in the nation.

Laramie's nickname, "Gem City of the Plains," is derived from James H. Hayford, editor of the *Laramie Sentinel*, who in 1869 described Laramie as a "gem on the high plains of Wyoming." Today the description is still appropriate. Laramie's appearance at night does resemble precious stones sparkling like gems.

"Fire in the Sky" Barbecue

Nothing announces summer in the high country better than Laramie's "Fire in the Sky" celebration on the Fourth of July. Live country-western music and a choreographed fireworks display form the perfect accompaniment to a traditional western barbecue on Independence Day.

The Menu

CRANBERRY MINT TEA

DILLED GREEN BEAN, BACON, AND
RED POTATO SALAD*

BLUEBERRY GOAT CHEESE SALAD*

BISTRO CARROTS*

SALMON WITH BACON, LEEKS, AND
CREAMY SCALLION SAUCE

LAMB SHISH KABOBS WITH
RED WINE SAUCE

RICE

LEMON PISTACHIO BARS

RED CHERRY LATTICE-TOP PIE

*pictured recipes

Salads & Dressings

BLUEBERRY VINAIGRETTE

MAKES ABOUT 1/4 CUP

2 tablespoons blueberries
2 tablespoons extra-virgin
    olive oil
1/2 garlic clove, crushed
1/4 teaspoon balsamic
    vinegar
Salt and freshly ground
    pepper to taste

Mash the blueberries in
a small bowl. Add the olive
oil, garlic, vinegar, salt, and
pepper and mix well.

PARSLEY VINAIGRETTE

MAKES ABOUT 1/2 CUP

1/4 cup vegetable oil
2 tablespoons vinegar
2 tablespoons sugar
1 tablespoon chopped
    parsley
1/2 teaspoon salt
1/4 teaspoon pepper
Dash of hot red pepper
    sauce

Whisk together the oil,
vinegar, sugar, parsley, salt,
pepper, and hot red pepper
sauce in a bowl until
combined.

BLUEBERRY GOAT CHEESE SALAD

*This salad is a real pleaser.
The sweet blueberries are offset by the tangy goat cheese.*

MAKES 4 SERVINGS

1/4 cup coarsely chopped pecans or hazelnuts
8 ounces mixed salad greens or romaine,
    rinsed and torn into bite-size pieces
1 avocado, finely chopped
1/2 cucumber, peeled and finely chopped
2 ounces goat cheese
1/2 cup fresh or frozen blueberries, thawed
Blueberry Vinaigrette

Preheat the oven to 350 degrees. Spread the pecans in a shallow
baking pan and toast for 5 to 10 minutes or until golden brown,
stirring occasionally. Combine the salad greens, avocado, and
cucumber in a large serving bowl. Crumble the goat cheese over the
top. Sprinkle with the warm pecans and the blueberries. Pour the
Blueberry Vinaigrette over the salad and toss just before serving.

ORANGE PICO DE GALLO SALAD

MAKES 8 SERVINGS

2 heads romaine, rinsed and torn into bite-size pieces
2 medium oranges, separated into sections and
    cut into bite-size pieces
1/2 cucumber, thinly sliced
1/2 red onion, thinly sliced into strips
1/2 green bell pepper, finely chopped
1 cup chopped jicama
Parsley Vinaigrette

Place the romaine in a large serving bowl. Arrange the oranges,
cucumber, onion, bell pepper, and jicama on top. Pour the Parsley
Vinaigrette over the salad and toss lightly. Serve with enchiladas,
grilled chicken, or beef.

CRISPY BACON AND MANDARIN ORANGE SALAD WITH POPPY SEED-ARTICHOKE DRESSING

MAKES 8 SERVINGS

1 head romaine, rinsed and torn into bite-size pieces
1 (8-ounce) can mandarin oranges, drained
1 avocado, chopped
1 small red onion, thinly sliced into rings
1 small green bell pepper, thinly sliced into rings
1/2 pound bacon, crisp-cooked and crumbled
1 cup walnut halves
1 cup finely grated Parmesan cheese
1 cup croutons
Poppy Seed-Artichoke Dressing

Combine the romaine, oranges, avocado, onion, and bell pepper in a large serving bowl. Top with the bacon, walnuts, cheese, and croutons. Pour the Poppy Seed-Artichoke Dressing over the salad and toss.

NOTE: *Other ingredients, such as carrots, celery, cauliflower, broccoli, or cubed cooked chicken, may be added to the salad.*

POPPY SEED-ARTICHOKE DRESSING

MAKES ABOUT 3 1/4 CUPS

2 cups mayonnaise
1/2 cup sugar
1/2 cup rice vinegar
3 or 4 marinated artichoke heart quarters, thinly sliced
1 tablespoon chopped parsley or parsley flakes
1 tablespoon poppy seeds
1/2 teaspoon celery salt
1/2 teaspoon seasoned pepper

Combine the mayonnaise, sugar, vinegar, artichokes, parsley, poppy seeds, celery salt, and pepper in a bowl and mix well. Chill, covered, until ready to use. The dressing can be made several days ahead. Store, covered, in the refrigerator.

LEMON VINAIGRETTE

MAKES ABOUT 2/3 CUP

2 tablespoons lemon juice
2 tablespoons white
    vinegar
1 tablespoon olive oil
1/3 cup sugar or sugar
    substitute (Splenda)

Whisk together the lemon juice, vinegar, olive oil, and sugar in a small bowl until the sugar is dissolved.

SPINACH CITRUS SALAD WITH FRESH BERRIES AND KIWI

MAKES 4 TO 6 SERVINGS

6 ounces baby spinach, rinsed
1 cucumber, peeled, seeded and
    thinly sliced
1 (8-ounce) can mandarin oranges,
    drained
2 kiwifruit, peeled and sliced
1/2 pint raspberries, or 1 cup
    sliced strawberries
1/4 cup slivered almonds, toasted
Lemon Vinaigrette

Combine the spinach, cucumber, oranges, kiwifruit, raspberries, and almonds in a large serving bowl. Pour the Lemon Vinaigrette over the salad and toss.

GRILLED ROMAINE WITH APPLES, BLUE CHEESE, AND BACON

MAKES 4 SERVINGS

2 heads romaine
1/4 cup olive oil
Salt and pepper to taste
10 slices bacon, crisp-cooked
   and crumbled

2 Granny Smith apples, sliced
1 cup crumbled blue cheese
Blue Cheese Vinaigrette

Preheat the grill. Slice the romaine heads in half vertically. Rinse, then dry in paper towels. Brush the romaine with the olive oil and season with salt and pepper. Grill for 1 to 2 minutes. Remove from the grill and place each romaine half on a serving plate. Cut out the core with a sharp knife. Top with the bacon, apple slices, and blue cheese. Serve with the Blue Cheese Vinaigrette.

CHRISTMAS PEAR SALAD

Quick & Easy

This salad has a sweet, fresh taste that can accompany any meal.

MAKES 6 SERVINGS

1 (16-ounce) can pear halves
1 (6-ounce) package red hot
   cinnamon candies
Curly red leaf lettuce, rinsed

4 ounces cream cheese,
   softened
1 to 2 tablespoons milk
Mint leaves

Drain the juice from the pears into a small saucepan, leaving the pears in the can. Add the red cinnamon candies to the juice and cook over low heat until the candies are dissolved, stirring occasionally. Pour the liquid over the pears in a bowl and chill, covered, for several hours. Drain the pears and arrange on lettuce-lined serving plates. Combine the cream cheese and milk in a small bowl and mix well. Shape the cheese mixture into 6 balls, using a melon ball scoop, if desired. Place a cheese ball in the center of each pear half and garnish with a mint leaf.

BLUE CHEESE VINAIGRETTE

MAKES ABOUT 2 1/2 CUPS

1/2 cup red wine vinegar
1 cup crumbled blue
   cheese
1/4 cup sliced green
   onions
3/4 cup olive oil
Salt and pepper to taste

Place the vinegar, blue cheese, and green onions in a food processor or blender. Add the olive oil gradually in a thin stream, processing constantly until combined. Season with salt and pepper.

Warm Goat Cheese Salad with Bacon, Dried Cherry, and Port Dressing

MAKES 4 SERVINGS

1 (11-ounce) log goat cheese, sliced into 8 rounds
Salt and pepper to taste
1 egg, beaten
1 1/4 cups plain bread crumbs
1/4 cup olive oil
5 ounces mixed salad greens or baby spinach
Bacon, Dried Cherry, and Port Dressing
1/2 cup pine nuts, toasted

Season the goat cheese rounds with salt and pepper. Dip in the egg, then in the bread crumbs, coating completely. Chill, covered, until ready to fry. Heat 1/4 cup olive oil in a heavy skillet over medium heat. Add the breaded cheese rounds, a few at a time, and fry for 1 to 2 minutes per side or until crisp and brown on the outside and soft on the inside. Toss the greens with the warm dressing in a large bowl. Divide the greens among 4 serving plates and top each with 2 cheese rounds. Sprinkle with the pine nuts.

Bacon, Dried Cherry, and Port Dressing

MAKES 2 1/2 CUPS

1 1/4 cups dried tart cherries or dried cranberries
1/2 cup tawny port
5 strips bacon, chopped
2 shallots, minced
1 garlic clove, minced
1/3 cup olive oil
1/3 cup red wine vinegar
3 to 5 tablespoons sugar

Combine the cherries and port in a small heavy saucepan and bring to a boil over medium heat. Remove from the heat and let stand for 15 minutes to plump the cherries.

Sauté the bacon in a large heavy skillet over medium heat until crisp. Add the shallots and garlic and cook for 2 minutes. Add the olive oil, vinegar, and sugar and cook until the sugar is dissolved, stirring constantly. Add the cherry mixture and season with salt and pepper. Cover and keep warm.

TRADITIONAL GREEK SALAD

MAKES 6 SERVINGS

1 large head romaine or other salad greens, rinsed and torn into bite-size pieces
1¹/2 cups finely shredded cabbage
1 cup chopped fresh Italian or flat-leaf parsley
6 Roma tomatoes, cut into wedges

1 large cucumber, sliced
36 Greek olives
1 large red onion, sliced
4 ounces (or more) feta cheese, crumbled
Greek Lemon Dressing

Place the romaine in a large serving bowl. Arrange the cabbage in the center of the bowl over the romaine, allowing the romaine to show around the side. Sprinkle the parsley over the cabbage. Arrange the tomato wedges around the side of the bowl with the points toward the center. Arrange the cucumber slices between the tomato wedges. Place the olives on top of the cucumber slices and in the center over the parsley. Top with the onion and cheese. Pour the Greek Lemon Dressing over the salad and let stand for 10 minutes before serving.

ROMAINE AND BACON SALAD WITH COTTAGE CHEESE DRESSING

MAKES 8 SERVINGS

¹/3 cup cider vinegar
¹/3 cup vegetable oil or olive oil
¹/4 cup sugar
1 teaspoon dry mustard
1 teaspoon salt
1 Bermuda onion, diced

1¹/2 cups cottage cheese
1 tablespoon poppy seeds
2 romaine hearts, or 1 large head romaine, rinsed and torn into bite-size pieces
1 pound bacon, crisp-cooked and crumbled

Combine the vinegar, oil, sugar, dry mustard, and salt in a blender and blend until smooth. Pour into a bowl. Add the onion, cottage cheese and poppy seeds and mix well. Chill, covered, until ready to use. Combine the romaine and bacon in a large serving bowl. Pour the dressing over the salad and toss.

DAY-AHEAD SPINACH SALAD

MAKES 6 TO 8 SERVINGS

8 to 12 ounces spinach, rinsed and torn into bite-size pieces
1/2 cucumber, thinly sliced
1/2 cup thinly sliced radishes
3 hard-cooked eggs, sliced
1/4 cup thinly sliced green onions
3/4 to 1 cup blue cheese salad dressing
5 slices bacon, crisp-cooked and crumbled
1/2 cup salted Spanish peanuts

Layer about 1/4 of the spinach in the bottom of a large serving
bowl. Layer with the cucumber, 1/4 of the spinach, the radishes,
1/4 of the spinach, the eggs, the remaining spinach, and the green
onions. Spread the dressing evenly over the top. Chill, covered, for
8 to 10 hours. Top with the bacon and peanuts just before serving.
To serve, lift out portions with a salad fork and spoon, being careful
to pick up all layers.

BISTRO CARROTS

MAKES 5 TO 6 SERVINGS

1 1/2 pounds carrots, peeled
    and shredded
3 tablespoons fresh lemon
    juice
2 teaspoons Dijon mustard
2 teaspoons sugar
1 tablespoon black sesame
    seeds

1/2 cup olive oil
Salt and pepper to taste
6 green onions, finely
    chopped
1/3 cup finely chopped fresh
    parsley

Blanch the carrots in boiling water for 1 minute. Plunge into ice water immediately to stop the cooking process; drain. Pat dry on paper towels. Whisk together the lemon juice, Dijon mustard, sugar, and sesame seeds in a small bowl. Add the olive oil gradually, whisking constantly until combined. Season with salt and pepper. Combine the carrots and the dressing in a large bowl and toss. Stir in the green onions and parsley. Serve slightly warm, at room temperature, or chilled, with small rounds of French bread.

GINGERED COLESLAW WITH LIME DRESSING

MAKES 4 SERVINGS

1/2 head Napa cabbage or bok
    choy, rinsed and shredded
2 carrots, shredded
3 green onions, sliced
3 tablespoons coarsely
    chopped cilantro

2 teaspoons grated fresh
    ginger
Dash of salt
1/4 teaspoon freshly ground
    pepper
Lime Dressing

Chop the shredded cabbage. Combine the cabbage, carrots, green onions, cilantro, ginger, salt, and pepper in a large serving bowl. Pour the Lime Dressing over the slaw and toss.

LIME DRESSING

MAKES ABOUT 1 3/4 CUPS

1 cup fresh lime juice
3/4 cup mayonnaise
1 1/2 tablespoons sugar

Whisk together the lime juice, mayonnaise, and sugar in a small bowl until blended.

Dilled Green Bean, Bacon, and Red Potato Salad

Makes 8 to 10 servings

1¹/₂ pounds green beans, cut into 2-inch pieces
1 cup water
¹/₂ teaspoon salt
1 tablespoon dill weed
1 teaspoon salt
1 teaspoon pepper
1 cup water
¹/₂ teaspoon salt
1¹/₂ pounds red potatoes, diced
1 beef bouillon cube
1 cup boiling water
10 to 12 slices bacon, crisp-cooked and crumbled
1 bunch green onions, sliced
2 teaspoons olive oil
2 teaspoons wine vinegar
Fresh dill weed

Place the green beans in a saucepan with 1 cup water and
¹/₂ teaspoon salt and bring to a boil. Cook, uncovered, for 5 minutes.
Cover and cook for 5 to 10 minutes longer; drain. Let stand until cool.
Season with the dill weed, 1 teaspoon salt, and the pepper.

Combine 1 cup water and ¹/₂ teaspoon salt in a saucepan and
bring to a boil. Add the potatoes and return to a boil. Reduce the heat
and cook, covered, for 15 minutes.

Dissolve the bouillon cube in the boiling water in a small bowl.
Toss the potatoes with the bouillon in a large bowl. Add the green
beans, bacon, green onions, olive oil, and vinegar and mix well. Chill,
covered, for several hours or overnight.

Prepare a day ahead for best flavor. Serve at room temperature.
Garnish with fresh dill weed.

PARSLIED POTATO SALAD

Best made twenty-four hours ahead.
Great for picnics because there's no mayonnaise.

MAKES 8 TO 10 SERVINGS

1¹/₂ pounds white or russet
   potatoes
¹/₄ teaspoon salt (optional)
1 cup chopped red onion
1 cup chopped parsley leaves

¹/₃ cup chopped fresh mint
   leaves
¹/₂ cup fresh lemon juice
1 cup extra-virgin olive oil
Salt and pepper to taste

Combine the potatoes, water to cover and ¹/₄ teaspoon salt in a medium saucepan. Bring to a boil. Reduce the heat and simmer, covered, for 20 to 25 minutes or just until tender. Drain and let cool slightly. Peel the potatoes and cut into thin wedges. Combine the remaining ingredients in a large bowl and mix well. Add the potatoes and toss to coat. Chill, covered, for 24 hours. Serve chilled or at room temperature.

FRESH TOMATO SALAD WITH AVOCADO BALLS AND HERB DRESSING

MAKES 6 SERVINGS

2 ripe avocados
1 medium cucumber, scored
   and sliced
Herb Dressing

Butter lettuce or other salad
   greens
6 tomatoes, cut into wedges,
   or cherry tomatoes

Use a melon ball scoop to make small avocado balls. Place the avocado balls and the cucumber in a large bowl and pour the Herb Dressing over the vegetables. Marinate, covered, for 3 to 5 hours in the refrigerator. Drain the dressing from the vegetables and pour into a small serving bowl. Line 6 salad plates with lettuce and arrange the avocado balls, cucumber, and tomato wedges on top. Drizzle with the Herb Dressing.

HERB DRESSING

MAKES ABOUT 1¹/₂ CUPS

1 cup olive oil
1 tablespoon lemon juice
¹/₃ cup vinegar
1 teaspoon sugar
1 teaspoon crushed basil
1 teaspoon crushed
   marjoram
1 teaspoon salt
1 teaspoon dry mustard
¹/₄ teaspoon cayenne
   pepper
Crushed garlic to taste

Combine the olive oil, lemon juice, vinegar, sugar, basil, marjoram, salt, dry mustard, cayenne pepper, and garlic in a jar with a tight-fitting lid and shake until blended.

BALSAMIC MARINADE

MAKES ABOUT
1 1/2 CUPS

1/2 cup sugar
1/2 cup balsamic
   vinegar or
   wine vinegar
1/2 cup olive oil
1 tablespoon water
1/2 teaspoon salt
1 teaspoon pepper

Combine the sugar,
vinegar, olive oil, water,
salt, and pepper in a
small bowl and whisk
until blended.

MARINATED VEGETABLE RELISH

MAKES 8 TO 10 SERVINGS

1 (15-ounce) can tiny green peas, drained
1 (14-ounce) can French-cut green beans, drained
1 (11-ounce) can white Shoe Peg corn, drained
1 yellow bell pepper, finely chopped
1 cup finely chopped celery
1 (4-ounce) jar diced pimentos
4 small green onions, sliced
Balsamic Marinade

Combine the peas, green beans, corn, bell pepper, celery, pimentos, and green onions in a large glass bowl. Pour the Balsamic Marinade over the vegetables and mix well. Marinate, covered, in the refrigerator for 8 to 12 hours to allow the flavors to blend.

SUMMER SAUERKRAUT SALAD

MAKES 8 SERVINGS

1 1/2 cups sugar
3/4 cup white or other vinegar
1/4 cup vegetable oil
1 (32-ounce) package crisp sauerkraut
3 to 4 cups shredded cabbage
1/2 cup diced celery
1 onion, thinly sliced
1/2 green bell pepper, diced
1 teaspoon celery seeds
Pepper to taste

Combine the sugar, vinegar, and oil in a small saucepan and bring to a boil. Cook for 5 minutes. Combine the sauerkraut, cabbage, celery, onion, bell pepper, celery seeds, and pepper in a large bowl. Pour the hot dressing over the sauerkraut mixture and mix well. Chill, covered, for 24 hours.

CURRIED CHICKEN SALAD

The homemade curry powder sets this salad apart.

MAKES 6 TO 8 SERVINGS

1 or 2 firm apples, finely
    chopped
2 to 3 tablespoons vinegar or
    lemon juice
3 pounds boneless skinless
    chicken breasts or thighs,
    cut into strips
1 to 2 garlic cloves, crushed
2 to 3 tablespoons minced
    onion

3 to 4 tablespoons olive oil
3 to 4 teaspoons Homemade
    Curry Powder
2 or 3 celery ribs, sliced
1 to 1¹/2 cups mayonnaise or
    plain yogurt
Lettuce leaves
Raisins, chopped walnuts,
    and shredded carrots

Toss the apples with the vinegar in a small bowl. Sauté the chicken with the garlic and onion in the olive oil in a large skillet until light brown, stirring frequently. Add the Homemade Curry Powder and stir to coat the chicken. Cook, covered, over medium-low heat until the chicken is cooked through, stirring occasionally. Remove from the heat and chill for several hours. Combine the chicken, celery, and apples in a large bowl and mix well. Stir in the mayonnaise. Serve over lettuce and garnish with raisins, walnuts, and carrots.

HOMEMADE CURRY POWDER

MAKES 3 TO 4 TEASPOONS

1/2 teaspoon cardamom
1/2 teaspoon coriander
1/2 teaspoon ground
    cumin
1/2 teaspoon ground
    ginger
1/2 teaspoon turmeric
1/4 teaspoon freshly
    ground black pepper
1/4 teaspoon chili powder
Generous dash of
    cayenne pepper
Generous dash of ground
    cinnamon
Generous dash of ground
    cloves

Combine the cardamom, coriander, cumin, ginger, turmeric, black pepper, chili powder, cayenne pepper, cinnamon, and cloves in a small bowl and mix with a fork.

NOTE: *If you lack 1 or more of these spices, substitute and experiment with what you have. The most critical ingredients are coriander, cumin, ginger, black pepper, chili powder, and cinnamon. This mixture is far superior to "grocery store" curry powders. But if you use a purchased curry powder instead of making your own, use at least 3 to 4 teaspoons for this recipe.*

SMOKED SALMON AND MANGO SALAD WITH HORSERADISH CREAM DRESSING

MAKES 6 SERVINGS

6 cups torn mixed salad greens, rinsed
Horseradish Cream Dressing
2 tablespoons olive oil
2 teaspoons raspberry vinegar
Salt and pepper to taste
1/2 cup thinly sliced red onion
1 cup canned mangoes, drained
9 ounces smoked salmon or smoked trout, flaked
3 avocados, sliced
1/2 cup pine nuts (optional)
Fresh dill weed

Combine the greens, 1/3 cup Horseradish Cream Dressing, the olive oil, and vinegar in a large bowl and toss. Season with salt and pepper. Divide the greens among 6 salad plates. Top each with the onion. Arrange the mangoes on top, fanning out from the center. Top with the salmon, then the avocado slices. Spoon the remaining Horseradish Cream Dressing over each salad. Sprinkle with the pine nuts, if desired. Garnish with fresh dill weed.

HORSERADISH CREAM DRESSING

MAKES ABOUT 1 2/3 CUPS

1 cup heavy cream
1/3 cup prepared horseradish
2 tablespoons olive oil
2 tablespoons raspberry or cider vinegar
2 teaspoons finely chopped fresh dill weed
1/8 teaspoon cayenne pepper
Salt and black pepper to taste

Whisk together the cream, horseradish, olive oil, vinegar, dill weed, and cayenne pepper in a small bowl until blended. Season with salt and black pepper.

ALBACORE SALAD WITH GOLDEN RAISINS AND ALMONDS

The raisins add a nice sweetness to this summer main dish salad.

MAKES 4 SERVINGS

1 onion, finely chopped
1 bunch parsley, finely
  chopped
3 or 4 sprigs of fresh tarragon,
  finely chopped, or
  2 teaspoons dried tarragon
2 to 3 celery ribs, finely
  chopped, or 1 (8-ounce) can
  sliced water chestnuts,
  drained and chopped
Juice of 1 lemon

1/4 cup slivered almonds
1 (12-ounce) can water-pack
  albacore tuna, drained
1/2 to 3/4 cup golden raisins
2 to 3 tablespoons
  mayonnaise, or to taste
1 teaspoon curry powder, or
  to taste
Dash of hot red pepper sauce,
  or to taste
Lettuce leaves

Combine the onion, parsley, tarragon, celery, and lemon juice in a large bowl. Add the almonds, tuna, and raisins and toss gently. Combine the mayonnaise, curry powder, and hot red pepper sauce in a bowl and add to the tuna mixture, stirring gently. Chill, covered, until ready to serve. Serve on a bed of lettuce.

LAYERED CRAB SALAD WITH LEMON CAPER VINAIGRETTE

MAKES 8 SERVINGS

8 ounces capers, drained
1 pound crab meat, flaked
2 bunches green onions,
  minced
1 yellow bell pepper, minced

2 tomatoes, finely chopped
1 cucumber, finely chopped
1 red onion, finely chopped
Lemon Caper Vinaigrette
Dried tarragon, crushed

Coat eight 4- to 6-ounce plastic cups or glasses with nonstick cooking spray. Layer an equal amount of the capers, crab meat, green onions, bell pepper, tomatoes, cucumber, and red onion in the prepared cups, pressing down firmly after each layer. Chill, covered, for 2 hours or longer. Invert the cups onto 8 salad plates and drizzle with Lemon Caper Vinaigrette. Sprinkle tarragon onto the plates to garnish.

LEMON CAPER VINAIGRETTE

MAKES ABOUT
2 1/4 CUPS

1 1/4 cups vegetable oil
1/2 cup white wine
  vinegar
1/4 cup fresh lemon juice
2 ounces capers, drained
2 tablespoons sugar
1 teaspoon paprika

Combine the oil, vinegar, lemon juice, capers, sugar, and paprika in a jar with a tight-fitting lid and shake until blended; chill.

Oriental Shrimp Salad

1/4 cup vegetable oil
1/4 cup lemon juice
2 tablespoons soy sauce
1 garlic clove, minced
1/4 teaspoon grated ginger
1/8 teaspoon pepper
1 pound mushrooms, sliced
1 pound green beans,
  julienned
1/2 cup water

1/2 teaspoon salt
1/2 cup water
1/2 teaspoon salt
1 pound snow peas, trimmed
8 ounces bean sprouts
1 (8-ounce) can sliced water
  chestnuts, drained
1 pound peeled cooked salad
  shrimp, chilled

Combine the oil, lemon juice, soy sauce, garlic, ginger, and pepper with the mushrooms in a large bowl and mix well. Combine the green beans, 1/2 cup water, and 1/2 teaspoon salt in a saucepan and bring to a boil. Cook, uncovered, for 5 minutes. Cook, covered, for 10 to 15 minutes; drain. Let stand until cool. Combine 1/2 cup water and 1/2 teaspoon salt in a saucepan and bring to a boil. Add the snow peas and cook, uncovered, for 1 to 2 minutes or until tender; drain. Let stand until cool. Add the green beans, snow peas, bean sprouts, and water chestnuts to the mushroom mixture and mix well. Chill, covered, for 1 hour. Add the shrimp and toss gently.

Sushi Salad

Supremely simple and delicious

8 ounces spinach, rinsed
4 cups cooked rice, at room
  temperature
1 1/2 pounds medium shrimp,
  peeled, cooked, and chilled

2 avocados, finely chopped
1 cucumber, julienned
3 tablespoons olive oil
2 tablespoons rice vinegar
Soy sauce and wasabi

Divide the spinach equally among 4 salad plates. Mound 1 cup of rice in the center of each plate. Combine the shrimp, avocados, and cucumber in a bowl. Sprinkle with the olive oil and vinegar and toss gently. Divide the shrimp mixture equally among the 4 plates, spooning it over the rice. Serve with soy sauce and wasabi (Japanese horseradish).

ARTICHOKE BOTTOMS WITH SHRIMP

MAKES 4 MAIN DISH OR 8 SIDE SERVINGS

3 tablespoons olive oil
1 1/2 tablespoons wine vinegar
Salt and freshly ground pepper to taste
8 canned artichoke bottoms, drained and patted dry
1 pound peeled cooked salad shrimp, chilled
1/3 cup mayonnaise
2 teaspoons lemon juice
Paprika to taste
1/2 green bell pepper, finely chopped
Lettuce

Whisk together the olive oil, vinegar, salt, and pepper in a bowl. Add the artichoke bottoms, stirring to coat with the olive oil mixture. Let stand for about 1 hour. Reserve 8 shrimp for garnish. Coarsely chop the remaining shrimp. Combine the mayonnaise, lemon juice, and paprika in a large bowl. Add the shrimp and bell pepper and mix well. Place a lettuce leaf on each of 4 salad plates. Top each with an artichoke bottom. Mound the shrimp mixture on the artichoke bottoms. Garnish with the reserved shrimp.

RASPBERRY VINEGAR

Makes a great holiday gift.

MAKES ABOUT 3 CUPS

12 to 16 ounces red or white wine vinegar
1 1/4 cups sugar
12 ounces frozen unsweetened raspberries,
    or 1 pint fresh raspberries

Combine the vinegar and sugar in a 3-quart saucepan. Add the raspberries and bring to a boil. Reduce the heat and simmer for 20 minutes. Cool slightly. Strain through a fine sieve, reserving the liquid. Discard the seeds and pulp. Pour into decorative bottles or jars and cover. Store in the refrigerator.

PORT WINE GLAZE

MAKES ABOUT 1 1/2 CUPS

1 (750-ml) bottle port (Portuguese port preferred)

Pour the port into a large saucepan and bring to a boil. Reduce the heat to low and simmer for 2 hours or until reduced to 1 1/2 cups. Cool. Store the glaze in a plastic squeeze bottle in the refrigerator. Drizzle on salad plates or use to garnish chicken, meat, or fish plates.

NOTE: *This glaze will keep indefinitely in the refrigerator. Bring to room temperature before using.*

Halloween Luncheon for the University Women's Club

Historically, it has been a tradition to host a luncheon at the University of Wyoming president's home for the University Women's Club, an organization that was formed in 1912. Part of the club's original mission, which continues to this day, was to welcome newcomers to the area and raise money for scholarships awarded to nontraditional female students at UW.

The Menu

SPICY BLACK BEAN AND
PUMPKIN CHIPOTLE SOUP*

STUFFED PUMPKIN*

ZUCCHINI MUFFINS*

PUMPKIN SPICE MOUSSE*

WYOMING PUMPKIN BARS*

HOT APPLE CIDER AND CINNAMON STICKS

pictured recipes

Soups & Stews

Gazpacho Andaluz

Makes 6 to 8 servings

1 (1-pound) loaf French bread, crusts removed
3 to 4 large ripe tomatoes, peeled and coarsely chopped
1/3 large green bell pepper, chopped
1/2 medium cucumber, peeled and coarsely chopped
1 large garlic clove, chopped
3 tablespoons red wine vinegar
2 tablespoons olive oil
1 tablespoon salt
Bread cubes, chopped onion, chopped green bell pepper,
  or chopped cucumber

Tear the loaf of bread into chunks and place in a large bowl. Add enough water to cover the bread and let stand until the bread is completely moistened. Add the tomatoes, bell pepper, cucumber, garlic, vinegar, olive oil, and salt. Ladle the tomato mixture, in batches, into a blender and blend until smooth. Pour the mixture into a bowl or other large container and add water to the desired consistency. Chill, covered, for several hours or until very cold. Adjust the seasonings to taste. Garnish with bread cubes, onion, green bell pepper, or cucumber.

Spicy Black Bean and Pumpkin Chipotle Soup

1 tablespoon olive oil
$1/2$ teaspoon to $11/2$ tablespoons ground
  New Mexico or Chimayo chile
$1/2$ teaspoon ground cumin
1 (14-ounce) can diced tomatoes
1 onion, chopped
3 garlic cloves
1 or 2 canned chipotle chiles in adobo sauce,
  patted dry
1 teaspoon adobo sauce
2 (15-ounce) cans black beans
2 cups chicken broth
1 (15-ounce) can pumpkin
Lime wedges
Sour cream
Cilantro sprigs

Heat the olive oil, ground chile, and cumin in a 6-quart saucepan over medium-high heat for 1 to 2 minutes or until the spices start to smoke, stirring constantly. Add the undrained tomatoes, onion, garlic, chipotle chiles, and adobo sauce and mix well. Pour into a blender or food processor and blend until smooth. Return the mixture to the pan and bring to a boil over medium-high heat. Reduce the heat and simmer for 6 to 7 minutes or until slightly thickened, stirring occasionally. Stir in the beans, broth, and pumpkin and return to a boil. Reduce the heat and simmer for 10 minutes to allow the flavors to blend. Ladle 2 cups of the soup into a blender or food processor and blend until smooth. Return to the pan and heat through. Ladle into soup bowls. Squeeze a lime wedge over each serving and garnish with a dollop of sour cream and the cilantro.

MINESTRONE

MAKES 10 SERVINGS

1 large onion, chopped
3 garlic cloves, finely chopped
3 tablespoons extra-virgin olive oil
4 cups chicken broth
1 (14-ounce) can diced tomatoes
1 cup vegetable juice cocktail
3 carrots, chopped
2 celery ribs, chopped
1 cup shredded cabbage, or to taste
3 stalks bok choy, chopped
Thyme leaves to taste

1/4 to 1/3 cup basil leaves, chopped, or to taste
Oregano leaves to taste
1 or 2 zucchini, chopped
2 (15-ounce) cans Great Northern beans, drained and rinsed
1 (16-ounce) package frozen Italian green beans
4 to 6 ounces small shell macaroni
3 cups water
Grated Parmesan cheese (optional)

Sauté the onion and garlic in the olive oil in an 8-quart stockpot. Add the broth, undrained tomatoes, vegetable juice cocktail, carrots, celery, cabbage, bok choy, thyme, basil, and oregano and mix well. Bring to a boil. Reduce the heat and simmer, covered, for 20 minutes. Stir in the zucchini, beans, macaroni and water and bring to a boil. Reduce the heat and simmer for 10 to 15 minutes or until the vegetables and macaroni are tender. Ladle into bowls and sprinkle with Parmesan cheese.

ESSENCE OF MUSHROOM SOUP

MAKES 4 TO 8 SERVINGS

You may start the preparation of the Essence of Mushroom Soup up to three days in advance. To serve, heat the soup on low until hot but not boiling. Fold in the parsley just before serving. This is a very rich soup and makes a superb first course if served in small portions. As a main course, this will serve 4.

1 small onion, diced
1 garlic clove, minced
1/2 cup (1 stick) butter
1 pound button mushrooms, sliced
3 tablespoons fresh lemon juice
3 cups beef broth

2 teaspoons Maggi seasoning sauce (optional)
1 1/2 cups sour cream
Pepper to taste
1/2 cup chopped parsley
Slivered almonds, toasted (optional)

Sauté the onion and garlic in the butter in a large saucepan for 5 minutes or until the onion is tender but not brown. Add the mushrooms and lemon juice and sauté until the mushrooms are tender. Add the broth and seasoning sauce and mix well. Remove from the heat and let cool for about 10 minutes. Whisk in the sour cream gradually. Season with pepper. Fold the parsley into the soup and ladle into bowls. Garnish with toasted almonds.

CREAM OF SPINACH SOUP

3 pounds baby spinach
4 tablespoons (1/2 stick) butter
4 garlic cloves, minced
2 beef or chicken bouillon cubes
2 cups cream or half-and-half
2 tablespoons rice wine vinegar
Salt to taste
Additional cream or chopped hard-cooked eggs

Steam the spinach in a small amount of water in a covered saucepan just until wilted. Drain, reserving the liquid. Put half the spinach, 2 tablespoons of the butter, half the garlic, and 1 bouillon cube in a blender and blend until smooth, adding reserved cooking liquid as needed for a smooth thick purée. Repeat with the remaining spinach, butter, garlic, and bouillon cube. Pour both batches of the spinach purée into a large saucepan and cook over high heat until hot but not boiling, stirring constantly. Stir in the cream and vinegar and heat through. Ladle into soup bowls and garnish with the cream or hard-cooked eggs. May be served warm or chilled.

FRESH TOMATO-BASIL SOUP

This is a rich, hearty, and satisfying soup.

MAKES 6 SERVINGS

3 cups water
4 large tomatoes
3 cups cold water
1/3 cup butter
1/4 cup all-purpose flour
1/4 teaspoon baking soda
3 cups milk
1 tablespoon basil
1 teaspoon salt
1 teaspoon sugar
1/4 teaspoon cayenne pepper
Grated Parmesan cheese

Bring 3 cups water to a boil in a medium saucepan. Cut an "X" in the bottom of each tomato and place in the boiling water. Boil for about 30 seconds. Remove the tomatoes and immediately place in the cold water. Peel off and discard the tomato skins. Purée the tomatoes in a blender, or by hand in a colander. Melt the butter in a large saucepan. Stir in the flour and cook for 1 to 2 minutes or until smooth, stirring constantly. Add the tomato purée and bring to a boil. Reduce the heat and stir in the baking soda until no longer bubbly. Add the milk, basil, salt, sugar, and cayenne pepper. Cook for 40 minutes, stirring occasionally. Serve immediately or refrigerate to serve later. Reheat chilled soup slowly before serving. Sprinkle each serving with Parmesan cheese.

NOTE: *For a spicier, Western flavor, add 1 seeded diced jalapeño chile. For a "New Orleans" flavor, add a teaspoon of Cajun seasoning.*

CHINESE HOT AND SOUR SOUP

MAKES 8 TO 16 SERVINGS

3 (49-ounce) cans
 chicken broth
3/4 pound lean pork, cooked
 and shredded
5 dried black mushrooms,
 soaked and shredded
5 dried wood ear mushrooms,
 soaked and shredded
6 slices fresh ginger
1 (12-ounce) package tofu,
 drained and cubed
1 (8-ounce) can bamboo
 shoots, drained and
 shredded
3 slices cooked ham,
 shredded

4 small mushrooms, sliced
1 cup rice vinegar, or to taste
2 tablespoons soy sauce
1 tablespoon chili oil, or
 to taste
1 tablespoon hot chili sauce,
 or to taste
2 1/2 teaspoons white pepper
2 teaspoons toasted sesame oil
1/2 teaspoon salt
1/2 teaspoon sugar
6 tablespoons cornstarch
1/2 cup cold water
4 eggs, lightly beaten
2 or 3 green onion tops, sliced
Additional chili oil

Bring the broth to a boil in a large stockpot. Add the pork, black
mushrooms, wood ear mushrooms, and ginger and cook for 4 minutes.
Remove and discard the ginger slices. Add the tofu, bamboo shoots,
ham, mushrooms, vinegar, soy sauce, chili oil, hot chili sauce, white
pepper, sesame oil, salt, and sugar. Simmer gently for 4 to 5 minutes.
Stir the cornstarch into the water in a small bowl until dissolved. Stir
the cornstarch mixture into the soup and cook until thickened and
clear, stirring constantly. Remove the pan from the heat and stir in the
eggs with a fork. Ladle into soup bowls and garnish with the green
onions and chili oil.

SOPA DE RECUERDOS
(SOUP OF MEMORIES)

MAKES 6 TO 8 SERVINGS

1 pound chorizo sausage or
    smoked kielbasa, casings removed and sausage sliced
1 onion, diced
6 garlic cloves, sliced
1/4 cup olive oil
1 teaspoon thyme
1 teaspoon fennel seeds
1/2 teaspoon ground celery seeds
1/2 teaspoon basil
1/2 teaspoon red pepper flakes
6 to 8 cups chicken stock
1/2 cup red wine
2 (15-ounce) cans cannellini beans, drained and rinsed
2 (15-ounce) cans garbanzo beans, drained and rinsed
1 (9-ounce) package frozen chopped spinach,
    or 1 bunch fresh spinach or kale, rinsed and chopped
1 (9-ounce) package cheese tortellini
Freshly grated Parmesan cheese

Cook the sausage, onion, and garlic in the olive oil in a stockpot, stirring constantly until the sausage is brown and crumbly. Add the thyme, fennel seeds, celery seeds, basil, and red pepper flakes and cook for 5 minutes. Add the stock and wine and bring to a boil. Reduce the heat and simmer for 10 minutes. Add the cannellini beans, garbanzo beans, and spinach and bring to a boil. Add the tortellini and return to a boil. Reduce the heat and simmer for 8 to 10 minutes or until the tortellini are tender, stirring occasionally. Ladle into bowls and serve with the Parmesan cheese.

NOTE: *To make the soup ahead of time, prepare as above but omit the tortellini. Cool the soup and refrigerate. When ready to serve, bring to a boil and add the tortellini. Continue to cook as directed above.*

PEPPER JACK CHOWDER WITH POPCORN

MAKES 12 SERVINGS

4 cups water
5 medium red potatoes, diced
1 cup sliced carrots
1 cup sliced celery
1/4 onion, diced
2 dashes of hot red pepper
   sauce, or to taste
2 teaspoons salt
1/4 teaspoon pepper

2 cups cubed cooked ham
1/2 cup (1 stick) butter or
   margarine
1/2 cup all-purpose flour
4 cups 1% milk
4 cups (16 ounces) shredded
   Pepper Jack cheese
Air-popped popcorn

Bring the water to a boil in a stockpot or large heavy pan. Add the potatoes, carrots, celery, onion, hot red pepper sauce, salt, and pepper. Reduce the heat and simmer, covered, for 10 minutes or until the vegetables are tender. Add the ham. Melt the butter in a large saucepan. Stir in the flour and cook for 1 to 2 minutes or until smooth. Stir in the milk and cook over medium heat until the mixture comes to a boil, stirring constantly. Reduce the heat and simmer for 1 minute. Stir in the cheese until melted. Pour the cheese mixture into the stockpot and mix well. Heat through but do not boil. Ladle into bowls and garnish with the popcorn.

NOTE: *This chowder freezes well.*

Mulligatawny Soup

This outstanding and unusual soup is a meal in itself.

Makes 8 servings

1/4 cup (1/2 stick) butter
1 onion, diced
1 carrot, peeled and diced
2 celery ribs with leaves, diced
1 green bell pepper, seeded and diced
1 apple, peeled and diced
1 1/2 cups diced chicken or beef (optional)
2 tablespoons butter
1/3 cup all-purpose flour
1 tablespoon curry powder
1/2 teaspoon ground nutmeg
6 cups chicken broth or beef broth
6 to 8 ounces cream cheese,
    at room temperature
1 cup chopped peeled tomatoes
2 whole cloves, crushed
1/8 teaspoon cayenne pepper, or
    black pepper to taste
Salt to taste
3 to 4 cups steamed white rice
Raisins
1 cup slivered almonds, toasted
4 bananas, chilled and sliced

Melt 1/4 cup butter in a stockpot. Add the onion, carrot, celery, bell pepper, apple, and chicken. Cook over medium-low heat for 15 minutes, stirring frequently. Add 2 tablespoons butter. Stir together the flour, curry powder, and nutmeg and stir into the vegetable mixture. Cook over medium heat for 5 minutes, stirring occasionally. Heat 1 to 2 cups of the broth in a saucepan and stir in the cream cheese until blended. Add the cream cheese mixture, the remaining broth, tomatoes, cloves, cayenne pepper, and salt to the soup and mix well. Simmer, partially covered, for 30 to 40 minutes. Adjust the seasonings to taste. Ladle into soup bowls. Serve the rice on the side, topped with raisins, almonds, and bananas.

TURKEY AND WILD RICE SOUP

*This is a great soup to make ahead and take to potlucks
in a slow cooker. It goes well with corn bread.*

MAKES 8 SERVINGS

3 (10-ounce) cans chicken broth
2 cups water
1/2 cup wild rice
3/4 cup finely chopped onion
3/4 cup finely chopped celery
1/2 cup (1 stick) butter or margarine
3/4 cup all-purpose flour
1/2 teaspoon salt
1/2 teaspoon poultry seasoning
1/4 teaspoon pepper
2 cups half-and-half
2 cups chopped cooked turkey
8 slices bacon, crisp-cooked and crumbled
Dried cranberries

Combine the broth, water, wild rice, onion, and celery in a 3-quart
saucepan and bring to a boil. Reduce the heat and simmer, covered,
for 20 minutes. Melt the butter in a small nonstick skillet over low heat.
Whisk in the flour, salt, poultry seasoning, and pepper until blended.
Cook over low heat until thickened and smooth, stirring constantly.
Whisk in the half-and-half slowly and cook for 2 to 4 minutes or until
thickened. Whisk the half-and-half mixture into the broth gradually
and cook until thickened and hot. Do not boil. Add the turkey and
bacon and heat through. Ladle into soup bowls and garnish with
the cranberries.

NOTE: *Roasted or baked turkey provides the best flavor.*

DUCK GUMBO

MAKES 6 TO 8 SERVINGS

1/2 cup (1 stick) butter
1/2 cup olive oil
1 cup all-purpose flour
1 cup finely chopped onion
1 cup finely chopped celery
2 garlic cloves, minced
1 (6-ounce) can tomato paste
2 (28-ounce) cans stewed
   tomatoes or diced tomatoes
2 cups chopped boiled duck
1/2 pound Italian sausage
   links, cooked and sliced

3/4 cup chopped green onions
1/2 cup chopped parsley
2 to 3 tablespoons
   Worcestershire sauce
1/2 teaspoon oregano leaves
1/2 teaspoon tarragon leaves
1/2 teaspoon salt
1/2 teaspoon black pepper
1/4 teaspoon red pepper flakes
1/2 cup (or more) water
1/4 cup chopped parsley
Filé powder

Prepare a roux by melting the butter in a large heavy skillet. Stir in the olive oil, then the flour. Cook over medium-high heat for 15 to 20 minutes or until the roux is a medium-dark nutty brown color, stirring constantly. The darker the color of the roux, the more flavorful the gumbo. Add the onion and celery and cook until tender. Stir in the garlic, tomato paste, and tomatoes. Bring to a boil over medium heat, stirring constantly. Stir in the duck, sausage, green onions, 1/2 cup parsley, Worcestershire sauce, oregano, tarragon, salt, black pepper, red pepper flakes, and water and bring to a boil. Reduce the heat to low and simmer for 20 to 30 minutes, stirring frequently. Add additional water as needed to thin the gumbo as it cooks. Ladle into bowls and sprinkle with the parsley and filé powder.

NOTE: *To boil duck, combine 1 (4-to 5-pound) thawed frozen duckling or cleaned fresh duck with water to cover in a stockpot and bring to a boil over medium heat. Reduce the heat to low and simmer, covered, for about 1 hour or until the skin is plump and the meat begins to separate from the bones. Remove the duck from the pan and cool before removing the meat from the bones.*

SHRIMP GUMBO

MAKES 4 TO 6 SERVINGS

1 quart water
2 medium onions, sliced
1/2 cup white vinegar
1 teaspoon salt
2 pounds rinsed unpeeled shrimp
1/4 cup instant flour (such as Wondra)
1/4 cup (1/2 stick) butter
8 small white onions, halved lengthwise
2 tablespoons chopped parsley
2 cups sliced fresh okra or frozen okra
3 large ripe tomatoes, peeled and chopped
1 tablespoon chopped green bell pepper
1 bay leaf
1 teaspoon salt
1 teaspoon ground thyme
1 1/2 teaspoons Worcestershire sauce
1/2 teaspoon black pepper
1/4 teaspoon red pepper flakes
1/4 teaspoon sugar
Additional chopped parsley

Combine the water, sliced onions, vinegar, and 1 teaspoon salt in a large stockpot and bring to a boil. Add the shrimp and return to a boil. Boil for 7 minutes or until the shrimp turn pink. Remove the shrimp, reserving the cooking liquid. Peel the shrimp and set aside.

Brown the flour in a large heavy skillet, stirring constantly. Melt the butter in a small skillet and add the onion halves and 2 tablespoons parsley. Cook until the onions are translucent. Stir the onions into the browned flour and mix well. Stir in the reserved cooking liquid. Cook for 5 minutes, stirring constantly.

Cook the okra in boiling salted water in a small saucepan for 5 minutes and drain, or thaw frozen okra and pat dry. Add the okra, tomatoes, bell pepper, bay leaf, 1 teaspoon salt, thyme, Worcestershire sauce, black pepper, red pepper flakes, and sugar to the skillet and mix well. Simmer, covered, for 15 minutes. Add the shrimp and simmer for 20 minutes. Remove and discard the bay leaf. Garnish with the parsley. Serve with hot cooked rice.

SHRIMP BISQUE

MAKES 4 TO 8 SERVINGS

1 pound large unpeeled
  shrimp
1/4 cup (1/2 stick) butter
1 cup finely chopped onion
1/2 cup finely chopped carrots
1/2 cup finely chopped celery
2 garlic cloves, chopped
1 rounded tablespoon
  tomato paste
1 cup white wine

Fish Velouté
1 bay leaf
2 sprigs of fresh thyme
1/2 teaspoon crushed black
  pepper
1 cup heavy cream, heated
  but not boiled
Salt and white pepper to taste
Tabasco sauce to taste
1/4 cup (1/2 stick) butter

Peel and rinse the shrimp, reserving the shells. Melt 1/4 cup butter in an 8-quart stockpot over medium-low heat. Add the onion, carrots, celery, and reserved shrimp shells and cook for 15 minutes or until caramelized, stirring occasionally. Stir in the garlic and tomato paste and sauté lightly. Add the wine, stirring to loosen the browned bits from the bottom of the pan. Cook until the liquid is reduced by 1/2. Add the Fish Velouté, bay leaf, thyme, and black pepper and mix well. Simmer for 30 minutes. Strain the mixture, discarding the solids. Return the liquid to a boil. Reduce the heat and stir in the hot cream, salt, white pepper, and Tabasco sauce. Sauté the shrimp in 1/4 cup butter in a skillet until the shrimp turn opaque. Reserve 8 shrimp for garnish. Coarsely chop the remaining shrimp and add to the soup. Heat through. Ladle the soup into bowls and garnish with the reserved shrimp.

FISH VELOUTÉ

MAKES 8 CUPS

1/2 cup (1 stick) butter
1/2 cup all-purpose flour

8 cups Fish Stock

Make a roux by melting the butter in a saucepan and stirring in the flour until smooth. Cook for 5 minutes or until thick and light brown, stirring constantly. Cool. Bring the Fish Stock to a boil in a 4-quart saucepan. Stir in 1 cup of the cooled roux and mix well. Return to a boil. Reduce the heat and simmer for 30 minutes or until the mixture is the consistency of heavy cream.

FISH STOCK

To make your own fish stock, combine 2 pounds white fish, 2 1/2 quarts water, 1 finely chopped celery rib, 1 finely chopped carrot, 1 finely chopped small onion, 1 bay leaf, and 2 peppercorns in a 6- to 8-quart saucepan and bring to a boil. Reduce the heat and simmer, covered, for 1 1/2 to 2 hours. Strain through several layers of cheesecloth and discard the solids.

CRAB SOUP

MAKES 6 SERVINGS

2 carrots, finely chopped
1 onion, finely chopped
2 tablespoons olive oil
3 cups chicken broth
3 cups beef broth
3 to 4 cups peeled diced
  potatoes
3 to 4 cups chopped tomatoes

2 teaspoons Old Bay
  seasoning
1 (10-ounce) package
  frozen peas
1 pound cooked crab meat
2 tablespoons chopped
  parsley

Sauté the carrots and onion in the olive oil in a stockpot until the vegetables are tender. Add the broths, potatoes, tomatoes, and Old Bay seasoning and bring to a boil. Reduce the heat and simmer for 15 to 20 minutes or until the potatoes are tender, adding the peas for the last 5 minutes. Add the crab meat and parsley and heat through. Serve with dark rye bread and beer or iced tea.

HOT CHICKEN CHILI

MAKES 12 SERVINGS

4 boneless skinless
  chicken breasts
1 1/2 cups water
1 teaspoon lemon pepper
1 teaspoon ground cumin
1 cup chopped onion
1 garlic clove, minced
1 tablespoon olive oil
2 (15-ounce) cans Great
  Northern beans,
  drained

2 (9-ounce) or 1 (16-ounce)
  package frozen white corn
2 (4-ounce) cans diced
  green chiles
2 to 3 teaspoons lime juice
1 teaspoon ground cumin
1 teaspoon red pepper flakes,
  or to taste
2/3 cup crushed tortilla chips
2/3 cup shredded Monterey
  Jack cheese

Combine the chicken, water, lemon pepper, and 1 teaspoon cumin in a large saucepan and bring to a boil. Reduce the heat and cook for 20 to 30 minutes or until the chicken is tender, stirring occasionally. Sauté the onion and garlic in the olive oil in a small nonstick skillet until tender. Add to the chicken mixture. Remove the chicken, reserving the liquid in the pan. Shred the chicken into 1- to 2-inch pieces and return to the pan. Add the beans, corn, green chiles, lime juice, 1 teaspoon cumin, and the red pepper flakes and bring to a boil. To serve, place the tortilla chips in the bottom of each soup bowl and top with the cheese. Ladle the chili into the bowls.

SIGMA CHI RING-OF-FIRE CHILI

MAKES 4 GALLONS, ABOUT 75 SERVINGS

6 pounds ground chuck
1/2 cup diced onion
1 tablespoon garlic salt
1 teaspoon garlic powder
1 jalapeño chile, minced

1 tablespoon minced pickled
 serrano chiles
1 teaspoon cayenne pepper
Chili Base

Combine the ground chuck, onion, garlic salt, garlic powder, jalapeño chile, serrano chiles, and cayenne pepper in a large stockpot and cook until the meat is browned, stirring until the meat is crumbly; drain. Add to the Chili Base and simmer for 30 minutes. Adjust the seasonings to taste.

CHILI BASE

MAKES 1 1/2 TO 2 GALLONS

2 tablespoons olive oil
1/2 large onion, chopped
1 pound diced green chiles, or
 4 (4-ounce) cans
1 tablespoon minced garlic
2 tablespoons chili powder
2 teaspoons cayenne pepper
1 teaspoon ground cumin
1 teaspoon each salt and
 black pepper

2 (28-ounce) cans diced
 tomatoes
3 cups tomato sauce
3 (15-ounce) cans chili beans
1/2 (4-ounce) bottle red hot
 cayenne pepper sauce
 (Frank's Original)
1 tablespoon minced pickled
 serrano chiles
4 (12-ounce) cans beer

Heat the olive oil in a large stockpot and add the onion, green chiles, and garlic. Sauté until the onion is tender. Stir in the chili powder, cayenne pepper, cumin, salt, and black pepper and mix well. Add the tomatoes, tomato sauce, beans, hot pepper sauce, and serrano chiles and mix well. Bring to a boil. Reduce the heat and simmer, covered, for 2 1/2 hours, stirring occasionally. Add the beer and mix well.

WYOMING WHITE CHILI

Quick & Easy

2 pounds ground chicken
1 small onion, chopped
Garlic salt to taste
1 (10-ounce) can cream of chicken soup
8 ounces cream cheese, at room temperature
2 (4-ounce) cans diced green chiles, or more to taste
1/2 to 1 cup sour cream
3 to 4 ounces Velveeta cheese (optional)
1 tablespoon minced pimento
Beer or water
Salt to taste
Chopped chives
Chopped tomatoes

Brown the chicken in a large nonstick skillet, stirring until crumbly. Stir in the onion and garlic salt and sauté until the onion is tender. Add the soup, cream cheese, green chiles, sour cream, Velveeta cheese, and pimento and mix well. Thin to the desired consistency with beer or water and season with salt. Cook over medium heat until the cheeses have melted and the mixture is hot, stirring occasionally. Do not boil. Ladle into soup bowls and garnish with the chives and tomatoes.

NOTE: *To make your own ground chicken, grind 2 pounds boneless skinless chicken breasts in a food processor until finely chopped.*

VEGETARIAN CHILI

MAKES 12 SERVINGS

1 eggplant, cut into
  1/2-inch pieces
1 tablespoon kosher salt
1/4 cup olive oil
2 onions, finely chopped
2 zucchini, chopped
1 jalapeño chile, seeded and
  chopped, or to taste
4 large garlic cloves, chopped
1/4 cup olive oil
8 ripe tomatoes, chopped
3 cups canned vegetable broth
1/2 cup chopped fresh cilantro
1/2 cup fresh basil leaves,
  julienned
3 tablespoons chili powder
1 1/2 tablespoons ground
  cumin

1 tablespoon dried oregano
1 teaspoon freshly ground
  black pepper
1 teaspoon red pepper flakes,
  or to taste
Salt to taste (optional)
2 cups cooked or canned
  black beans or pinto beans
1 1/2 cups corn kernels
1/2 cup chopped fresh
  dill weed
1/4 cup fresh lemon juice
1/2 cup chopped fresh cilantro
Sour cream, shredded
  sharp Cheddar or
  Monterey Jack cheese,
  and sliced green onions

Toss the eggplant with the kosher salt in a colander and let stand for 1 hour to remove the moisture. Pat dry on paper towels. Heat 1/4 cup olive oil in a stockpot and add the onions, zucchini, jalapeño chile, and garlic. Sauté over medium-low heat for 10 minutes. Heat 1/4 cup olive oil in a skillet and add the eggplant. Cook over medium-high heat for 10 minutes or until the eggplant is tender, stirring occasionally. Transfer the eggplant to the stockpot with a slotted spoon. Add the tomatoes, broth, 1/2 cup cilantro, basil, chili powder, cumin, oregano, black pepper, red pepper flakes, and salt and bring to a boil. Reduce the heat to low and cook for 30 minutes or until thickened and reduced to about 1 1/2 cups, stirring occasionally. Add the beans, corn, dill weed, and lemon juice. Cook for 15 minutes. Adjust the seasonings to taste. Stir in 1/2 cup cilantro. Ladle into bowls and garnish with the sour cream, cheese, and green onions.

AMAZING STEW

MAKES 4 TO 6 SERVINGS

1 pound beef chuck roast or
   sirloin tip roast,
   cut into 1-inch cubes
1 (14-ounce) can consommé
5 ounces red wine
1 onion, sliced
1/4 cup dry bread crumbs
1/4 cup all-purpose flour
1 tablespoon Kitchen Bouquet
   seasoning (optional)

1/2 teaspoon Worcestershire
   sauce
Salt and pepper to taste
2 cups sliced carrots
2 cups chopped peeled
   potatoes
Chopped parsley

Preheat the oven to 350 degrees. Combine the beef, consommé, wine, onion, bread crumbs, flour, Kitchen Bouquet, Worcestershire sauce, salt and pepper in a large bowl and mix well. Spoon into a large roasting pan and bake, covered, for 1 hour. Add the carrots, potatoes, and additional wine or water if needed. Roast for 1 to 2 hours longer or until the meat and vegetables are tender. Garnish with the parsley. This recipe may be doubled.

NOTE: *For a clever garnish, use a wooden pick to poke a hole in the end of a baby carrot and insert a small sprig of parsley.*

COMFORT STEAK STEW

1/2 cup all-purpose flour
1 tablespoon Mrs. Dash seasoning
5 pounds round steak, cut into cubes
2 pounds link sausage, cut into thirds
1 cup olive oil
4 large sweet onions, quartered
1 (46-ounce) can tomato juice
1 tablespoon rubbed sage
12 potatoes, peeled and halved
12 large carrots, cut into chunks
6 tart apples, halved and cored
1 package brown gravy mix
1 cup cold water

Combine the flour and seasoning in a sealable plastic bag.
Add the steak and sausage pieces, a few at a time, and shake to coat.
Heat the olive oil in a large roasting pan. Add the steak and sausage
and cook until brown, stirring frequently. Add the onions and cook
for 3 to 4 minutes; drain. Add the tomato juice and sage and bring
to a boil. Reduce the heat and simmer, covered, for 2 hours, stirring
occasionally. Add the potatoes, carrots, and apples and cook for
10 minutes. Combine the gravy mix and water in a bowl and stir until
blended. Add to the stew and mix well. Cook for 10 to 15 minutes or
until the vegetables are tender.

END-OF-THE-GARDEN STEW

This is a great way to use up all those vegetables from your garden, or take a trip to the local farmers' market at the end of summer. The meatballs and vegetables can be prepared ahead of time.

MAKES 10 SERVINGS

Steak Meatballs
$1/3$ cup vegetable oil
1 large onion, sliced
2 garlic cloves, crushed
1 eggplant, peeled and cubed
4 medium zucchini, sliced
Flour to coat vegetables
2 green bell peppers,
   cut into strips

5 large ripe tomatoes, peeled
   and seeded, or $3^1/2$ cups
   canned tomatoes
   with liquid
1 teaspoon salt, or to taste
$1/2$ to 1 teaspoon pepper, or
   to taste

Brown the Steak Meatballs in a large heavy stockpot or Dutch oven coated with vegetable oil or nonstick cooking spray, stirring occasionally. Remove the meatballs and set aside. Add the oil and heat. Add the onion and garlic and cook over low heat until tender, stirring occasionally. Coat the eggplant and zucchini with the flour. Add the eggplant and bell pepper to the pan. Cook, covered, over low heat for 30 to 40 minutes, stirring frequently. Add the tomatoes and zucchini and cook over low heat for 15 to 20 minutes, stirring frequently. Do not boil. Season with the salt and pepper. Add the meatballs and heat for 15 to 20 minutes or until the vegetables are tender. Serve with coleslaw, corn sticks, and fresh fruit, if desired.

NOTE: *The vegetables may be prepared ahead of time. Store, covered, in separate containers in the refrigerator.*

STEAK MEATBALLS

MAKES ABOUT 40 MEATBALLS

$1^1/2$ cups soft bread cubes
$1/3$ cup milk
1 pound ground round
   or chuck steak
$1/2$ onion, minced
1 tablespoon vegetable oil
1 egg, lightly beaten
1 teaspoon salt
$1/4$ teaspoon pepper

Soak the bread in the milk until absorbed, then squeeze dry and combine with the beef in a large bowl. Sauté the onion in the oil in a small skillet until tender and add to the beef mixture. Add the egg, salt, and pepper and mix well. Shape into 1-inch meatballs. Store, covered, in the refrigerator until ready to use.

PATHFINDER GREEN CHILE STEW

This stew is for those who like their food hot and spicy.

MAKES 10 TO 12 SERVINGS

2 pounds pork cubes, diced
1 pound ground beef
2 large onions, chopped
2 tablespoons chopped garlic, or to taste
1 bunch cilantro, chopped
8 cups pork, beef, or chicken stock
12 ounces beer
2 cups peeled, seeded and chopped green chiles (Hatch's preferred)
4 large potatoes, diced
2 carrots, sliced
1 (8-ounce) can corn

2 tomatoes, diced
2 tablespoons ground cumin
1 tablespoon garlic powder
1 tablespoon onion powder
1 tablespoon oregano, crushed
1 tablespoon parsley flakes, crushed
1 tablespoon pepper
1 tablespoon Tabasco sauce
1 to 3 teaspoons chipotle chile powder
1 to 3 teaspoons ancho chile powder
1/2 cup all-purpose flour
1 cup water

Brown the pork and ground beef in an 8-quart stockpot, stirring occasionally; drain. Add the onions, garlic, and cilantro and sauté over medium-high heat for about 3 minutes. Add the stock, beer, green chiles, potatoes, carrots, corn, tomatoes, cumin, garlic powder, onion powder, oregano, parsley, pepper, Tabasco sauce, chipotle chile powder, and ancho chile powder and mix well. Bring to a boil. Reduce the heat and simmer, uncovered, for 30 minutes, stirring occasionally. Combine the flour and water in a bowl and stir until blended. Stir the flour mixture into the stew. Return to a boil. Reduce the heat and simmer, uncovered, for 30 minutes or until thickened, stirring occasionally.

WILD GAME STEW

4 carrots, sliced
2 onions, quartered
1 cup sliced celery
1 (8-ounce) can sliced mushrooms,
    drained
1 small garlic clove, minced
1/4 cup (1/2 stick) butter
    or margarine
1/2 cup all-purpose flour
2 teaspoons salt
1/4 teaspoon paprika
Pepper to taste
11/2 to 2 pounds venison, antelope, elk,
    or beef, cubed
2 tablespoons butter or margarine
13/4 cups dry red wine
11/2 cups water
11/2 teaspoons thyme
1/2 teaspoon marjoram
1/2 teaspoon salt

Sauté the carrots, onions, celery, mushrooms, and garlic in
1/4 cup butter in a large stockpot for 10 minutes. Remove the
vegetables to a bowl and set aside. Combine the flour, 2 teaspoons
salt, paprika, and pepper in a sealable plastic bag. Add the meat, a
few pieces at a time, and shake to coat. Add 2 tablespoons butter
to the stockpot and heat. Add the meat and cook until brown, stirring
frequently. Add the wine, water, thyme, marjoram, and 1/2 teaspoon
salt and bring to a boil. Reduce the heat and simmer, covered, for
2 hours. Add the sautéed vegetables and cook for 40 minutes,
stirring occasionally. Serve with hot cooked noodles and pass the
pepper grinder.

The western states have a rich tradition of raising livestock on the open range and also hunting wild game that roams here. Wyoming is known for its abundant herds of elk, pronghorn antelope, and deer. It is not uncommon to find meat from one or more of these animals in the typical Wyoming family's freezer. There is nothing more delicious than grilled elk, venison steak, or well-spiced antelope chili.

Black Tie & Boots: An Elegant Dinner for Ten

The spirit of The Virginian *lives on in the American West. Like the legendary character in Owen Wister's book, today's cowboy can choose a life that is rugged yet refined, enjoying the smell of saddle leather, cattle, and sagebrush by day and the aroma of a sophisticated dining experience by night.*

The Menu

SOUR APPLE MARTINIS

BLUE CHEESE AND WALNUT SHORTBREAD

JAPANESE EGGPLANT CRISPS WITH TOMATO RELISH

SMOKED SALMON AND CRAB PÂTÉ

BLACK MAGIC CAVIAR MOLDS

CREAM OF SPINACH SOUP

TENDERLOIN STEAKS WITH MUSHROOM SAUCE*

COWBOY ONION RINGS*

ASPARAGUS CHINOIS*

RASPBERRY ROUSSE

CRANBERRY MARSH ICE

*pictured recipes

Meats

PULL-OFF-THE-BONE
BARBECUED BEEF BRISKET

*This brisket recipe won the 2004 People's Choice Award at the
Ivinson Memorial Hospital Grill-off in Laramie, Wyoming.*

MAKES 12 TO 15 SERVINGS

1 (12-ounce) can cola
1 (12-ounce) bottle chili sauce
1 envelope dry onion soup mix
Chopped onion (optional)
1 teaspoon liquid smoke (optional)
1/2 teaspoon garlic salt (optional)
1 (5- to 6-pound) beef brisket

Preheat the oven to 325 degrees. Combine the cola, chili sauce,
soup mix, onion, liquid smoke, and garlic salt in a bowl and mix well.
Place the brisket, fat side up, in a foil-lined roasting pan. Pour the cola
mixture over the meat. Roast, tightly covered, for 2 1/2 to 3 hours.

NOTE: *The brisket may also be baked all day at 220 degrees.*

SMOKED BRISKET

*Don't rush it! Brisket needs to be slow cooked and smoked;
otherwise, you'll be chewing for days.*

MAKES 45 TO 50 SERVINGS

1 (10- to 15-pound)
   untrimmed beef brisket
1 tablespoon black pepper
1 tablespoon paprika
1 1/2 teaspoons white pepper

1 teaspoon cayenne pepper
1 teaspoon ground cumin
1 teaspoon oregano
Barbecue sauce

Preheat the oven to 200 degrees. Place the brisket, meat side up,
in a large roasting pan. Stir together the black pepper, paprika, white
pepper, cayenne pepper, cumin, and oregano. Sprinkle the pepper
mixture evenly over the meat surface and rub in, coating completely.
Turn the brisket over. Roast, tightly covered, for 8 to 10 hours or until
the meat is tender but not falling apart. Remove the meat from the
pan and cool. Drain and reserve the drippings. Prepare charcoal for a
smoker or outdoor grill. Soak 2 to 4 cups wood chips (hickory, oak,
mesquite, or combination) in water for 20 minutes or longer. Place the
hot coals to 1 side of the grill and top with half the drained wood
chips to produce a generous amount of smoke. Immediately place the
brisket on the grill rack on the side away from the coals. Cover the
grill and vent as little as possible. Add more wood chips after 1 hour.
Smoke the meat for 2 to 4 hours, turning and basting with the reserved
drippings every half hour. Remove the meat to a cutting board and
separate the top cap of meat and fat from the bottom of the brisket.
Trim the fat and slice the meat diagonally against the grain. Heat the
barbecue sauce separately to serve alongside. The meat can also be
"pulled" and mixed with hot barbecue sauce for great sandwiches.

NOTE: *Refrigerate any remaining drippings in a small bowl. Remove and discard
the fat that solidifies on top. Use the remaining drippings as a base for gravy or soup.
Freeze if not using right away.*

ROASTED TENDERLOIN OF BEEF WITH HIGH PLAINS BÉARNAISE SAUCE

MAKES 8 SERVINGS

5 unpeeled garlic cloves
1/2 teaspoon extra-virgin
    olive oil
1 tablespoon extra-virgin
    olive oil
1 tablespoon bacon drippings
1 teaspoon dry mustard
1/2 teaspoon kosher salt or
    sea salt
1/2 teaspoon white pepper

1/4 teaspoon paprika
1/4 teaspoon rubbed sage
Dash of cayenne pepper
1 (4-pound) beef tenderloin,
    trimmed
1 tablespoon extra-virgin
    olive oil
High Plains Béarnaise Sauce
    (page 131)

Soak 2 cups of mesquite, hickory, or alder wood chips in water for 20 minutes to overnight. Prepare an outdoor charcoal grill with an aluminum foil drip pan in the center and the briquettes around the side of the grill. Preheat the oven to 425 degrees. Place the garlic in a small baking dish or on a piece of foil and drizzle with 1/2 teaspoon olive oil. Bake, covered, for 5 minutes. Turn off the oven and leave the garlic in the oven for 45 minutes. Cool slightly, then remove and discard the garlic skins. Mash the garlic to a paste in a small bowl. Whisk in 1 tablespoon olive oil, bacon drippings, dry mustard, salt, white pepper, paprika, sage, and cayenne pepper.

Place the tenderloin in a baking dish and rub the garlic mixture evenly over the surface. Let stand, covered, at room temperature for 20 minutes. Drizzle the meat with 1 tablespoon olive oil and brush evenly over the surface. Coat the grill rack with nonstick cooking spray, if desired. Preheat the grill to 350 degrees and place the tenderloin in the center of the rack. Grill over indirect heat for 30 to 40 minutes, turning often with tongs until a meat thermometer reads 135 degrees for medium-rare. Remove the meat to a clean baking dish or cutting board and let stand, loosely covered with foil, for 10 to 15 minutes. Cut the meat into 1-inch-thick slices and serve each slice with a tablespoon of the High Plains Béarnaise Sauce. Pass the remaining sauce.

HIGH PLAINS BÉARNAISE SAUCE

MAKES 1 CUP

4 teaspoons white wine vinegar
2 tablespoons minced shallots
1 tablespoon minced cooked bacon
1¹/₂ teaspoons chopped fresh tarragon
1¹/₂ teaspoons chopped fresh parsley
2 teaspoons white wine vinegar
4 egg yolks, at room temperature
1 cup (2 sticks) butter, at room temperature
¹/₂ teaspoon dry mustard
¹/₄ teaspoon white pepper
¹/₄ teaspoon rubbed sage
¹/₄ teaspoon paprika
Dash of salt
Dash of cayenne pepper

Combine 4 teaspoons vinegar, shallots, bacon, tarragon and parsley in the top of a double boiler. Cook over boiling water for 1 minute. Reduce the heat and simmer for about 5 minutes or until reduced by ¹/₂. Strain and discard the solids and return the liquid to the top of the double boiler. Add 2 teaspoons vinegar and heat. Whisk the egg yolks in a bowl. Whisk about 2 teaspoons of the vinegar mixture into the egg yolks, stirring constantly. Add the egg yolks slowly to the vinegar mixture, whisking constantly and vigorously. Quickly whisk in the butter, 2 tablespoons at a time, stirring after each addition until melted. Stir in the dry mustard, white pepper, sage, paprika, salt, and cayenne pepper. Continue to cook over the hot water for 1 minute, whisking constantly.

MOCK PRIME RIB

Quick & Easy

MAKES 6 TO 8 SERVINGS

1 (3- to 4-pound) beef roast
1 package Italian salad
   dressing mix

1 package au jus mix
2 cups canned beef broth

Place the roast in a slow cooker. Combine the dressing mix, au jus mix, and broth in a bowl and mix well. Pour over the roast. Cook on Low for 8 to 10 hours. Use the broth for French dip sandwiches or thicken for gravy.

GRILLED STEAK WITH BLUE CHEESE, TOMATOES, AND PENNE PASTA

MAKES 6 SERVINGS

1 pound penne or other
   pasta
3 tablespoons cornstarch
1/2 cup water
3 cups beef broth
1 cup milk
8 ounces blue cheese,
   crumbled

1 1/2 pounds New York strip
   or boneless rib-eye steak,
   about 1 inch thick
Salt and pepper to taste
1 (28-ounce) can tomatoes,
   chopped
1/2 cup fresh basil leaves,
   chopped

Preheat the grill and coat the grill rack with nonstick cooking spray, if desired. Cook the pasta using the package directions; drain and keep warm. Combine the cornstarch and water, stirring until dissolved. Combine the broth and milk in a 3-quart saucepan and bring to a boil. Reserve about 1/3 cup cheese for garnish. Stir the remaining cheese into the broth mixture until melted. Stir in the cornstarch mixture and cook until thickened, stirring constantly. Reduce the heat and keep the sauce warm. Season the steak with salt and pepper. Grill the steak to desired doneness. Add the pasta, tomatoes, and basil to the cheese sauce and mix well. Slice the steak into strips and add to the pasta. Garnish each serving with the reserved blue cheese.

STEAK WITH
PICO DE GALLO MARINADE

Quick & Easy

MAKES 2 SERVINGS

1 pound round steak or
    London broil, trimmed
8 ounces (1 cup) medium-hot
    pico de gallo

2 ounces Parmesan cheese,
    grated
2 ounces mozzarella cheese,
    shredded

Combine the steak and pico de gallo in a large sealable plastic bag.
Marinate in the refrigerator for 3 hours. Preheat the broiler and coat
the broiler pan with nonstick cooking spray. Place the steak on the
broiler pan and spoon half the marinade evenly over the top. Broil for
9 minutes. Turn the steak over and top with the remaining marinade.
Broil the steak for 8 minutes or until medium-rare. Combine the
cheeses and sprinkle on the steak. Broil until the cheese is bubbly and
light brown. Let the steak stand for 5 minutes before thinly slicing
diagonally across the grain.

NOTE: *Pico de gallo is available refrigerated in most supermarket produce
departments.*

BEEF TENDERLOIN WITH
GREEN PEPPERCORN SAUCE

MAKES 6 SERVINGS

6 (6- to 8-ounce) beef
    tenderloin steaks
Ground black pepper
2 tablespoons butter
1/2 cup Cognac or brandy
1 cup beef stock

2 tablespoons green
    peppercorns
1 cup heavy cream
Salt and freshly ground
    pepper to taste

Rub the steaks on both sides with black pepper. Melt the butter
in a large skillet over medium-high heat and add the steaks. Sauté
for 4 minutes per side or until brown. Remove the steaks to a platter
and keep warm. Drain the fat from the skillet and add the Cognac,
stirring to loosen the browned bits from the bottom of the skillet.
Add the stock and peppercorns and cook until the liquid is reduced
by 1/2. Add the cream and cook until thickened, stirring constantly.
Season with salt and pepper. Spoon the sauce over the steaks.

TENDERLOIN STEAKS WITH MUSHROOM SAUCE

MAKES 4 SERVINGS

4 (1-inch-thick) beef
   tenderloin steaks
Olive oil
1/4 teaspoon salt
1/2 teaspoon pepper
1 tablespoon olive oil
8 to 10 ounces sliced
   mushrooms

1 tablespoon minced shallots
2 tablespoons red wine
1/2 teaspoon beef bouillon
   granules
3/4 cup water
1 tablespoon butter,
   at room temperature
1 tablespoon all-purpose flour

Brown the steaks in a small amount of olive oil in a large skillet for about 4 minutes. Turn the steaks and season with the salt and pepper. Cook for 5 minutes longer for rare or to desired doneness. Remove to a platter and keep warm. Add 1 tablespoon olive oil to the skillet and heat. Add the mushrooms and shallots and cook for about 5 minutes over medium-high heat until golden brown. Stir in the wine, bouillon granules, and water and bring to a boil. Reduce the heat to low and simmer for 3 minutes. Stir the butter and flour together in a bowl to make a paste and stir into the mushroom mixture. Cook until slightly thickened, stirring constantly. To serve, spoon the sauce over the steaks.

———◆◆◆———

MULE SHOE STEAK SAUCE

MAKES ABOUT 1/2 CUP

3 garlic cloves
2 tablespoons kosher salt
1/2 teaspoon dry mustard
1 teaspoon pepper

1 teaspoon thyme
3 to 4 tablespoons
   vegetable oil

Smash the garlic with the side of a broad-bladed knife. Remove the thin skins from the garlic. Sprinkle the salt on the garlic and mash with the knife. Combine the salt and garlic by alternately mincing and mashing with the knife. Place the mixture into a small bowl. Stir in the dry mustard, pepper, and thyme. Drizzle with the oil and whisk until of a thin paste consistency. Spread onto steaks before grilling.

FANTASTIC BEEF STROGANOFF

The dill really sets off this stroganoff, which has been a family recipe for almost forty years. All the ingredients can be readied in advance, leaving only the final combination to be done just before serving.

MAKES 6 TO 8 SERVINGS

2 pounds sirloin or tenderized round
   steak, trimmed
4 tablespoons (1/2 stick) butter or margarine
1 cup chopped onion
1 garlic clove, finely chopped
8 ounces mushrooms, sliced
3 tablespoons all-purpose flour
1 tablespoon soy sauce
1 tablespoon Worcestershire sauce
1 tablespoon ketchup
1/2 teaspoon salt
Freshly ground pepper to taste
1 (10-ounce) can beef bouillon
1/4 cup dry white wine
1 tablespoon snipped fresh dill weed, or
   1 teaspoon dried dill weed, or to taste
11/2 cups sour cream, at room temperature
6 cups cooked rice (4 cups white rice and
   2 cups wild rice)

Cut the steak crosswise across the grain into 1/2-inch slices. Melt 1 tablespoon of the butter in a large heavy skillet or electric skillet. Add the beef strips, a few at a time, and sear quickly to brown on both sides. The strips should still be rare in the center. Remove the beef strips to a platter. Add the remaining 3 tablespoons butter to the skillet and heat. Add the onion, garlic, and mushrooms and sauté until golden brown. Remove from the heat and stir in the flour, soy sauce, Worcestershire sauce, ketchup, salt, and pepper and mix well. Add the bouillon gradually and bring to a boil, stirring constantly. Reduce the heat and simmer for 5 minutes. Stir in the wine, dill weed, and sour cream until combined. Add the beef and heat through. Transfer to a serving dish and serve immediately. Serve the rice separately. With a simple salad and a good bread, this makes an excellent meal.

NOTE: *This recipe doubles easily.*

SHEPHERD'S PIE FOR WYOMING COWBOYS

MAKES 8 SERVINGS

2 cups chopped carrots
2 cups chopped onions
2 cups chopped broccoli
2 cups green peas
2 pounds cooked round steak,
   coarsely chopped
1 to 2 tablespoons cornstarch
1 to 2 tablespoons water
6 beef bouillon cubes

1 tablespoon basil
1 tablespoon thyme
1¹/2 teaspoons pepper,
   or to taste
2 eggs
1/2 cup milk
1/2 cup vegetable oil
2 cups all-purpose flour
2 tablespoons baking powder

Cook the carrots and onions in boiling water in a large saucepan for 5 minutes. Add the broccoli and return to a boil. Cook for 5 minutes. Add the peas and cook for 1 minute. Add the meat and additional water if needed to make 1 cup liquid in the pan. Combine the cornstarch and 1 tablespoon water, stirring until dissolved. Add the bouillon cubes, basil, thyme, pepper, and cornstarch mixture to the meat mixture and mix well. Cook until thickened and the bouillon cubes are dissolved, stirring constantly. Remove from the heat. Preheat the oven to 350 degrees. Whisk the eggs in a medium bowl. Whisk in the milk and oil. Add the flour and baking powder, mixing to form a sticky dough. Turn the dough onto a lightly floured surface and roll out to a 9¹/2×13¹/2-inch rectangle. Spread the meat mixture evenly in a 9×13-inch baking dish. Top with the dough, sealing to the edges of the dish. Cut several slits in the dough. Use the leftover dough to make leaf cut-outs and arrange on the top of the pie. Bake on the middle oven rack for 30 minutes or until the topping is golden brown.

DIVINELY EASY MEAT LOAF

Quick & Easy

MAKES 4 TO 6 SERVINGS

2 eggs
1¹/2 pounds ground beef
¹/2 cup chopped green
   bell pepper
¹/2 cup ketchup
1 cup Italian-seasoned dry
   bread crumbs

1 package dry onion soup mix
1 teaspoon prepared mustard
¹/2 teaspoon basil, crushed
¹/2 teaspoon oregano, crushed
1¹/2 teaspoons minced garlic
¹/2 cup ketchup

Preheat the oven to 325 degrees. Beat the eggs in a large bowl. Add the ground beef, bell pepper, ¹/2 cup ketchup, bread crumbs, soup mix, mustard, basil, oregano, and garlic and mix well. Shape into a loaf and place in an 8×12-inch loaf pan or other shallow baking pan. Spread the remaining ¹/2 cup ketchup over the top. Bake for 1 hour and 35 minutes. Let stand for 15 minutes before serving.

LAYERED SIRLOIN AND POTATO BAKE

Quick & Easy

MAKES 8 SERVINGS

8 large potatoes, peeled
3 onions
4 pounds ground sirloin
Salt and pepper to taste

5 (10-ounce) cans tomato
   soup
3 cups sour cream

Preheat the oven to 350 degrees. Cut the potatoes into ¹/4-inch-thick slices. Cut the onions into ¹/4-inch-thick slices. Layer ¹/2 of the potatoes and ¹/2 of the onions in a greased 6- to 8-quart Dutch oven or large casserole. Shape the meat into 3-inch-round patties about ¹/2 inch thick. Arrange ¹/2 of the patties over the onions. Season with salt and pepper. Combine the soup and sour cream in a large bowl and mix well. Pour about ¹/3 of the soup mixture over the patties. Layer with the remaining potatoes, onions, and meat patties. Season with salt and pepper. Pour the remaining soup mixture over the top. Bake, covered, for 3¹/2 hours.

LAYERED ENCHILADAS—
NEW MEXICO STYLE

In northern New Mexico, enchiladas are layered instead of rolled.

MAKES 4 SERVINGS

1 pound ground pork or beef
4 garlic cloves, minced
3 tablespoons chili powder
1 tablespoon onion powder
2 teaspoons ground cumin
1 teaspoon oregano
Salt and pepper to taste
1 to 1 1/2 cups (about) water

8-inch corn tortillas
2 cups (8 ounces) shredded
    Cheddar cheese
1 head iceberg lettuce,
    shredded
4 tomatoes, diced
1 onion, finely chopped
1 cup sour cream

Cook the pork in a large saucepan until brown, stirring until crumbly. Add the garlic, chili powder, onion powder, cumin, oregano, salt, and pepper and mix well. Cook over medium-high heat for several minutes to blend the flavors, stirring frequently. Add the water and bring to a boil. Reduce the heat and simmer for 10 to 15 minutes, adding additional water as needed to keep the chili mixture moist. Place the tortillas, 1 at a time, in the simmering chili mixture. Spoon the chili over the tortilla and cook until softened. Place the tortilla on an individual serving plate and top with additional chili, cheese, lettuce, tomatoes, and onion. Repeat the layering of the softened tortilla, chili, cheese, lettuce, tomatoes, and onion once or twice on each plate. Garnish with the sour cream.

EAST MEETS WEST HAMBURGERS

MAKES 6 SERVINGS

1 1/2 pounds ground chuck
1 1/2 pounds ground sirloin
3/4 cup salted peanuts,
    chopped
1 onion, chopped
2 tablespoons Worcestershire
    sauce

6 tablespoons ketchup
2 teaspoons ground ginger
2 teaspoons dry mustard
2 teaspoons pepper
1 1/2 teaspoons turmeric
    (optional)
1/2 cup sesame seeds (optional)

Combine the ground chuck, ground sirloin, peanuts, onion, Worcestershire sauce, ketchup, ginger, dry mustard, pepper, and turmeric in a large bowl and mix well. Shape into 6 patties. Coat the patties with the sesame seeds, if desired. Grill, pan-fry, or broil the burgers to desired doneness.

STUFFED PUMPKIN

*It always seems to snow in Laramie, Wyoming, on
Halloween night. This is a wonderful meal to come home
to for trick-or-treaters large or small.*

MAKES 8 SERVINGS

1 (4- to 5-pound) fresh pumpkin
1 pound extra-lean ground beef
1 onion, chopped
2 cups corn
2 cups diced tomatoes
1/4 cup chopped black olives
(optional)
Salt and pepper to taste
Vegetable oil

Cut the top off the pumpkin and
scoop out the seeds. If using a leftover
jack-o-lantern, remove any smoky areas
and cover the openings with foil. Preheat
the oven to 350 degrees. Brown the
ground beef in a large skillet, stirring until
crumbly. Add the onion and cook until
translucent. Stir in the corn, tomatoes, and
olives. Season with salt and pepper, if
desired. Fill the pumpkin cavity with the
meat mixture and replace the pumpkin
top. Coat the outside of the pumpkin with
oil. Place on a heavy baking sheet and
bake for 2 to 4 hours or until the pumpkin
is tender. Scoop out the meat mixture and
cut the pumpkin into wedges. To serve,
place a pumpkin wedge on each plate and
top with the meat mixture.

NOTE: *The pumpkin can also be cooked in
a large slow cooker. Cook on High for 1 hour.
Reduce the setting to Low and cook for 4 hours
or longer.*

BEEF OR WILD GAME JERKY

MAKES 1 POUND

1 (2-pound) beef chuck or game meat steak,
   partially frozen
$^1/_2$ cup red wine
$^1/_3$ cup soy sauce or teriyaki sauce
$^1/_4$ cup water
2$^1/_2$ tablespoons dark brown sugar
1 tablespoon Montreal steak seasoning
1$^1/_2$ tablespoons lemon juice or lime juice
1 tablespoon liquid smoke
1$^1/_2$ teaspoons hickory-smoked salt
2 teaspoons garlic powder or crushed garlic
1 teaspoon onion powder or onion salt
$^1/_2$ to 1 teaspoon pepper
Dash of hot red pepper sauce (optional)

Slice the meat diagonally across the grain into $^1/_4$-inch-wide strips.
Combine the wine, soy sauce, water, brown sugar, steak seasoning,
lemon juice, liquid smoke, salt, garlic powder, onion powder, pepper,
and hot red pepper sauce in a large glass bowl or other nonmetallic
container. Add the meat, stirring to coat well. Marinate, covered, in
the refrigerator for 2 to 8 days, stirring daily. Remove the meat from
the marinade and place in a dehydrator, or arrange on foil-lined oven
racks and bake in a preheated 150-degree oven with the door held ajar
with a metal knife. Dry for 6 to 8 hours, turning every 2 hours. Cool
and store in sealable plastic bags in the freezer.

VEAL CUTLETS WITH MUSHROOM SAUCE

MAKES 4 SERVINGS

1/2 cup all-purpose flour
1/2 teaspoon salt
1/8 teaspoon black pepper
1/8 teaspoon paprika
4 veal cutlets
1 egg, beaten
2 tablespoons vegetable oil
1 tablespoon butter
2 onions, diced
8 ounces portobello
  mushrooms, sliced

8 ounces white mushrooms,
  sliced
1 cup light cream or fat-free
  half-and-half
1/4 cup dry white wine
Dash of white pepper
Dash of paprika
2 to 4 tablespoons beef stock
1 teaspoon minced parsley
1 tablespoon chopped chives
  (optional)

Combine the flour, salt, black pepper, and 1/8 teaspoon paprika in a shallow dish. Dip the cutlets into the egg, then coat with the flour mixture. Heat the oil and butter in a large heavy skillet and add the cutlets. Brown over medium-high heat for about 2 minutes per side. Remove the cutlets to a platter and cover with foil. Keep warm in a low oven. Add the onions to the skillet and cook until brown. Add the mushrooms and cook slightly. Add the cream and wine and mix well. Cook over low heat until the mixture is reduced by 1/2, stirring occasionally. Season with white pepper and paprika. Stir in the stock and heat through. Remove from the heat and stir in the parsley and chives. To serve, pour the sauce over the cutlets.

You may be surprised to learn that Wyoming has a small selection of wineries. Extensive testing conducted at the University of Wyoming Research and Extension Center in Sheridan assists local vintners in determining the best varieties of grapes to grow in Wyoming.

BRAISED TUSCAN LAMB SHANKS

MAKES 4 SERVINGS

2 tablespoons vegetable oil
4 small lamb shanks
3 carrots, diced
3 celery ribs, diced
4 to 5 garlic cloves, sliced
1 large onion, diced
2 cups dry red wine

1 teaspoon thyme
1 teaspoon marjoram
3 tomatoes, chopped
1/3 cup tomato paste
Salt and pepper to taste
10 mushrooms
Hot cooked polenta

Preheat the oven to 325 degrees (400 degrees if using a clay baker). Heat the oil in a heavy ovenproof skillet. Add the lamb shanks and brown well on all sides; remove from the skillet. Add the carrots, celery, garlic, and onion to the skillet and sauté for 3 to 4 minutes or until tender. Add the wine, thyme, and marjoram and bring to a boil. Reduce the heat and simmer until reduced by 1/2. Stir in the tomatoes, tomato paste, salt, and pepper and cook until hot, stirring constantly. Return the shanks to the skillet or place the shanks in a water-soaked 4-quart clay baker or heavy roasting pan. Pour the vegetable mixture over the meat. Bake for 3 to 3 1/2 hours, adding the mushrooms during the last 45 minutes. Serve over polenta or add 4 medium potatoes, cut into wedges, to the baking dish with the mushrooms.

LAMB SHANK AND EGGPLANT CASSEROLE

This is a great one-dish meal.

MAKES 6 SERVINGS

3 lamb shanks
1 large eggplant, peeled
  and cubed
1/2 to 1 head cabbage, sliced
1 (28-ounce) can diced
  tomatoes

1 teaspoon salt
1 teaspoon Maggi seasoning
  (optional)
1 1/2 cups uncooked rice

Preheat the oven to 325 degrees. Place the lamb shanks in a very large casserole. Add the eggplant, then the cabbage. Pour the tomatoes over the top and season with the salt and Maggi seasoning. Bake, covered, for 3 to 3 1/2 hours. Stir the rice into the liquid around the shanks. Bake, uncovered, for 30 minutes longer.

NOTE: *If you do not have a large enough casserole, divide the shanks and ingredients between 2 smaller casseroles.*

LAMB SHISH KABOBS WITH RED WINE SAUCE

MAKES 8 SERVINGS

1 cup dry red wine
3/4 cup vegetable oil
1/4 cup ketchup
2 tablespoons vinegar
2 garlic cloves, crushed
2 teaspoons each sugar and
    Worcestershire sauce
1 teaspoon salt
1 teaspoon marjoram, crushed
1 teaspoon rosemary, crushed

4 pounds lean boneless lamb,
    cut into 1 1/2-inch cubes
30 large mushroom caps
3 large red bell peppers,
    cut into squares
3 large yellow bell peppers,
    cut into squares
16 cherry tomatoes
Hot cooked rice
Red Wine Sauce

Combine the first 10 ingredients in a bowl and mix well. Combine the lamb and mushrooms with the marinade in a large sealable plastic bag or a shallow glass dish. Marinate, covered, in the refrigerator for 2 hours. Remove the meat and mushrooms from the marinade, reserving the marinade. Preheat the grill or broiler and coat the grill rack or broiler pan with nonstick cooking spray. Alternate the meat cubes, mushrooms, red and yellow peppers, and cherry tomatoes on 8 large metal skewers. Boil the marinade for 1 minute in a small saucepan. Grill or broil the kabobs to the desired degree of doneness, turning and basting frequently with the marinade. Remove the meat and vegetables from the skewers and serve over hot cooked rice. Top with the Red Wine Sauce.

MEDITERRANEAN GRILLED LEG OF LAMB

MAKES 6 TO 8 SERVINGS

1/2 cup olive oil
1/2 cup fresh lemon juice
2 tablespoons oregano
1 teaspoon salt
Pepper to taste

1 (6-pound) leg of lamb,
    boned and butterflied
8 garlic cloves, peeled
Sliced garlic and lemon wedges
    sprinkled with oregano

Combine the first 5 ingredients in a small bowl and mix well. Combine the lamb and lemon juice mixture in a large sealable plastic bag or a shallow baking dish. Marinate, covered, in the refrigerator for 24 hours or longer, turning the meat occasionally. Cut small slits in the meat and insert the garlic cloves. Grill over hot coals for 15 to 20 minutes per side. Let stand for 10 minutes before slicing. Garnish each serving with the sliced garlic and a lemon wedge.

RED WINE SAUCE

MAKES 3 1/2 TO 4 CUPS

4 teaspoons chopped
    onion
1/2 tablespoon butter
1 1/2 cups dry red wine
2 (14-ounce) cans beef
    broth
1/2 cup (1 stick) butter,
    softened
1/4 cup all-purpose flour
2 teaspoons chopped
    parsley
1/2 teaspoon pepper

Sauté the onion in 1/2 tablespoon butter in a large skillet until tender. Add the wine and simmer until reduced to 1 cup. Stir in the broth. Stir 1/2 cup butter and the flour together in a bowl to make a smooth paste or roux. Stir the roux, parsley, and pepper into the broth mixture and cook until thickened, stirring constantly. Serve hot.

LAMB MARRAKECH

MAKES 8 SERVINGS

3¹/2 pounds lean boneless
    lamb, cut into
    1¹/2-inch cubes
2 large onions, finely chopped
5 garlic cloves, chopped
1 tablespoon salt
5 large ripe tomatoes, peeled,
    seeded, and chopped

1 cup raisins, soaked in sherry
1 teaspoon red pepper flakes
1/2 teaspoon ground allspice
1 teaspoon turmeric
1¹/2 cups slivered almonds,
    toasted
Chopped parsley and
    additional almonds

Preheat the oven to 350 degrees. Place the lamb, onions, garlic, and salt in a 5- to 6-quart casserole. Bake, covered, for 1¹/2 hours or until brown. Add the tomatoes, raisins, red pepper flakes, allspice, turmeric, and slivered almonds. Bake, covered, for 1¹/2 hours longer or until the lamb is tender. Skim off the fat and refrigerate or freeze for later use. Garnish with the parsley and almonds. Serve with Rice with Pine Nuts on page 217.

BRINED AND RUBBED PORK LOIN

MAKES 12 SERVINGS

1 cup packed brown sugar
1 cup kosher salt
Water
1 (5-pound) boned and tied
    pork loin roast
2 teaspoons kosher salt
1 teaspoon pepper

1 teaspoon dry mustard
1 teaspoon ground ginger
1 teaspoon granulated garlic
    or garlic powder
1/2 teaspoon hot Hungarian
    paprika (optional)
Wine or apple juice (optional)

Combine the brown sugar, 1 cup salt and enough water to cover the roast in a very large bowl or other nonmetallic container, stirring until the sugar and salt are dissolved. Add the roast. Brine, covered, in the refrigerator for 24 hours. Preheat the oven to 425 degrees. Remove the roast from the brine and cut off the string, separating the meat into 2 portions. Combine 2 teaspoons salt, the pepper, dry mustard, ginger, garlic, and paprika and rub over the entire surface of the meat. Place the pork on a rack in a shallow baking pan and place in the oven. Turn the oven temperature down to 325 degrees and roast, uncovered, for 2 hours or until a meat thermometer reads 155 to 160 degrees. Let the meat stand for 10 minutes before slicing. Serve on a heated platter. Deglaze the pan with wine to serve with the roast, if desired.

Fiji Island Pork Tenderloin

Makes 6 servings

2 cups dry sherry
$1/2$ cup soy sauce
$1/4$ cup dark rum
$1/4$ cup lime juice
2 tablespoons brown sugar
2 tablespoons minced garlic
$1^1/2$ to 2 teaspoons finely chopped
    fresh ginger
2 to $2^1/2$ pounds pork tenderloin
    (2 or 3 tenderloins)

Combine the sherry, soy sauce, rum, lime juice, brown sugar, garlic, and ginger in a large sealable plastic bag and add the tenderloins. Marinate in the refrigerator for 1 to 2 days, turning the bag occasionally. Remove the meat from the marinade, reserving the marinade. Boil the marinade for 1 minute in the microwave or a small saucepan. Grill or broil the pork over medium-high heat for 25 to 30 minutes or until a meat thermometer reads 155 to 160 degrees, turning and basting frequently with the marinade. Remove to a cutting board. Let stand, covered with foil, for 10 minutes before slicing. Slice and serve with the remaining marinade, if desired.

APPLE MUSTARD SAUCE

MAKES 2¹/₂ TO 3 CUPS

2 tablespoons butter
1 onion, coarsely
  chopped
4 to 6 Jonathan apples,
  coarsely chopped
1 cup heavy cream
1 tablespoon Dijon
  mustard
¹/₄ teaspoon salt
¹/₄ teaspoon pepper
¹/₄ teaspoon ground
  nutmeg

Melt the butter in a
large heavy saucepan over
medium heat. Add the
onion and cook until tender.
Add the apples and cook
for about 5 minutes or just
until tender. Stir in the
cream and bring to a boil.
Reduce the heat and simmer,
uncovered, for 5 minutes,
stirring constantly. Stir in the
Dijon mustard. Season with
the salt, pepper, and nutmeg.

ROAST PORK LOIN WITH APPLE MUSTARD SAUCE

MAKES 4 TO 6 SERVINGS

1 (2- to 2¹/₂-pound) boneless pork loin roast
¹/₄ teaspoon salt
¹/₄ teaspoon pepper
Apple Mustard Sauce

Preheat the oven to 325 degrees. Rub the roast with the salt and
pepper and place on a rack in a shallow roasting pan. Roast for 1¹/₄ to
1¹/₂ hours or until a meat thermometer reads 155 to 160 degrees.
Remove the roast to a cutting board and let stand, covered with foil,
for 15 minutes before serving. Slice the meat and arrange on a platter.
Pour the Apple Mustard Sauce over the meat and serve.

PORK CHOPS AND SAUERKRAUT IN CREAMY CARAWAY GRAVY

Quick & Easy

*So easy, so good! This recipe was originally from the
director and producer of* True Grit *made while on location in
Montrose, Colorado, in 1967.*

MAKES 4 SERVINGS

1 tablespoon vegetable oil
  or butter
4 (³/₄-inch-thick) boneless
  pork chops, trimmed
1 (10-ounce) jar sauerkraut,
  drained

1 teaspoon caraway seeds
2 cups sour cream, at room
  temperature
Paprika

Preheat the oven to 350 degrees. Heat the oil in a large skillet
over medium-high heat. Add the chops and brown well, about 3 to
4 minutes, turning once. Transfer the chops to a baking dish. Divide
the sauerkraut evenly over the chops and sprinkle with the caraway
seeds. Top each chop with about ¹/₂ cup sour cream. Sprinkle
generously with paprika. Bake for 25 to 30 minutes or until
golden brown on top. Serve hot.

GARLIC-AND-BASIL-GRILLED PORK TENDERLOIN

Quick & Easy

MAKES 6 SERVINGS

8 garlic cloves
1 (1$\frac{1}{2}$- to 2-pound) package pork tenderloins
   (2 tenderloins)
8 to 10 fresh basil leaves, julienned
$\frac{1}{4}$ cup olive oil

Slice the garlic, then cut into thin strips. Cut small slits about 1 inch apart in the tenderloins and insert the garlic. Place the tenderloins in a shallow glass dish and top with the basil. Drizzle with the olive oil and rub over the surface of the meat. Let stand, covered, for 20 minutes at room temperature or 3 to 6 hours in the refrigerator. Return to room temperature before cooking. Preheat the grill and coat the grill rack with nonstick cooking spray, if desired. Grill over high heat for about 5 to 6 minutes per side, or until a meat thermometer reads 155 to 160 degrees, turning frequently. Remove to a cutting board and let stand, covered, for 10 minutes before slicing.

NOTE: *Fruit sauces such as rhubarb, raspberry, or apple are a good accompaniment to the pork. Simply cook the fruit to proper thickness and add sugar to taste.*

Mountain-Grilled Country Ribs

Makes 6 to 8 servings

3 to 5 pounds country-style
  pork ribs
1/2 cup water
1/4 cup red wine vinegar
1/4 cup (1/2 stick) butter
1 onion, sliced
1 lemon, sliced
2 tablespoons sugar

1 tablespoon prepared
  mustard
1 1/2 teaspoons salt
1/2 teaspoon black pepper
1/4 teaspoon cayenne pepper
1/2 cup ketchup
2 tablespoons Worcestershire
  sauce

Preheat the oven to 350 degrees. Place the ribs in a shallow baking dish or roasting pan and cover with foil, piercing the foil with a fork to allow the steam to escape. Bake for 1 to 1 1/2 hours or just until tender. Combine the water, vinegar, butter, onion, lemon, sugar, mustard, salt, black pepper, and cayenne pepper in a saucepan and mix well. Bring to a boil. Reduce the heat and simmer for 20 minutes. Add the ketchup and Worcestershire sauce and bring to a boil. Remove from the heat. Drain the ribs after baking and place in a glass bowl or baking dish. Pour the sauce over the ribs and marinate, covered, in the refrigerator for 24 hours. Preheat the grill and coat the grill rack with nonstick cooking spray, if desired. Remove the ribs from the marinade and boil the marinade in a small saucepan for several minutes. Place the ribs on the grill rack and grill over medium-high heat for 5 to 10 minutes, turning and basting frequently with the sauce. Serve the remaining sauce alongside the ribs.

Sweet-and-Sour Pork Ragout

Makes 10 to 12 servings

3 pounds boneless pork loin, cut into 1-inch cubes
24 dried apricots
1 cup raisins
1 cup dry red wine
1 cup red wine vinegar
3 tablespoons chopped fresh dill weed, or 1 tablespoon dried dill weed
3 tablespoons chopped fresh mint
1 tablespoon dried thyme
1 teaspoon ground cumin

1 teaspoon freshly ground pepper
Salt to taste
1/2 cup all-purpose flour
1/3 cup olive oil
4 shallots, minced
1/2 cup dry white wine
2 cups chicken stock
2 bay leaves
1/4 cup honey
Additional dry white wine
Additional chicken stock

Combine the pork, apricots, raisins, red wine, vinegar, dill weed, mint, thyme, cumin, pepper, and salt in a large sealable plastic bag or glass bowl and mix well. Marinate, covered, in the refrigerator for 24 hours, stirring occasionally. Preheat the oven to 350 degrees. Remove the pork from the marinade and reserve the fruit and the liquid in separate bowls. Pat the pork dry on paper towels, then coat with the flour.

Heat the olive oil in a large skillet. Add the pork, a few pieces at a time, and cook until brown. Place the pork in a large baking dish. Drain all but 1 tablespoon oil from the skillet. Add the shallots and sauté over medium heat for 5 minutes. Add the reserved liquid, white wine, stock, bay leaves, and honey and bring to a boil, stirring to loosen the browned bits from the bottom of the pan. Cook until reduced by about 1/4. Stir in the reserved fruit. Pour over the pork.

Bake, covered, for 1 hour and 15 minutes, stirring occasionally and adding additional white wine or chicken stock, if needed. Bake, uncovered, for 30 to 45 minutes longer or until thickened. Remove the bay leaves.

CAMPFIRE DINNER

A very hearty, satisfying campfire meal

MAKES 2 TO 4 SERVINGS

3 russet potatoes, cubed
4 carrots, sliced
1 celery rib, sliced
1 onion, chopped
4 garlic cloves, minced
1 tablespoon oregano
1 tablespoon marjoram
1 tablespoon thyme
1 teaspoon basil
1 teaspoon paprika
1 teaspoon salt
1 teaspoon pepper
3 tablespoons butter, cut into 6 pieces
1 to 2 pounds link smoked sausage or kielbasa,
    casings removed and sausage cut into 1-inch pieces

Combine the potatoes, carrots, celery, onion, and garlic in a bowl. Stir together the oregano, marjoram, thyme, basil, paprika, salt, and pepper in a small bowl. Place three 36-inch-long sheets of heavy foil on top of each other to create a triple layer. Rub the top sheet of foil with 2 pieces of the butter. Place 2 more pieces of the butter on the foil and top with about half the sausage, then half the vegetables. Sprinkle with half the seasoning mixture. Repeat the layering of the sausage, vegetables, and seasonings. Place the remaining 2 pieces of butter on top. Wrap the foil around the vegetables, double folding the edges to seal tightly. Place the foil packet in a bed of hot campfire coals, completely covering with the coals. Cook for 20 minutes. Stir the coals and turn the packet over, being careful not to puncture the foil. Cover with hot coals and cook for 20 minutes longer.

NOTE: *Cut the sausage, prepare the vegetables, measure and combine the seasonings at home, and pack in sealable plastic bags.*

BEEF, BLACK BEAN, AND SAUSAGE ENCHILADAS

Quick & Easy

MAKES 6 SERVINGS

1 pound bulk pork sausage
1 pound ground beef
Salt to taste
1 1/2 cups cooked black beans
1 1/2 cups taco sauce
1 (15-ounce) can enchilada sauce
6 large flour tortillas
1/2 cup chopped onion
16 ounces cheese, shredded
1/2 head iceberg lettuce, shredded
Sour cream
Salsa
Sliced green onions

Cook the sausage and ground beef in a large skillet until brown, stirring until crumbly; drain. Season with salt. Add the beans and taco sauce and bring to a boil. Reduce the heat and simmer for a few minutes.

Preheat the oven to 350 degrees. Pour 2 to 3 tablespoons of the enchilada sauce into a 9×13-inch baking dish and spread over the bottom. Pour the remaining enchilada sauce into a pie plate. Dip a tortilla in the sauce, completely covering the tortilla. Place the tortilla on a plate and top with the meat mixture, onion, cheese, and lettuce. Roll to enclose the filling and place in the baking dish. Repeat the process with the remaining tortillas, meat, onion, cheese, and lettuce, first dipping each tortilla into the enchilada sauce. Pour the remaining enchilada sauce over the rolled tortillas. Bake for 20 minutes. Serve with sour cream, salsa, and green onions.

CASSOULET

This recipe was originally made for the Colorado Chapter of the American Institute of Wine and Food's 1994 Beaujolais Nouveau dinner.

MAKES 15 SERVINGS

BOUQUET GARNI

To make a bouquet garni, place 4 unpeeled garlic cloves, 2 bay leaves, 6 sprigs of parsley, and 1/2 teaspoon thyme in a cheesecloth bag and tie.

The cassoulet can be frozen in convenient meal-size portions without the crumb topping. Bring to room temperature before heating and add the topping just before baking.

SPICE RUB

MAKES 2 1/2 TO 3 CUPS

1 garlic clove, mashed
1 teaspoon salt
1/4 teaspoon rubbed sage
1/8 teaspoon pepper
1/8 teaspoon ground
   bay leaf
Pinch of ground allspice

Combine the garlic, salt, sage, pepper, bay leaf, and allspice in a bowl and mix well.

---

1 (1 1/2-pound) boneless pork
   loin roast
2 1/2 quarts water
1 1/4 pounds dried white beans
6 ounces salt pork, rinsed
1/4 cup sliced onion
1 Bouquet Garni
1 frozen duckling, thawed
   and cut into pieces
1 1/4 pounds boneless lamb,
   cubed
1 carrot, chopped
1/2 large onion, chopped
1/2 pound link chorizo,
   kielbasa or andouille
   sausage, casings removed
1 1/4 cups beef stock
1 (8-ounce) can tomatoes
1/4 cup dry white vermouth
3 tablespoons tomato purée
1/4 teaspoon thyme
1 bay leaf
Salt and pepper to taste
1 cup dry bread crumbs
1/4 cup chopped fresh parsley
2 tablespoons butter, melted

Rub the Spice Rub over the pork loin. Chill, covered, overnight. Bring the water to a boil in a saucepan. Add the beans and boil for 10 minutes. Remove from the heat and soak for 3 hours. Preheat the oven to 325 degrees. Roast the pork loin in a baking pan for 1 1/2 hours or until a meat thermometer reads 155 to 160 degrees. Remove the pork to a cutting board and let stand, covered, for 10 minutes. Cut the pork into cubes. Reserve the pork drippings. Place the salt pork in a saucepan with water and boil for 1 minute. Cut into 1-inch cubes. Add the salt pork, 1/4 cup onion, and the Bouquet Garni to the beans and cook for 1 hour. Drain, reserving the liquid; discard the Bouquet Garni.

Broil or grill the duck for 10 minutes per side or just until brown and the fat is rendered. Brown the lamb with the carrot and onion half in a large skillet. Cut the sausage into 1-inch pieces. Add a small amount of the reserved liquid, reserved pork drippings, sausage and the next 6 ingredients to the lamb and bring to a boil. Pour into a 6-quart stockpot and add the cubed pork, duck, beans, and enough reserved liquid to cover. Cook until the duck falls off the bone. Remove the duck and let stand until cool. Remove the duck meat from the bones and return the meat to the stockpot. Season with salt and pepper. Remove the bay leaf.

Preheat the oven to 375 degrees. Spoon the cassoulet into a large baking dish or roasting pan. Sprinkle a mixture of the bread crumbs, parsley, and butter over the cassoulet. Bake in the upper third of the oven for 20 minutes or until a light crust has formed. Break the crust and baste the crust with liquid from the cassoulet. Decrease the oven temperature to 350 degrees and bake for 20 minutes or until a light crust has formed.

FAMOUS BUCKHORN
ELK ROAST

This recipe was submitted for all the students who enjoyed the
elk dinners at the Buckhorn in Laramie, Wyoming.

MAKES 12 SERVINGS

1 (5- to 8-pound) elk, venison, or antelope roast
1 to 2 tablespoons olive oil
1 (10-ounce) can tomato soup
1 (10-ounce) can cream of mushroom soup
1/2 cup ketchup
1/2 cup Heinz 57 steak sauce
1/2 cup A.1. steak sauce
1/4 cup Worcestershire sauce
1 teaspoon salt
1 teaspoon pepper
1 large onion, sliced into rings
1 cup chopped carrots
1 cup chopped celery

During the 1970s, the owner of a local establishment in Laramie prepared a free elk roast dinner for UW students. The students looked forward to this annual event and still talk about it when they get together for reunions.

Preheat the oven to 350 degrees. Brown the roast in the olive oil in a large heavy roasting pan, searing on all sides. Combine the soups, ketchup, Heinz 57 sauce, A.1. sauce, Worcestershire sauce, salt, and pepper in a bowl and mix well. Pour over the roast and add the onion, carrots, and celery. Roast, covered, for 2 to 3 hours, or until very tender, basting every 30 minutes with the sauce.

NOTE: *The roast can be cooked in a slow cooker on Low for 8 hours. Serve with mashed potatoes. The sauce makes perfect gravy.*

Après a Day in the Snowies: A Mexican Supper with Friends

Rising regally from the high plains of southeastern Wyoming are the Snowy Range Mountains, affectionately known as the "Snowies." This is the perfect place to snowshoe, ski, snowmobile, or hike in a pristine winter landscape, warming body and spirit afterward with a zesty Mexican supper with friends.

The Menu

EASY MARGARITAS

TEX-MEX AVOCADO EGG ROLLS WITH
SPICY BLACK OLIVE SALSA

SHRIMP CEVICHE WITH TORTILLA CHIPS

SOUTHWEST CHICKEN AND CHORIZO WITH
BLACK BEAN SAUCE*

ORANGE FLAN

*pictured recipes

Poultry

FLORENTINE CHICKEN WITH CURRY SAUCE

1 cup uncooked rice
1/2 cup hot water
2 tablespoons butter or margarine
3 tablespoons all-purpose flour
1/2 cup nonfat dry milk
1 (14-ounce) can low-fat chicken broth
2 tablespoons curry powder
3 garlic cloves, minced
1/2 teaspoon salt
1/2 teaspoon pepper
1/4 cup low-fat mayonnaise
4 cups baby spinach
1 pound boneless skinless chicken breast tenders
1/3 cup freshly grated Parmesan cheese

Preheat the oven to 350 degrees. Spread the rice in a 9×13-inch baking dish coated with nonstick cooking spray. Pour the water over the rice and cover. Melt the butter in a large saucepan over medium heat. Add the flour and cook until thickened, stirring constantly. Stir in a mixture of the dry milk and broth. Bring to a boil, stirring constantly. Add the curry powder, garlic, salt, and pepper. Cook for 1 minute. Remove from the heat and stir in the mayonnaise. Place the spinach on top of the rice. Spoon half the sauce over the spinach, spreading evenly. Top with the chicken, remaining sauce, and the cheese. Bake, covered with a sheet of foil coated with nonstick cooking spray, for 45 minutes. Bake, uncovered, for 15 minutes longer or until the rice is tender and the chicken is cooked through.

HONEYED CHICKEN TERIYAKI
WITH EGG FOO YUNG

MAKES 4 SERVINGS

4 boneless skinless chicken
  breasts
2 eggs, beaten
1/2 cup all-purpose flour
Vegetable oil for frying
1/3 cup soy sauce
1/3 cup honey

1 tablespoon dry sherry
1 tablespoon minced garlic
1 tablespoon minced fresh
  ginger
2 tablespoons sesame seeds
Egg Foo Young

Cut the chicken into 1-inch chunks. Dip the chicken into the eggs,
then the flour, coating completely. Preheat the oven to 250 degrees. Pour
about 1 inch of oil into a large heavy skillet and heat over medium-
high heat. Add the chicken, 6 to 8 chunks at a time, to the hot oil and
fry for 3 to 4 minutes per side. Remove to paper towels to drain.
Combine the soy sauce, honey, sherry, garlic, and ginger in a small
saucepan and cook over medium heat for 5 minutes, stirring
occasionally. Place a wire rack on a foil-lined baking sheet and arrange
the chicken chunks on the rack. Brush with the soy sauce mixture.
Bake for 10 minutes. Remove from the oven and brush with the soy
sauce mixture again. Sprinkle with the sesame seeds. Bake for
10 minutes longer. Serve with Egg Foo Yung.

EGG FOO YUNG

MAKES 4 SERVINGS

1/4 cup chicken broth
1 tablespoon cornstarch
3/4 cup chicken broth
3 tablespoons soy sauce
2 teaspoons sugar
1 teaspoon vegetable oil
1 carrot, finely chopped

3 scallions, finely chopped
1/4 pound bean sprouts
2 tablespoons all-purpose
  flour
5 eggs, beaten
1 teaspoon vegetable oil

Combine 1/4 cup broth with the cornstarch in a small bowl and
stir until the cornstarch is dissolved. Combine 3/4 cup broth, the soy
sauce, and sugar in a small saucepan and bring to a boil. Stir in the
cornstarch mixture. Reduce the heat and simmer until thickened,
stirring frequently. Keep warm. Heat 1 teaspoon oil in a skillet. Add
the carrot and half the scallions and sauté for 2 minutes. Add the bean
sprouts and sauté for 3 minutes. Combine the vegetables with the
flour and eggs in a bowl and mix well. Heat 1 teaspoon oil in a skillet.
Pour enough batter into the skillet to form a 3-inch pancake. Cook for
2 minutes on each side. Repeat the procedure with the remaining
batter. Serve with the sauce and remaining scallions.

EASY PARTY CHICKEN

Quick & Easy

You can put this in the oven and go enjoy your guests.

MAKES 6 TO 8 SERVINGS

1 (5-ounce) jar chipped
    dried beef
6 to 8 boneless skinless
    chicken breasts

2 (10-ounce) cans cream
    of mushroom soup
2 cups sour cream
1 teaspoon tarragon, crushed

Preheat the oven to 275 degrees. Layer the beef in a 9×13-inch baking dish coated with nonstick cooking spray. Arrange the chicken over the beef. Stir together the remaining ingredients in a large bowl and pour over the chicken. Bake, uncovered, for 3 hours.

BASQUE CHICKEN

MAKES 4 TO 5 SERVINGS

1 garlic clove, crushed
1/4 cup olive oil or butter, or a
    combination
1 whole chicken, or 3 to
    4 pounds chicken pieces
Salt and pepper to taste
1 (14-ounce) can diced
    tomatoes, drained,
    or 1 pound fresh tomatoes,
    peeled and chopped

1 large red bell pepper,
    cut into strips
1 large jalapeño chile,
    cut into strips
1/4 pound diced ham
2 garlic cloves, minced
1/4 cup dry white wine
    or vermouth
Tabasco sauce to taste
Chopped fresh parsley

Rub the inside of a 5-quart stockpot with the crushed garlic. Add the olive oil and heat. Season the chicken with salt and pepper and add to the stockpot. Sauté until brown on all sides. Add the tomatoes, bell pepper, jalapeño chile, ham, minced garlic, and wine. Bring to a boil. Reduce the heat and simmer, covered, for about 20 minutes. Simmer, uncovered, for 20 minutes longer or until the sauce is reduced by 1/2. Taste and add Tabasco sauce, if desired. Remove the chicken to a serving platter and garnish with parsley. Pour the sauce into a bowl to serve alongside. Serve with Basque Bread (page 54).

NOTE: *This recipe is easily doubled, using chicken pieces. May also be frozen.*

ITALIAN CHICKEN "CORDON BLEU"

MAKES 6 SERVINGS

6 boneless skinless chicken
  breasts
6 thin slices boiled ham
6 slices mozzarella cheese
1 tomato, seeded and chopped
1 teaspoon rubbed sage
3 tablespoons grated
  Parmesan cheese

$2/3$ cup dry bread crumbs
2 tablespoons snipped fresh
  parsley
6 tablespoons butter, melted
Hot cooked orzo
Cherry tomatoes
Additional fresh parsley

Preheat the oven to 350 degrees. Place the chicken between 2 pieces
of plastic wrap. Pound each piece lightly from the center out to about
a 5x5-inch square. Remove the top piece of plastic wrap. Place a ham
slice and a mozzarella slice on top of each chicken piece, trimming to
fit. Top each with tomato and sage. Roll up, tucking in the sides and
securing with wooden picks. Combine the Parmesan cheese, bread
crumbs, and 2 tablespoons parsley. Dip each roll-up in the melted
butter. Roll in the crumb mixture, coating completely. Place the roll-ups
in a shallow baking pan, seam side down. Pour any remaining butter
over the chicken and sprinkle with any remaining crumb mixture.
Bake for 40 to 45 minutes. Serve on a bed of orzo. Garnish with the
cherry tomatoes and parsley.

JUST PEACHY CHICKEN

MAKES 6 SERVINGS

1¼ to 1½ pounds boneless skinless
   chicken breast tenders
Salt and pepper to taste
1 tablespoon butter
1 tablespoon vegetable oil
1 large onion, halved and thinly sliced
1 large green bell pepper, cut into strips
1 (29-ounce) can syrup-pack peach slices
1 tablespoon cornstarch
2 tablespoons soy sauce
3 tablespoons vinegar
2 medium tomatoes, cut into wedges
Hot cooked rice

Season the chicken with salt and pepper. Heat the butter and oil in a large skillet. Add the chicken and brown lightly on all sides. Remove the chicken and keep warm. Add the onion and bell pepper to the skillet and cook until the onion is translucent. Drain the peaches, reserving the syrup. Add water to the reserved syrup to equal 1 cup. Combine the syrup, cornstarch, soy sauce, and vinegar in a bowl and stir until the cornstarch is dissolved. Return the chicken to the skillet. Add the syrup mixture and bring to a boil. Reduce the heat and cook until the sauce is thickened and clear, stirring constantly. Add the peach slices and tomatoes and cook over low heat for 5 minutes or until heated through, stirring occasionally. Serve over hot cooked rice.

WHOLE ROASTED CHICKEN WITH SWEET BASIL-GARLIC RUB

MAKES 4 TO 6 SERVINGS

Sweet Basil-Garlic Rub
1 (4- to 5-pound) whole chicken, rinsed and patted dry
2 to 3 tablespoons all-purpose flour (optional)
2 tablespoons water (optional)

Preheat the oven to 325 degrees. Rub the Sweet Basil-Garlic Rub on the outside and under the skin of the chicken, loosening the skin gently with your fingers. Place the chicken, breast side up, in a shallow roasting pan coated with nonstick cooking spray. Roast for 1½ hours (20 minutes per pound) or until the leg moves easily.

Remove the chicken from the pan and reserve the pan drippings. Let the chicken stand for 10 minutes before slicing. Combine the flour and water in a bowl and stir until of a paste consistency. Whisk into the pan drippings. Bring to a boil. Reduce the heat and simmer until thickened, stirring to loosen the browned bits from the bottom of the pan. Serve the gravy alongside the chicken.

NOTE: *You may bake the chicken on parchment paper to prevent sticking.*

SWEET BASIL-GARLIC RUB

MAKES ½ CUP

¼ cup extra-virgin olive oil
1 heaping tablespoon sugar
1 to 2 tablespoons salt
1 tablespoon fresh lemon juice
3 garlic cloves, minced
2 teaspoons basil
2 teaspoons tarragon
1 teaspoon pepper
½ teaspoon paprika

Combine the olive oil, sugar, salt, lemon juice, garlic, basil, tarragon, pepper, and paprika in a small bowl and mix to form a paste.

Mediterranean-Stuffed Chicken Breasts

Makes 4 servings

1 tablespoon olive oil
1/2 cup finely chopped onion
1 1/2 teaspoons minced garlic
1/2 cup pitted kalamata olives,
  cut into thin strips
1/4 cup pine nuts
1/2 cup oil-pack sun-dried
  tomatoes, drained and
  cut into thin strips

4 ounces feta cheese,
  crumbled
2 tablespoons freshly grated
  Parmesan cheese
1 tablespoon dried crumbled
  marjoram
1 tablespoon olive oil
4 boneless skinless
  chicken breasts

Preheat the oven to 350 degrees. Heat 1 tablespoon olive oil in a large ovenproof skillet over medium heat. Add the onion and sauté until tender. Add the garlic and cook for 1 minute, stirring constantly. Spoon the mixture into a bowl and let stand until cool. Add the olives, pine nuts, tomatoes, cheeses, and marjoram to the onion mixture, stirring until combined. Slit the chicken lengthwise to form a pocket and fill each with 1/4 cup of the onion mixture. Heat 1 tablespoon olive oil in the skillet over medium-high heat. Add the prepared chicken and cook until brown on all sides. Mound any remaining onion mixture around the chicken. Place the skillet in the oven and bake for 12 to 15 minutes or until the chicken is cooked through. Do not overbake. Serve with penne pasta. Johannisberg riesling is a good wine choice.

Chicken with Capers, Olives, and Dried Plums

Makes 10 servings

5 boneless skinless chicken breasts
5 boneless skinless chicken thighs
1/2 cup red wine vinegar or rice vinegar
1/2 cup olive oil
10 garlic cloves, minced
1 1/4 cups pitted dried plums, chopped
3/4 cup pitted or pimento-stuffed green olives
1/2 cup capers plus 1 tablespoon liquid
3 1/2 tablespoons oregano
5 large bay leaves
Salt and pepper to taste
3/4 cup packed brown sugar
1 cup dry white wine
1/4 cup chopped fresh cilantro

Combine the chicken, vinegar, olive oil, garlic, dried plums, olives, capers, oregano, bay leaves, salt, and pepper in a large sealable plastic bag. Marinate in the refrigerator overnight, turning occasionally. Preheat the oven to 350 degrees. Remove the chicken from the marinade and arrange in a large baking dish. Pour the marinade over the chicken and sprinkle with the brown sugar. Pour the wine around the chicken. Bake for 30 minutes or until the chicken is cooked through. Serve with brown rice or basmati rice and garnish with the cilantro.

Whatever happened to prunes? The California Dried Plum Board is banking on a new term, *dried plum*, instead. Consumer tests have indicated that the latter term makes the product sound better tasting, fresher, and more contemporary than the traditional term, *prune*. But don't worry about finding this wholesome product at the supermarket—to avoid confusion, both terms appear on the labeling.

SOUTHWEST CHICKEN AND CHORIZO WITH BLACK BEAN SAUCE

MAKES 8 TO 10 SERVINGS

BLACK BEAN SAUCE

MAKES ABOUT 5 CUPS

2 (15-ounce) cans
    Southwest-seasoned
    black beans, drained
1 1/2 cups chicken stock
2 tablespoons oyster
    sauce
1 tablespoon brown sugar
2 tablespoons hoisin
    sauce
1/8 to 1/4 teaspoon ancho
    chile powder
Dash of Mexican-style
    chili powder
3 tablespoons
    vegetable oil

Combine the beans,
stock, oyster sauce, sugar,
hoisin sauce, ancho chile
powder, and chili powder
in a blender and purée.
Heat the oil in a large
skillet and add the bean
mixture. Cook over low
heat for about 10 minutes
or until thickened, stirring
constantly.

8 to 10 boneless skinless chicken breasts
1 cup olive oil
1 cup light soy sauce
1 cup marsala
2 tablespoons dry mustard
2 teaspoons lemon pepper
2 teaspoons ground ginger
2 teaspoons diced green onions
    (optional)
Black Bean Sauce
4 to 5 chorizo sausage links, grilled,
    sliced, and kept warm
1 (16-ounce) jar chunky green chile salsa
8 ounces Monterey Jack cheese, shredded
8 ounces Cheddar cheese, shredded
Lime slice twists, avocado slices, chopped
    fresh cilantro, chopped fresh chives,
    green onion frills

Combine the chicken, olive oil, soy sauce, marsala, dry mustard,
lemon pepper, ginger, and 2 teaspoons green onions in a large sealable
plastic bag. Marinate in the refrigerator for 4 hours or overnight, turning
occasionally. Preheat the grill and coat the grill rack with nonstick
cooking spray, if desired. Remove the chicken from the marinade,
reserving the marinade. Grill the chicken for 5 minutes per side or
until the juices run clear, turning and brushing frequently with
the marinade.

Preheat the broiler. Spoon several tablespoons of the Black Bean
Sauce onto 8 to 10 ovenproof plates. Top each with a chicken breast
and several chorizo slices. Spoon 3 tablespoons of the green chile
salsa over each chicken breast. Sprinkle generously with the cheeses.
Place the plates on a large baking sheet and broil until the cheeses
melt. Garnish each plate with lime, avocado, cilantro, chives, and a
frilled green onion.

CHICKEN IN CHILI SAUCE

MAKES 4 TO 6 SERVINGS

1 (3- to 4-pound) whole
   chicken, cut up
1/4 cup shortening or lard
1/4 cup all-purpose flour

1/4 cup chili powder
1/2 teaspoon garlic powder
1/4 teaspoon ground cumin
Salt to taste

Place the chicken in a large Dutch oven or other large pan and cover with water. Bring to a boil and simmer for 40 minutes. Remove the chicken and reserve 4 cups of the liquid. Heat the shortening in a large skillet or Dutch oven. Add the flour and cook until brown, stirring constantly. Stir in the chili powder and reserved liquid and mix well. Add the garlic powder, cumin, and salt and bring to a boil. Reduce the heat and cook until thickened, stirring constantly. Simmer for 20 minutes, stirring occasionally. Add the chicken pieces and simmer until heated through. Serve with refried beans, hot cooked rice, or fideos pasta.

CHICKEN MADEIRA

MAKES 4 SERVINGS

1 rounded tablespoon
   sesame seeds
2 tablespoons olive oil
1 small onion, coarsely
   chopped
4 mushrooms, coarsely
   chopped

4 boneless skinless chicken
   breasts, cut into 8 pieces
2 tablespoons all-purpose flour
2 tablespoons olive oil
1 cup madeira
Chopped fresh parsley
Orange slices

Toast the sesame seeds in a dry pan over medium heat, stirring constantly. Heat 2 tablespoons olive oil in a large skillet. Add the onion and mushrooms and sauté over medium-high heat until golden brown. Remove the mixture to a bowl. Pound the chicken to 1/4-inch thickness. Coat with the flour. Heat 2 tablespoons olive oil in the skillet and sauté the chicken until golden brown on all sides and cooked through. Return the onion mixture to the skillet and add the sesame seeds and wine. Cook until hot and slightly thickened. Garnish with parsley and orange slices. Serve immediately with steamed rice.

DRUNKEN CHICKEN

MAKES 8 SERVINGS

8 boneless skinless
   chicken breasts
Salt and pepper to taste
1 cup all-purpose flour
3 tablespoons butter
2 tablespoons olive oil
1 large onion, finely chopped
1 (14-ounce) can diced
   tomatoes
2 tablespoons minced fresh
   parsley

1/2 teaspoon ground
   cinnamon
1/4 teaspoon ground cloves
1/2 cup packed light
   brown sugar
1/2 cup golden raisins
1 1/2 cups dry sherry or
   vermouth
1/2 cup slivered almonds

Season the chicken with salt and pepper and coat with the flour. Heat the butter and olive oil in a large skillet and brown the chicken on all sides. Remove the chicken to a 3-quart casserole. Preheat the oven to 375 degrees. Cook the onion in the skillet until translucent. Stir in the tomatoes, parsley, cinnamon, cloves, brown sugar, raisins, and sherry and bring to a boil. Reduce the heat and simmer, uncovered, for 20 minutes, stirring occasionally. Pour over the chicken and sprinkle with the almonds. Bake for 25 to 30 minutes or until the chicken is cooked through. Serve with couscous.

CHICKEN PARMESAN

An easy tasty recipe that smells delicious while baking

MAKES 6 TO 8 SERVINGS

2 cups bread crumbs
3/4 cup grated Parmesan
   cheese
1/4 cup parsley flakes
1 garlic clove, crushed

1 teaspoon salt
1/4 teaspoon pepper
6 to 8 chicken breasts
1/2 cup (1 stick) or more
   butter, melted

Preheat the oven to 350 degrees. Combine the bread crumbs, cheese, parsley, garlic, salt, and pepper in a shallow dish. Dip the chicken in the butter, then in the crumb mixture, coating completely. Place in a 9×13-inch baking dish and pour any remaining butter over the chicken. Bake for 1 hour or until the chicken is cooked through, basting occasionally with the drippings.

NOTE: *If boneless skinless chicken breasts are used, reduce the baking time to 40 minutes.*

CHICKEN WITH A TANG OF TUSCANY

Much of the preparation for this recipe can be done in advance, allowing you to sit and chat with your guests.

MAKES 6 SERVINGS

6 boneless skinless chicken breasts
1 cup soft garlic herb cheese
6 fresh basil leaves
1 (8-ounce) jar oil-pack sun-dried tomatoes, drained
2 cups Alfredo Sauce
1/2 cup freshly grated Parmesan cheese
Additional fresh basil leaves

Preheat the oven to 375 degrees. Place the chicken between 2 pieces of waxed paper and pound until very flat. Place 2 generous tablespoons of the herb cheese, 1 basil leaf, and 2 sun-dried tomatoes at 1 end of each breast. Roll tightly and place, seam side down, in a shallow baking dish coated with nonstick cooking spray. Pour the Alfredo Sauce over the roll-ups. Bake for 25 minutes or until the chicken is cooked through. Serve with angel hair pasta and sprinkle with the Parmesan cheese. Garnish with basil leaves.

ALFREDO SAUCE

MAKES ABOUT 2 CUPS

5 tablespoons butter
1/4 cup all-purpose flour
1 cup light cream
1/4 cup dry white wine
1/4 cup (1 ounce) shredded Swiss cheese
Salt and pepper to taste

Melt the butter in a large skillet over low heat and stir in the flour until smooth. Add the cream and wine and cook until the sauce thickens and begins to bubble, stirring constantly. Stir in the cheese until melted. Season with salt and pepper.

Coq au Vin
(Chicken in Wine)

MAKES 6 SERVINGS

6 slices bacon, diced
2 tablespoons butter
6 chicken breasts
1 onion, thinly sliced into rings
1 garlic clove, minced
1 pound mushrooms, quartered
2 tablespoons all-purpose flour
2 tablespoons water
2 cups good-quality red wine
1 cup chicken broth
1/2 teaspoon thyme
1 bay leaf
Salt and freshly ground pepper to taste
12 small red potatoes
12 ounces baby carrots
Chopped fresh parsley
Chopped fresh tarragon

Cook the bacon in a Dutch oven or large heavy ovenproof skillet until crisp. Remove to a paper towel-lined plate with a slotted spoon. Add the butter to the drippings in the pan and heat. Add the chicken and brown on all sides. Remove the chicken to a platter. Add the onion and garlic to the pan and sauté over medium heat for 5 minutes or until the onion is tender. Add the mushrooms and sauté for 5 minutes. Combine the flour and water, stirring to make a paste. Stir into the mushroom mixture. Stir in the wine and broth. Add the thyme, bay leaf, salt, and pepper and mix well. Add the bacon, chicken and juices from the platter, potatoes, and carrots and bring to a boil. Reduce the heat and simmer, covered, for 1 hour or until the potatoes and carrots are tender and the chicken is cooked through. Remove the bay leaf. Sprinkle with parsley and tarragon just before serving.

CHICKEN POTPIE

MAKES 8 SERVINGS

2 or 3 small to medium red potatoes,
    peeled and finely chopped
1 cup thinly sliced carrots
1 cup cauliflower florets
1 cup broccoli florets
1 cup frozen peas
3 cups diced cooked chicken
1/3 cup butter or margarine
1/4 cup chopped onion
1/3 cup all-purpose flour
13/4 cups chicken broth
1 cup milk
Salt and pepper to taste
Dash of hot red pepper sauce
Pastry

Cook the potatoes, carrots, and cauliflower in a small amount of water in a large saucepan for 5 minutes. Add the broccoli and cook for 5 minutes. Add the peas and cook for 1 to 2 minutes longer or until all the vegetables are tender; drain. Stir the chicken into the vegetables. Spoon the mixture into a 9×13-inch baking dish coated with nonstick cooking spray. Melt the butter in a medium saucepan. Add the onion and cook for 2 to 3 minutes or until tender. Stir in the flour. Add the broth, milk, salt, pepper, and hot red pepper sauce and mix well. Bring to a boil. Reduce the heat to medium and cook until thickened, stirring constantly. Pour over the chicken and vegetables.

Preheat the oven to 425 degrees. Roll out 1 ball of the pastry on a lightly floured surface to a 9 1/2×13 1/2-inch rectangle and place over the baking dish, sealing to the edges of the dish. Crimp, if desired. Pierce the pastry with a fork in several places. Bake for 30 minutes, covering the edge of the crust with foil during the last few minutes if needed to prevent over-browning.

NOTE: *If a bottom crust is desired for the potpie, roll out 1 dough ball and line the baking dish before adding the chicken mixture. Proceed as directed above. Bake on the lowest oven rack.*

PASTRY

MAKES ENOUGH DOUGH
FOR 3 CRUSTS

3 3/4 cups all-purpose
    flour
1/2 teaspoon salt
1 1/4 cups cold butter or
    margarine, cut into
    pieces
1/3 cup shortening
1 egg yolk, beaten
1/2 to 1 cup ice water

Combine the flour and salt in a mixing bowl. Cut in the butter and shortening until crumbly. Stir together the egg yolk and water. Add to the flour mixture gradually. Knead lightly to form a dough. Shape into 3 balls. Use immediately or freeze in a sealable plastic bag for later use.

TERIYAKI-GLAZED CHICKEN WINGS

MAKES 45 TO 60 WINGS

5 pounds chicken wings,
   rinsed and patted dry
2 tablespoons vegetable oil
Salt and pepper to taste
1 cup honey

1/2 cup soy sauce
2 tablespoons ketchup
1 teaspoon garlic powder
1/2 teaspoon ground ginger

Preheat the oven to 375 degrees. Divide the chicken wings between two 9×13-inch baking pans coated with nonstick cooking spray. Brush the chicken wings with the oil and season with salt and pepper. Combine the honey, soy sauce, ketchup, garlic powder, and ginger in a bowl and mix well. Pour over the chicken wings. Bake for 1 hour. Remove from the oven and transfer to a slow cooker set on Low until ready to serve.

SLOW-COOKER CHICKEN À LA KING

MAKES 6 SERVINGS

2 cups chopped cooked
   chicken
1 cup finely chopped celery
1 cup croutons
1 cup mayonnaise
3/4 cup (3 ounces) shredded
   Cheddar cheese
3 tablespoons grated
   Parmesan cheese

1/2 cup slivered almonds
1 tablespoon lemon juice
1/2 teaspoon salt
1/4 teaspoon curry powder
3/4 cup (3 ounces) shredded
   Cheddar cheese
1 cup crushed potato chips
Toasted croissants

Combine the chicken, celery, croutons, mayonnaise, 3/4 cup Cheddar cheese, the Parmesan cheese, almonds, lemon juice, salt, and curry powder in a large saucepan and mix well. Cook over medium heat until the center is warm, 120 degrees on an instant-read thermometer.

Spoon into a slow cooker and cook on Low for 2 hours. Top with 3/4 cup Cheddar cheese and the potato chips and cook on High for 30 minutes longer. If cooking longer, add a small amount of milk if needed to keep the mixture moist. Serve over toasted croissants.

BEER CAN GAME HENS

MAKES 4 SERVINGS

1 tablespoon kosher salt
1 tablespoon freshly ground pepper
1 tablespoon paprika
1 tablespoon brown sugar
1 teaspoon garlic powder
4 (1-pound) game hens
4 (8-ounce) cans beer (Tecate preferred)
2 limes, halved

Soak 1 cup hickory or pecan wood chips in beer or water for 1 hour. Combine the salt, pepper, paprika, brown sugar, and garlic powder in a small bowl. Rinse the birds and remove any excess fat from the cavities and pat dry. Rub about 2/3 of the salt mixture over the birds, inside and out.

Pop the tabs on the beer cans and use a punch can opener to make 2 additional holes in the top of each can. Pour off half the beer from each can. Squeeze a lime half into each can and divide the remaining salt mixture among the 4 cans.

Preheat a gas grill to 350 degrees for indirect grilling, or prepare a charcoal grill with a foil drip pan surrounded by hot coals. Stand the beer cans on a sturdy surface. Stretch each cavity and fit it over a can. Drain the wood chips and add to the coals. Place the bird-topped cans on the grill and cook until the birds are cooked through. Remove from the cans to serve.

BERRY-ROASTED POULTRY

MAKES 4 TO 6 SERVINGS

3 celery ribs, finely chopped
1 small onion, chopped
1 apple, chopped
1 (15-ounce) can blueberries, drained,
    or 1 (16-ounce) package frozen
    blueberries, thawed
1 (12-ounce) can whole cranberry sauce
1 1/2 tablespoons poultry seasoning
1/4 cup dry white wine
2 tablespoons frozen orange juice
    concentrate, thawed
1 whole goose, chicken, or small turkey, or
    2 whole ducks, or 4 Cornish game hens
1/4 cup dry white wine
1 tablespoon frozen orange juice
    concentrate, thawed
1 1/2 teaspoons minced garlic
1/4 teaspoon thyme
1/4 teaspoon rubbed sage

Preheat the oven to 500 degrees. Combine the celery, onion, apple, half the blueberries, half the cranberry sauce, the poultry seasoning, 1/4 cup wine, and 2 tablespoons orange juice concentrate in a large bowl and mix well. Remove and discard the giblets, neck, and excess fat from the bird. Rinse and pat dry. Prick the skin with a fork several times. Fill the poultry cavities with the fruit mixture. Place the bird, back side up, in a large roasting pan. Bake for 20 minutes. Turn the bird over and bake for 20 minutes longer. Reduce the oven temperature to 350 degrees and roast for 20 minutes per pound or until cooked through. Let stand for 15 minutes before carving. Combine the remaining blueberries and cranberry sauce, 1/4 cup wine, 1 tablespoon orange juice concentrate, the garlic, thyme, and sage in a small saucepan and cook over medium heat until slightly thickened. Serve the sauce over the sliced poultry.

"PHABULOUS" PHEASANT

MAKES 6 SERVINGS

1 (6-ounce) package mixed long grain and wild rice
3/4 pound bulk pork sausage
1 large onion, finely chopped
8 ounces mushrooms, sliced
1 (8-ounce) can sliced water chestnuts,
   drained and chopped
Juice of 1/2 lemon
2 tablespoons butter
1/4 cup all-purpose flour
1 teaspoon salt
1/8 teaspoon pepper
1/2 cup milk
1 3/4 cups chicken broth
2 cups chopped cooked pheasant
1/2 cup sliced almonds

Cook the rice using the package directions. Sauté the sausage in a large skillet until brown, stirring until crumbly. Remove the sausage from the skillet and drain on paper towels, reserving the drippings in the skillet. Sauté the onion and mushrooms in the drippings. Stir in the water chestnuts and heat through. Add the lemon juice to the mixture. Preheat the oven to 350 degrees.

Melt the butter in a small saucepan and stir in the flour, salt, and pepper. Stir in the milk slowly. Add the broth and cook over medium heat until thickened, stirring constantly. Add the sausage, rice and pheasant to the onion mixture in the skillet and mix well. Spoon into a 2-quart baking dish. Pour the sauce over the top and sprinkle with the almonds. Bake for 1 hour.

CREAMED PHEASANT IN A BAG

MAKES 4 TO 6 SERVINGS

2 tablespoons butter
1 onion, thinly sliced
1/2 cup dry sherry
1 cup heavy cream
1/4 cup Dijon mustard
1/2 teaspoon white pepper
1/2 teaspoon dry mustard

1/2 teaspoon Hungarian
   paprika
1/2 teaspoon seasoned salt or
   Cajun seasoning
2 tablespoons all-purpose
   flour
4 boned pheasant breasts

Preheat the oven to 325 degrees. Melt the butter in a large skillet and add the onion. Sauté for 15 minutes or until golden brown. Combine the sherry, cream, Dijon mustard, white pepper, dry mustard, paprika, and seasoned salt in a bowl and mix well. Stir into the caramelized onions. Coat the inside of an oven cooking bag with the flour and place the pheasant breasts inside. Pour the onion mixture over the pheasant. Close the bag and place on a baking sheet. Make 6 small slits in the top of the oven bag. Bake for 1 1/2 hours. Remove the pheasant from the bag to serving plates.

WATER GAME PILLOWS

MAKES 8 SERVINGS

2 cups chopped cooked
   duck, goose, pheasant,
   or sage hen
1 (10-ounce) can cream of
   mushroom soup
8 ounces cream cheese,
   softened
1/4 cup finely chopped carrots
1/4 cup finely chopped onion
2 tablespoons heavy cream

4 green onions, chopped
1 teaspoon prepared
   horseradish
1/2 teaspoon dry mustard
1/2 teaspoon white pepper
2 (8-count) cans refrigerator
   crescent rolls
1/2 cup (1 stick) butter, melted
Cracker crumbs or crushed
   potato chips

Preheat the oven to 350 degrees. Combine the chopped poultry, soup, cream cheese, carrots, onion, cream, green onions, horseradish, dry mustard, and white pepper in a large bowl and mix well. Unroll and separate the crescent roll dough into triangles on a large ungreased baking sheet. Divide the poultry mixture among the triangles, placing a small mound on the wide side of each triangle. Roll up and brush with the melted butter. Sprinkle with the cracker crumbs. Bake for 20 minutes or until golden brown.

A Sushi Get-Together ~ Wyoming Style

———

Today, UW students can enjoy traditional Japanese sushi rolls and other Asian dishes in the Washakie Dining Center on campus. However, sushi rolls are not always readily available in many parts of Wyoming, and the technique is difficult to master at home. Equally as delicious as their more splashy counterparts, sushi sandwiches are made by folding sushi rice and selected toppings inside a seaweed (nori) wrapper. Then, bite by bite, the sushi sandwich is dipped in a bowl of soy sauce mixed with wasabi to taste. Pickled ginger is a refreshing accompaniment. Now anyone can enjoy sushi anytime at home!

The Menu

SUSHI, WYOMING STYLE*

SUSHI RICE*

NORI SEAWEED WRAPPERS*

SUSHI TRAY SELECTIONS*

SUSHI CONDIMENTS*

*pictured recipes

———

Fish & Seafood

BLUE CHEESE FLOUNDER

MAKES 6 SERVINGS

6 flounder fillets
3 tablespoons butter
1 small onion, chopped
1/4 cup all-purpose flour
1/2 teaspoon salt
1/2 teaspoon pepper

1/2 teaspoon celery seeds
2 cups half-and-half
3/4 cup crumbled blue cheese
2 to 4 tablespoons capers,
   drained
2 tablespoons A.1. steak sauce

Preheat the oven to 375 degrees. Arrange the fillets in a buttered shallow baking dish. Melt the butter in a skillet. Add the onion and sauté until tender. Stir in the flour. Add the salt, pepper, celery seeds, and half-and-half and cook until thickened, stirring constantly. Remove from the heat and stir in the cheese, capers, and steak sauce. Pour the sauce over the fish. Bake for 10 to 15 minutes or until the sauce is bubbly and the fish is brown.

GRILLED SALMON WITH HONEY MUSTARD ZEST

In spite of the ingredients, there is almost no mustard flavor in the cooked fish. The sauce greatly reduces the "oily" texture of the salmon.

MAKES 4 SERVINGS

1/4 cup grated lemon zest
1/4 cup Dijon mustard
2 tablespoons olive oil
2 tablespoons honey

2 tablespoons lemon juice
2 (8- to 12-ounce) salmon
   fillets

Preheat the grill and coat the grill rack with nonstick cooking spray, if desired. Combine the lemon zest, Dijon mustard, olive oil, honey, and lemon juice in a small bowl and mix well. Place the salmon, skin side down, on the grill rack and spread about 1/3 of the lemon zest mixture on top. Cook until the skin is brown. Turn the fillets and remove the skin. Top the skinned side with 1/3 of the zest mixture and cook just until grill lines appear. Turn the fillets and top with the remaining lemon zest mixture. Grill just until the salmon flakes easily. Total cooking time should be about 10 minutes for a 1-inch-thick fillet.

Salmon with Bacon, Leeks, and Creamy Scallion Sauce

Makes 4 servings

2 cups fish stock or bottled
  clam juice
3 tablespoons frozen apple juice
  concentrate
2 scallions, chopped
1¹/₂ teaspoons black peppercorns
1¹/₂ teaspoons ground coriander
1 bay leaf
1 cup heavy cream
3 leeks (white part only),
  sliced
8 slices bacon, diced
¹/₂ cup dry white wine
4 (6- to 8-ounce) salmon fillets
2 tablespoons butter
Salt and pepper to taste

Combine the fish stock, apple juice concentrate, scallions, peppercorns, coriander, and bay leaf in a large saucepan and bring to a boil. Boil until reduced by ¹/₂. Add the cream and return to a boil. Simmer until thickened; keep warm. Combine the leeks and bacon in a large skillet and cook until golden brown, stirring occasionally; drain. Add the wine and cook until nearly all the wine has evaporated. Cover and keep warm. Preheat the broiler and coat the broiler pan with nonstick cooking spray, if desired. Place the salmon fillets on the broiler pan and broil for 4 minutes per side or until the flesh flakes easily. Divide the leek mixture among 4 individual plates and top each with a fillet. Bring the sauce to a simmer and stir in the butter. Taste and season with salt and pepper. Remove the bay leaf. Spoon the sauce over the salmon and leeks.

COLD POACHED SALMON

This makes a beautiful presentation for a buffet, whether a brunch or dinner. There'll be nothing left but the bones!

MAKES 80 SERVINGS

1 (10- to 12-pound) whole
   dressed salmon with head
   on, slit to the back fin
Cold water
6 lemons, sliced

6 limes, sliced
2 pounds salt
20 bay leaves
1/2 cup white wine

Stovetop Method: Spread the salmon open on a wire rack and tie loosely onto the rack. Place in a large shallow baking pan or roaster. Add cold water to completely cover the fish. Add the lemons, limes, salt, bay leaves, and wine. Slowly heat the water to approximately 170 degrees on an instant-read thermometer. Poach for about 1 1/2 hours or until the thermometer reads 150 degrees in the thickest part of the salmon. Remove from the water to a sheet pan.

Oven Method: Omit the lemons, limes, salt, and bay leaves. Place the salmon, skin-side down, on a heavy sheet pan and place in the oven. Add 2 to 3 cups cold water, 1/2 cup wine, and 1 tablespoon lemon juice. Place a piece of cheesecloth across the salmon. Bake at 250 degrees until the thermometer reads 150 degrees in the thickest part of the salmon. Pour off or spoon the liquid from the pan before removing from the oven.

Chill the poached salmon for 6 hours. To serve, lift the sides of the salmon with large spatulas, sliding between the flesh and skin. Split the skin down the back and peel off the skin slowly. Remove the fat above the backbone and the bones. Arrange on a large mirror, tray, or serving platter and garnish with cooked shrimp, cucumber and lemon slices, capers, sliced pimento-stuffed green olives, and/or lettuce leaves. Serve with water crackers or rye toast.

NOTE: *A side of salmon can be poached in the same manner.*

PECAN DIJON SALMON

MAKES 4 SERVINGS

1/4 cup dry bread crumbs or crushed saltines
1/4 cup finely chopped pecans
4 teaspoons chopped fresh parsley
1/4 cup (1/2 stick) butter, melted
3 tablespoons Dijon mustard
1 1/2 tablespoons honey
4 (4- to 6-ounce) salmon fillets
Salt and pepper to taste

Preheat the oven to 400 degrees. Combine the bread crumbs, pecans, and parsley. Stir together the butter, Dijon mustard, and honey in a small bowl. Place the fillets in a shallow baking pan and brush each with the butter mixture. Top with the crumb mixture. Bake for 10 to 15 minutes or until the flesh flakes easily. Season with salt and pepper. Serve with lemon wedges, if desired.

WEST COAST CANADIAN SALMON

MAKES 4 SERVINGS

1/4 cup soy sauce
1/4 cup rye whiskey
1/2 cup olive oil
1 tablespoon brown sugar
1/2 teaspoon salt
1/4 teaspoon pepper
1 whole dressed salmon, or 4 salmon fillets

Combine the soy sauce, whiskey, olive oil, brown sugar, salt, and pepper in a small bowl and mix well. Place the salmon in a sealable plastic bag or shallow glass dish and pour the soy sauce mixture over it. Marinate, covered, in the refrigerator overnight, turning occasionally. Preheat the grill and coat the grill rack with nonstick cooking spray, if desired. Place the salmon, skin-side down, on the rack and grill over low heat for 15 to 20 minutes or until the flesh flakes easily.

BACON-GRILLED TROUT WITH GREEN ONION YOGURT SAUCE

MAKES 6 SERVINGS

GREEN ONION YOGURT SAUCE

MAKES ABOUT 2 1/2 CUPS

1 1/2 cups plain yogurt
3/4 cup shredded
   cucumber
6 green onions,
   thinly sliced
1 tablespoon sugar
1 teaspoon white pepper

Combine the yogurt, cucumber, green onions, sugar, and white pepper in a small bowl and mix well.

6 slices bacon
3 large or 6 small fresh trout, cleaned and
   with head and tail left on
1 teaspoon seasoned salt
1 teaspoon white pepper
Fresh basil leaves or other fresh herb sprigs
Seasoned salt and white pepper to taste
Green Onion Yogurt Sauce

Cook the bacon in a large skillet until crisp; remove and crumble, reserving the drippings. Brush the inside of each trout generously with the bacon drippings. Season with 1 teaspoon seasoned salt and 1 teaspoon white pepper. Place basil leaves inside each cavity. Brush the outside of the trout with the bacon drippings and sprinkle with additional seasoned salt and white pepper. The trout may be refrigerated, covered, at this point for up to 24 hours. Preheat the grill or broiler and coat the grill rack or broiler pan with nonstick cooking spray, if desired. Place the trout on the rack and cook for about 5 minutes. Turn the fish carefully and cook for 5 to 8 minutes longer or until the flesh is opaque and flakes easily. Do not overcook. Serve with the Green Onion Yogurt Sauce and sprinkle with the crumbled bacon.

A terrific variety of wild mushrooms springs up every summer in Wyoming, and many make for savory eating. A great time to look for mushrooms is while fly-fishing for trout; knowledge of edible mushrooms is essential, however. Particularly hardy souls might consider roasting both trout and mushrooms on sticks over an open fire before heading home. With the simple seasonings of salt, pepper, and butter, you can create a scrumptious meal.

RAINBOW TROUT WITH APPLE BUTTER SAUCE

MAKES 4 SERVINGS

2 tablespoons butter or
  margarine
2 apples, cut into thin wedges
1 (16-inch) dressed rainbow
  trout
2 cups (about) apple juice
  or apple cider

1 tablespoon butter or
  margarine
1 green onion, thinly sliced
1 tablespoon all-purpose flour
1/2 cup milk
1 tablespoon Dijon mustard
1 tablespoon snipped parsley

Preheat the oven to 350 degrees. Melt 2 tablespoons butter in a medium skillet. Add the apples and cook over medium-high heat for about 1 minute or until light brown, turning the apples once. Remove from the heat. Place the trout in a large shallow baking dish and add the apples. Add enough apple juice to half cover the fish. Bake, covered with foil, for about 30 minutes or until the flesh flakes easily. Remove the fish and apples to a serving platter, reserving 1/4 cup of the cooking liquid. Cover the platter and keep warm. Melt 1 tablespoon butter in the skillet. Add the green onion and cook until tender but not brown. Stir in the flour. Add the reserved cooking liquid, milk, and Dijon mustard. Bring to a boil. Reduce the heat to medium and cook until thickened and bubbly, stirring constantly. Cook and stir for 1 minute longer and then stir in the parsley. Serve the sauce with the trout.

BACON-WRAPPED TUNA STEAKS WITH BALSAMIC GLAZE

MAKES 2 SERVINGS

2 slices bacon, partially
  cooked
2 thick tuna steaks

Salt and pepper to taste
Balsamic Glaze

Wrap the bacon around the steaks and secure with wooden picks. Season with salt and pepper. Preheat the grill or a heavy nonstick skillet and coat the grill rack or skillet with nonstick cooking spray, if desired. Grill or pan-fry the steaks for 4 minutes per side. Spoon the Balsamic Glaze onto 2 individual serving plates and top each with a tuna steak.

BALSAMIC GLAZE

MAKES ABOUT 3/4 CUP

6 tablespoons beef
  bouillon or broth
1/2 cup balsamic vinegar
1/3 cup soy sauce
1 tablespoon sesame
  seeds
1 tablespoon honey

Cook the bouillon in a small saucepan until reduced by 1/2. Add the vinegar, soy sauce, sesame seeds, and honey and cook over medium-high heat until reduced by 1/2.

GRILLED AHI TUNA WITH MUSTARD GINGER SAUCE

2 tablespoons grapeseed oil, or other vegetable oil
4 (3-ounce) pieces sushi-grade ahi tuna,
    about 3/4-inch thick, at room temperature
1 tablespoon Szechwan pepper blend
Mustard-Ginger Sauce

Pour the grapeseed oil onto a plate and coat both sides of the tuna pieces. Sprinkle all over with the pepper. Preheat the grill and coat the grill rack with nonstick cooking spray, if desired. Grill over high heat for 1 1/2 minutes per side. Serve with the Mustard-Ginger Sauce.

MUSTARD GINGER SAUCE

MAKES ABOUT 1 CUP

2 1/2 tablespoons Dijon
    mustard
2 1/2 tablespoons soy
    sauce
2 1/2 tablespoons fresh
    lime juice
1 1/2 tablespoons grated
    fresh ginger
1 1/2 tablespoons minced
    green onions or
    shallots
1/3 cup grapeseed oil or
    other light oil

Whisk together the Dijon mustard, soy sauce, lime juice, ginger, and green onions. Add the grapeseed oil in a steady stream, whisking constantly until combined.

FISH TACOS WITH
MANGO SALSA

2 tablespoons vegetable oil
Juice of 1 lime
4 garlic cloves, minced
1 teaspoon ground cumin
3 pounds flounder or other firm white fish
12 to 20 flour tortillas, warmed
Finely shredded savoy cabbage
Mango Salsa

Combine the oil, lime juice, garlic, and cumin in a small bowl and mix well. Place the fish in a large shallow glass dish and pour the lime juice mixture over it. Marinate, covered, in the refrigerator for 1 hour. Preheat the grill and coat the grill rack with nonstick cooking spray, if desired. Grill the fish for 4 to 5 minutes per side or until the flesh flakes easily. Remove the fish from the grill and flake into a large bowl. Divide the fish among the tortillas and top with cabbage. Serve with the Mango Salsa.

MANGO SALSA

MAKES ABOUT 3 1/4 CUPS

1 mango, chopped
2 cups chopped pineapple
1 onion, chopped
3 tablespoons chopped fresh cilantro
2 jalapeño chiles, chopped
Juice of 1 lime
Pinch of salt

Combine the mango, pineapple, onion, cilantro, jalapeño chiles, lime juice, and salt in a bowl and mix well.

SUSHI, WYOMING STYLE

Good sushi depends on good sushi rice. The time is worth the effort.

MAKES 6 TO 8 SERVINGS

1/2 pound cooked crab meat
1/2 pound cooked jumbo
   shrimp, peeled and
   deveined
1/2 pound yellowfin tuna,
   thinly sliced
1/2 pound smoked salmon,
   thinly sliced
1/2 English cucumber, peeled
   and julienned
1/2 red onion, thinly sliced
2 avocados, thinly sliced

1 (3½-ounce) bag enoki
   mushrooms, trimmed
1 bunch green onions,
   thinly sliced
1 (1-ounce) package roasted
   nori (dried seaweed)
Sushi Rice
Wasabi Paste
Sesame Sauce
Pickled ginger, toasted
   sesame seeds, and
   soy sauce

Arrange the crab meat, shrimp, tuna, salmon, cucumber, red onion, avocados, mushrooms, and green onions on a large serving tray. You may do this in advance and chill, tightly covered, for up to 2 hours. Remove from the refrigerator and let stand until room temperature. Cut each nori sheet into 4 squares. To make a sushi "sandwich," spread a nori square with Sushi Rice. Top with your choice of seafood and vegetables, Wasabi Paste, Sesame Sauce, pickled ginger, and sesame seeds to taste. Bring the corners of the nori square together to enclose the filling. Dip in soy sauce. Serve with hot-and-sour soup, Japanese beer or sake, and lemon sorbet with sliced kiwifruit.

SUSHI RICE

3 cups fancy short grain rice
3½ cups water
1/2 cup rice vinegar

1/4 cup sugar
1 tablespoon sea salt

Place the rice in a fine mesh strainer in a bowl. Pour water over the rice, stirring to release the starch. Drain and rinse with water 5 to 10 times or until the water is clear. Combine the rice and 3½ cups water in a 3- to 4-quart saucepan. Bring to a boil, covered, over high heat. Reduce the heat to low and simmer, covered, for 15 minutes or until the water is absorbed. Remove from the heat. Fluff with a fork and let stand, covered, for 10 minutes. Combine the vinegar, sugar, and salt in a small saucepan and cook over medium heat until the sugar and salt are dissolved, stirring constantly. Spread the rice in a 9×13-inch glass dish. Pour the vinegar mixture over the rice and stir quickly so that the rice does not become sticky. You may prepare the rice to this point and let stand, tightly covered, at room temperature for up to 1 day.

WASABI PASTE

3 tablespoons wasabi
   powder (Japanese
   horseradish)
3½ teaspoons water

Combine the wasabi powder and water in a bowl and stir until blended. Spoon into a small serving bowl.

SESAME SAUCE

1 cup mayonnaise
2 tablespoons honey
2 teaspoons oriental
   sesame oil
Toasted sesame seeds

Combine the mayonnaise, honey, and sesame oil in a bowl and stir until blended. Spoon into a small serving bowl and sprinkle with the sesame seeds.

COQUILLES ST. JACQUES

MAKES 6 SERVINGS

12 sea scallops
1/2 cup chardonnay
1/2 cup water
2 tablespoons butter
2 tablespoons lemon juice
1/2 cup sliced mushrooms
1/4 cup chopped onion
1 garlic clove, minced
3 tablespoons butter

5 tablespoons
  all-purpose flour
1 egg yolk
1/4 cup heavy cream
Dash of salt and pepper
3 tablespoons butter, melted
1/2 cup dry bread crumbs
1 tablespoon lemon juice

Combine the scallops, wine and water in a large skillet and bring
to a boil. Reduce the heat and simmer, covered, for 10 to 15 minutes
or until the scallops are tender. Remove the scallops from the skillet.
Pour off and reserve the cooking liquid. Cut the scallops into
small pieces.

Melt 2 tablespoons butter in the skillet and add 2 tablespoons
lemon juice. Add the mushrooms, onion, and garlic and cook over low
heat for 10 minutes or until tender but not brown. Add 3 tablespoons
butter and melt. Stir in the flour. Cook for 1 to 2 minutes, stirring
constantly. Stir in the reserved scallop cooking liquid and simmer for
3 minutes. Remove from the heat.

Whisk together the egg yolk and cream in a small bowl until
blended. Stir a little of the hot mushroom sauce into the egg mixture
and mix well. Add the egg mixture to the skillet, stirring constantly.
Fold in the scallops and season with salt and pepper. Heat through,
but do not boil.

Brush 6 baking shells or other small baking dishes with 1 tablespoon
of the melted butter. Preheat the broiler. Divide the scallop mixture
among the shells and place them on a large baking sheet. Combine
the remaining 2 tablespoons melted butter with the bread crumbs and
1 tablespoon lemon juice and sprinkle over the shells. Broil until brown.

SEAFOOD EN CROÛTE

MAKES 9 TO 12 SERVINGS

2 tablespoons butter
2 tablespoons all-purpose flour
1 (8-ounce) bottle clam juice
1 cup heavy cream
1 cup sliced mushrooms
1 onion, chopped
2 tablespoons butter
2 cups cooked rice
4 hard-cooked eggs, coarsely chopped
1/2 cup chopped fresh parsley
2 cups cooked shrimp
2 cups coarsely chopped cooked haddock
1/2 teaspoon curry powder
Salt and pepper to taste
Pastry for a double-crust 9-inch pie
1 egg, beaten

Preheat the oven to 350 degrees. Melt 2 tablespoons butter in a large saucepan. Stir in the flour and cook until light brown, stirring constantly. Add the clam juice and cream and cook over medium heat until thickened. Sauté the mushrooms and onion in 2 tablespoons butter in a skillet until tender.

Spread half the rice in a greased 9×13-inch baking dish. Layer with half the mushroom mixture, half the hard-cooked eggs, half the parsley, half the shrimp, half the haddock, and half the curry powder. Season with salt and pepper. Layer with the remaining rice, mushroom mixture, hard-cooked eggs, parsley, shrimp, haddock, and curry powder. Season with salt and pepper. Roll out the pastry to a 9¹/₂×13¹/₂-inch rectangle and place over the baking dish, sealing to the edges of the dish. Crimp, if desired. Brush the egg over the pastry. Cut several small slits in the pastry. Bake for 30 minutes or until the pastry is a light golden brown. Let stand for 20 minutes before serving.

GRILLED GARLIC SHRIMP ON THE BARBIE

If you love garlic, you will love these shrimp. They go great with pasta.

MAKES 6 TO 8 SERVINGS

12 to 16 unpeeled whole garlic cloves
2/3 cup olive oil
1/2 cup tomato sauce
1/4 cup red wine vinegar
1/4 cup chopped fresh basil
3 garlic cloves, minced
1 teaspoon salt
1 teaspoon cayenne pepper
2 pounds uncooked jumbo shrimp,
   peeled and deveined

Place the whole garlic cloves in a saucepan of rapidly boiling water. Boil for 3 to 5 minutes or until partially cooked but still firm; drain. Combine the olive oil, tomato sauce, vinegar, basil, minced garlic, salt, cayenne pepper, and shrimp in a large sealable plastic bag. Marinate in the refrigerator for 30 minutes, turning occasionally. Preheat the grill and coat the grill rack with nonstick cooking spray. Remove the shrimp from the marinade, reserving the marinade. Alternate the shrimp and whole garlic cloves on skewers and grill, 4 to 6 inches above the coals, for 8 to 10 minutes or until the shrimp turn pink, turning and brushing frequently with the marinade.

EASY SHRIMP AND WILD RICE CASSEROLE

Quick & Easy

This casserole can be prepared in the morning and baked in time for dinner. If refrigerated, add fifteen minutes to the baking time.

MAKES 12 SERVINGS

2 (6-ounce) packages mixed long grain and wild rice
1/4 cup (1/2 stick) butter
1 garlic clove, minced
1/2 cup chopped onion
1/2 cup chopped red bell pepper
1/2 cup chopped celery
1 (8-ounce) can sliced water chestnuts, drained
1 1/2 pounds mushrooms, sliced
2 pounds cooked medium shrimp, peeled
1 (10-ounce) can cream of shrimp soup
1 cup sour cream
Salt and pepper to taste
1/4 cup (1 ounce) shredded Cheddar cheese
Chopped fresh parsley (optional)

Cook both packages of the rice using the package directions. Preheat the oven to 325 degrees. Melt the butter in a large skillet and add the garlic, onion, bell pepper, celery, water chestnuts, and mushrooms. Sauté for about 5 minutes, then remove from the heat. Stir in the shrimp, soup and sour cream and mix well. Stir in the rice and season with salt and pepper. Pour into a buttered 9×13-inch baking dish. Bake for 30 to 40 minutes. Sprinkle with the cheese and bake for 5 minutes longer or until the cheese is melted. Sprinkle with parsley before serving.

SPICY SHRIMP FAJITAS

MAKES 6 SERVINGS

12 fajita-size flour tortillas
1 teaspoon black pepper
1/2 teaspoon salt
1/2 teaspoon cayenne pepper
1/2 teaspoon thyme leaves, crushed
1/2 teaspoon red pepper flakes
1/2 teaspoon rosemary leaves, crushed
1/8 teaspoon oregano leaves, crushed
1 pound uncooked shrimp, peeled and deveined
1/4 cup (1/2 stick) unsalted butter
1 cup red bell pepper strips
1 cup sliced onion
1 to 2 garlic cloves, minced
1/4 cup (1/2 stick) unsalted butter
1 teaspoon Worcestershire sauce
1/2 cup water
1 cup flat beer

Preheat the oven to 200 degrees. Separate the tortillas onto a large baking sheet. Cover with a clean towel and place in the oven. Stir together the black pepper, salt, cayenne pepper, thyme, red pepper flakes, rosemary, and oregano. Rinse the shrimp and pat dry. Melt 1/4 cup butter in a large skillet. Add the bell pepper, onion, and garlic and cook over medium-high heat for about 1 minute. Add the shrimp and seasoning mixture. Cook for 2 minutes or until the shrimp curl and turn pink, shaking the pan without stirring. Add 1/4 cup butter, the Worcestershire sauce, and water. Cook for about 2 minutes, shaking the pan. Add the beer and cook for about 1 minute to evaporate the liquid, shaking the pan. To serve, spoon about 1/3 cup shrimp mixture onto each warm tortilla.

CAJUN-BARBECUED SHRIMP

These shrimp are messy to eat, but worth the effort.

MAKES 4 TO 6 SERVINGS

3 pounds uncooked shrimp
  in the shell, rinsed and
  patted dry
1³/4 cups (3¹/2 sticks) unsalted
  butter, melted
Juice of 1 lemon
1 tablespoon olive oil
6 bay leaves
2 garlic cloves, chopped

1¹/2 teaspoons seasoned salt
1 teaspoon garlic powder
1 teaspoon onion salt
1 teaspoon Cajun seasoning
¹/4 teaspoon Worcestershire
  sauce
1 to 3 dashes of hot red
  pepper sauce

Preheat the oven to 350 degrees. Place the shrimp in a large bowl and add the butter, lemon juice, olive oil, bay leaves, chopped garlic, seasoned salt, garlic powder, onion salt, Cajun seasoning, Worcestershire sauce, and hot red pepper sauce. Mix well to completely coat the shrimp. Remove the shrimp and seasonings to an oiled 9×13-inch baking dish. Bake for 15 minutes and stir the shrimp. Bake for 5 to 10 minutes longer or until the shrimp turn pink. Remove the bay leaves. Cool the shrimp slightly before serving.

HOT CHILI PRAWNS

MAKES 6 TO 8 SERVINGS

1¹/2 cups soy sauce
¹/4 cup vegetable oil
¹/4 cup honey
3 to 6 garlic cloves, minced
2 tablespoons toasted
  sesame oil
1 tablespoon hot chili oil
1 tablespoon chili garlic paste

1 tablespoon Worcestershire
  sauce
2 teaspoons minced fresh
  ginger
2 to 3 pounds uncooked
  jumbo shrimp or prawns,
  peeled

Combine the soy sauce, vegetable oil, honey, garlic, sesame oil, chili oil, garlic paste, Worcestershire sauce, and ginger in a bowl and mix well. Combine with the shrimp in a large sealable plastic bag. Marinate in the refrigerator for 30 minutes or longer. Remove the shrimp from the marinade, reserving the marinade. Preheat the grill or broiler and coat the grill rack or broiler pan with nonstick cooking spray, if desired. Grill or broil until the shrimp curl and turn pink, turning and basting frequently with the marinade.

INDIAN STIR-FRIED SHRIMP

MAKES 4 SERVINGS

1/2 cup grated fresh or dried
    unsweetened coconut
1 tablespoon minced garlic
1/4 teaspoon red pepper flakes
1/2 teaspoon curry powder
2 to 3 tablespoons water
1 tablespoon rice vinegar
3 tablespoons hot water
2 tablespoons olive oil
1/4 teaspoon mustard seeds
1 teaspoon uncooked basmati rice
1 cup minced onion
1 tablespoon minced green chile
1 1/2 teaspoons minced fresh ginger
1 1/2 pounds uncooked large shrimp,
    peeled and deveined
1/2 teaspoon coarsely ground black pepper
1/4 teaspoon cayenne pepper

Combine the coconut, garlic, red pepper flakes, and curry powder in a bowl. Stir in 2 to 3 tablespoons water to make a crumbly paste. Combine the vinegar and 3 tablespoons water in a small bowl. Heat the olive oil in a large wok or heavy pan until very hot. Add the mustard seeds and rice and stir-fry briefly. Reduce the heat to medium-high and add the onion, green chile, and ginger. Stir-fry for 3 to 4 minutes or until the onion is tender. Remove to a bowl and keep warm.

Reheat the wok over medium heat and add the coconut paste. Stir-fry until the color changes. Add the shrimp and stir-fry briefly. Add the vinegar mixture and increase the heat to medium-high. Steam, covered, for 3 minutes. Uncover and stir-fry for 20 seconds over medium heat. Stir in the onion mixture and cook for 1 minute over medium heat or until all the shrimp have turned pink. Stir in the black pepper and cayenne pepper. Serve with basmati rice.

OVEN-BAKED OYSTERS

MAKES 4 SERVINGS

1 (10-ounce) jar raw oysters,
   or 1 pint shucked fresh oysters
1 1/2 cups all-purpose flour
2 teaspoons baking powder
1/2 teaspoon salt
1/4 teaspoon baking soda
1/3 cup shortening
1 tablespoon cornmeal
1/4 teaspoon paprika
1/4 teaspoon garlic salt
1/4 teaspoon pepper
3 eggs, lightly beaten
1/2 cup (1 stick) butter, melted

Preheat the oven to 425 degrees. Drain the oysters and pat dry on paper towels. Stir together the flour, baking powder, salt, and baking soda in a large bowl. Cut in the shortening until well mixed. Add the cornmeal, paprika, garlic salt, and pepper and mix well. Dip the oysters in the eggs, then in the flour mixture, and then in the melted butter, coating completely. Place on a parchment paper-lined baking sheet. Bake for about 15 minutes or until golden brown. Serve immediately.

SCALLOPED OYSTERS

MAKES 12 SERVINGS

3 (8-ounce) cans raw oysters, undrained
1/4 pound (1 sleeve) saltines, crushed
1/2 cup (1 stick) butter, melted

Preheat the oven to 350 degrees. Combine the oysters, crushed crackers, and melted butter in a large bowl and mix gently, adding a small amount of water if needed to moisten the mixture. Spoon into a buttered baking dish. Bake for 1 1/2 hours. Cool for 10 minutes before serving.

Ladies-Only Christmas Luncheon: If We Don't Pamper Ourselves, Who Will?

What better way to relieve the hustle-and-bustle stress of the holidays than with a women's-only "pampering" luncheon, an annual tradition hosted at the University of Wyoming president's home? When hosting your own, don't forget to remind each guest to bring a pampering gift to exchange with a secret friend.

The Menu

COLD POACHED SALMON WITH RICE CRACKERS

GOLDEN MINIATURE CRAB CAKES WITH
CURRIED RÉMOULADE SAUCE*

FRESH TOMATO SALAD WITH
AVOCADO BALLS AND HERB DRESSING*

SPINACH AND ITALIAN SAUSAGE LASAGNA*

CHRISTMAS GUMDROP BREAD*

WINTER TUMBLEWEEDS*

GINGERBREAD BOYS AND GIRLS*

CHRISTMAS RUM CAKE

IRISH CREAM LIQUEUR*

*pictured recipes

Pasta & Rice

Angel Hair Pasta with Shrimp, Mushrooms, and Creamy Tomato Sauce

Makes 6 to 8 servings

2 tablespoons unsalted butter
1½ pounds uncooked shrimp, peeled and deveined
1½ pounds mushrooms, sliced
10 Roma tomatoes, peeled and finely chopped
2 large garlic cloves, minced
1 quart heavy cream
1 teaspoon red pepper flakes

Salt and freshly ground black pepper to taste
1 teaspoon capers
1½ pounds angel hair pasta, cooked
1 cup freshly grated Parmigiano-Reggiano or other Parmesan cheese

Melt the butter in a large skillet over medium-high heat. Add the shrimp and sauté over high heat just until they begin to turn pink. Remove the shrimp from the skillet to a bowl. Add the mushrooms to the skillet and cook over medium-high heat for 8 minutes, stirring occasionally. Add the tomatoes and cook just until tender. Add the garlic and cream and bring to a boil. Reduce the heat and simmer until the mixture is reduced by about 1/3. Remove from the heat and add the shrimp, red pepper flakes, salt, black pepper, and capers. Stir in the pasta and heat through. Serve with the Parmigiano-Reggiano cheese.

Asparagus and Ham Confetti Fettuccini

Makes 4 to 6 servings

12 ounces fettuccini
1 small bunch green onions, white part only, thinly sliced
8 ounces mushrooms, sliced
1 pound asparagus, cut into 2-inch pieces

2 to 3 tablespoons butter
2 cups chopped cooked ham
2 cups heavy cream
2 tablespoons ketchup
2 teaspoons Italian seasoning
1 cup grated Parmesan cheese

Cook the fettuccini using the package directions; drain and keep warm. Sauté the green onions, mushrooms, and asparagus in the butter in a skillet until tender. Add the ham, cream, ketchup, Italian seasoning, and cheese. Cook over medium heat until hot and slightly thickened, stirring constantly. Serve over the fettuccini.

CLASSIC FETTUCCINE ALFREDO

MAKES 4 TO 6 SERVINGS

8 to 12 ounces fettuccini
1/2 cup butter
1 teaspoon (or more) minced
   fresh garlic
1/2 cup heavy cream

3/4 cup grated Parmesan
   cheese
1/2 teaspoon salt
Dash of white pepper
Dash of ground nutmeg

Cook the fettuccini using the package directions; drain and keep warm. Melt the butter with the garlic in a large skillet over low heat. Add the cream and bring to a gentle boil, stirring constantly. Reduce the heat to low. Simmer for 5 to 7 minutes or until slightly thickened, stirring frequently. Remove from the heat and stir in the cheese, salt, and white pepper. Pour over the fettuccini and sprinkle with the nutmeg.

PARMA FETTUCCINI IN VERMOUTH SAUCE

MAKES 6 SERVINGS

8 ounces fettuccini
1/2 cup grated Parmesan
   cheese
1/3 cup olive oil
1/4 cup sliced mushrooms
3 tablespoons minced onion
2 garlic cloves, minced
1/4 cup all-purpose flour
2 cups light cream

1/2 teaspoon oregano
Salt and pepper to taste
1/4 cup grated Parmesan
   cheese
1/2 cup vermouth
1 pound cooked ham or
   prosciutto, julienned
1/3 cup sliced green olives

Preheat the oven to 200 degrees. Cook the fettuccini using the package directions; drain. Toss the fettucini with 1/2 cup cheese in a bowl. Spoon into a large buttered baking dish and keep warm, covered, in the oven. Heat the olive oil in a large skillet. Add the mushrooms, onion, and garlic and sauté briefly. Remove the vegetables with a slotted spoon and add to the pasta in the oven. Stir the flour into the oil remaining in the skillet until blended. Add the cream, oregano, salt, pepper, and 1/4 cup cheese gradually, stirring constantly. Cook over low heat until thickened and bubbly, stirring constantly. Stir in the vermouth. Stir in the ham and olives and heat through. Remove the pasta from the oven. Pour the sauce over the pasta and vegetables and toss gently. Serve with crusty bread and a dry white wine.

SPINACH AND ITALIAN SAUSAGE LASAGNA

MAKES 16 SERVINGS

18 lasagna noodles
1 pound bulk hot Italian sausage
2 tablespoons olive oil
4 garlic cloves, finely chopped
1 pound portobello mushroom caps, sliced
6 to 8 ounces baby spinach
1 (26- to 28-ounce) jar red pepper pasta sauce
1 (32-ounce) jar chunky pasta sauce
2 cups whole-milk ricotta cheese
6 cups (24 ounces) shredded mozzarella cheese
1/2 cup grated Parmesan cheese

Cook the lasagna using the package directions; drain and rinse
with cold water. Preheat the oven to 350 degrees. Brown the sausage
in a large skillet, stirring until crumbly. Remove the sausage from
the skillet and drain off the fat. Add the olive oil and garlic to the
skillet and sauté for a few minutes. Add the mushrooms and sauté
until tender. Add the spinach and cook for 1 to 2 minutes, stirring
occasionally. Combine the pasta sauces in a large bowl.

Spread a thin layer of the sauce in two 9×13-inch baking dishes.
Place 3 lasagna noodles on top of the sauce in each dish. Mound equal
amounts of the ricotta cheese over the lasagna noodles. Spoon equal
amounts of the mushroom mixture between the ricotta mounds. Spoon
1/2 cup sauce evenly over the top of each dish. Sprinkle 1 1/2 cups of the
mozzarella cheese over each dish. Layer 3 lasagna noodles in each
dish. Divide the sausage equally between the 2 dishes and spread
evenly over the top. Spoon 1/2 cup sauce evenly over the top of each
dish. Sprinkle 1 1/2 cups mozzarella cheese over each dish. Layer
3 lasagna noodles in each dish. Divide the remaining sauce between
the 2 dishes and spread evenly over the tops. Sprinkle 1/4 cup
Parmesan cheese over each dish. Bake for 50 minutes or until bubbly
and light brown on top. Let stand for 10 minutes before serving.

LINGUINI WITH CHICKEN, CARAMELIZED ORANGES, SCALLIONS, AND PISTACHIOS

MAKES 6 SERVINGS

2 oranges
2 tablespoons butter
2 tablespoons sugar
8 ounces linguini
4 tablespoons olive oil
2 whole boneless skinless chicken breasts, split and
    cut into 1/4-inch-wide strips
2 shallots, chopped
6 scallions, cut into 3/4-inch pieces
3/4 cup raw pistachio nuts, toasted and chopped
1 teaspoon red pepper flakes
1/2 cup grated Parmigiano-Reggiano cheese or
    other Parmesan cheese
1/4 cup raw pistachio nuts, toasted and chopped
Salt and black pepper to taste

Slice the top and bottom off the oranges and discard. Cut the orange zest from the top to the bottom of each orange in 1-inch wide strips with a sharp knife. Remove any pith from the zest strips, and then cut into long thin strips. Squeeze the juice from the oranges into a small bowl. Bring a small amount of water to a boil in a saucepan and add the orange strips. Boil for 2 minutes. Remove the strips and rinse with cold water.

Melt the butter in a large skillet over medium-high heat. Add the sugar and orange juice and simmer for 5 minutes. Add the orange zest strips and simmer until the liquid is reduced by 1/2 to a syrupy glaze. Cook the linguini in a large pot of boiling water until al dente; drain. Toss gently with 2 tablespoons of the olive oil in a large bowl and keep warm. Heat the remaining 2 tablespoons olive oil in a large skillet over high heat. Add the chicken and sauté for 5 to 7 minutes. Add the shallots, scallions, and glazed orange strips and sauté for 2 minutes. Stir in 3/4 cup pistachios and the red pepper flakes and heat through. Divide the linguini among 6 plates. Sprinkle with the Parmigiano-Reggiano cheese. Top with the chicken mixture. Garnish with 1/4 cup pistachios and season with salt and black pepper.

Linguini with Cajun Shrimp and Feta Cheese

Makes 2 servings

6 ounces linguini
2 tablespoons olive oil
1/2 pound uncooked shrimp,
   peeled and deveined
1/2 cup white wine or cooking wine
1 tomato, chopped
1/2 cup sliced mushrooms
4 or 5 green onions, chopped
2 teaspoons Cajun seasoning, or to taste
3/4 cup crumbled feta cheese
2 tablespoons chopped garlic

Cook the linguini using the package directions; drain and keep warm. Heat the olive oil in a saucepan over medium heat. Add the shrimp and cook just until the shrimp turn pink, stirring occasionally. Add the wine, tomato, mushrooms, green onions, and Cajun seasoning and mix well. Cook until the liquid is reduced by 1/2. Add the cheese and garlic, stirring until the cheese is melted. Divide the linguini between 2 plates and top with the shrimp sauce.

PENNE, WILD MUSHROOMS, BROCCOLI, AND CHICKEN IN GARLIC BUTTER

MAKES 4 TO 6 SERVINGS

1 cup dried wild mushrooms
8 ounces penne pasta
6 tablespoons butter
1 to 1¹/₂ cups broccoli florets
3 tablespoons chicken broth
   or white wine

1 tablespoon minced garlic
¹/₄ teaspoon red pepper flakes
1 to 2 cups chopped cooked
   chicken
¹/₃ cup grated asiago, Romano,
   or Parmesan cheese

Soak the mushrooms in warm water for 30 minutes; rinse and pat dry on paper towels. Remove and discard any tough stems. Cook the pasta using the package directions; drain and keep warm. Melt the butter in a large skillet. Add the mushrooms and sauté over medium heat until tender. Add the broccoli and cook until tender. Add the broth, garlic, red pepper flakes, and chicken and sauté over high heat until heated through, stirring constantly. Remove from the heat and add the pasta, tossing gently. Sprinkle with the cheese.

NOTE: *For those who like anchovies, a can of drained and mashed anchovies is a wonderful addition.*

Sicilian-Baked Sedanini with Béchamel Sauce

Makes 8 servings

2 tablespoons olive oil
1 garlic clove, minced
3 or 4 fresh basil leaves, chopped
1/4 cup diced sweet onion (optional)
2 1/2 cups diced zucchini
1/2 cup white wine
2/3 cup tomato sauce
16 ounces sedanini or other short round pasta
Béchamel Sauce
1/2 cup grated Parmesan cheese
1/2 cup (2 ounces) shredded mozzarella cheese
1/3 cup tomato sauce

Heat the olive oil in a large skillet. Add the garlic, basil, and onion and sauté briefly. Add the zucchini and wine and cook over medium heat until the zucchini is tender and the wine has evaporated, stirring occasionally. Add 2/3 cup tomato sauce and simmer for 15 minutes. Preheat the oven to 300 degrees. Cook the pasta in boiling salted water for 15 minutes or until tender; drain. Add to the zucchini mixture. Stir in the Béchamel Sauce, Parmesan cheese, and mozzarella cheese and mix well. Pour into a large baking dish and spread 1/3 cup tomato sauce over the top. Bake for 10 minutes. Serve hot.

Béchamel Sauce

Makes 3 1/2 to 4 cups

1/4 cup (1/2 stick) butter
1/4 cup all-purpose flour
1/2 teaspoon salt
1/8 teaspoon pepper
4 cups milk

Melt the butter in a large saucepan over low heat. Stir in the flour, salt, and pepper until blended. Stir in the milk and cook over medium heat until thickened and bubbly, stirring constantly. Cook for 1 minute longer.

SPAGHETTI AND HOMEMADE MEATBALLS

MAKES 4 SERVINGS

3 eggs
1 pound ground beef, or
   equal parts ground beef,
   pork, and veal
1 1/2 slices bread, soaked in
   2 tablespoons water,
   then squeezed dry
1/3 cup grated Parmesan
   cheese

2 tablespoons bread crumbs
1/2 teaspoon salt
1/4 teaspoon pepper
1 (26-ounce) jar pasta sauce,
   or 3 cups homemade
   spaghetti sauce
8 ounces spaghetti
Fresh basil

Preheat the oven to 400 degrees. Beat the eggs in a large bowl and add the ground beef, bread, cheese, bread crumbs, salt, and pepper. Mix by hand until combined. Shape into meatballs of desired size and place in a 9×13-inch baking pan lightly coated with olive oil. Bake for 20 minutes or until brown. Heat the pasta sauce in a large saucepan and add the meatballs. Simmer for 30 minutes. Cook the spaghetti using the package directions; drain. Serve the meatballs and sauce over the spaghetti. Garnish with basil.

NOTE: *The meatballs can be pan-fried in olive oil instead of browned in the oven.*

SPAGHETTI WITH ARTICHOKE RED SAUCE

MAKES 4 SERVINGS

1 (6-ounce) jar marinated artichoke hearts
8 ounces mushrooms, sliced
1 (15-ounce) can tomato sauce
$1/2$ cup dry white wine
1 (2-ounce) can sliced black olives, drained
2 teaspoons basil
2 teaspoons oregano
1 teaspoon minced onion
1 teaspoon minced garlic
1 teaspoon brown sugar
$1/2$ teaspoon fennel seeds
$1/2$ teaspoon salt
$1/4$ teaspoon pepper
1 pound thin spaghetti, cooked and drained
Grated Parmesan cheese

Drain the marinade from the artichoke hearts into a large saucepan. Coarsely chop the artichokes. Heat the marinade. Add the mushrooms and sauté until tender. Add the artichokes, tomato sauce, wine, olives, basil, oregano, onion, garlic, brown sugar, fennel seeds, salt, and pepper and bring to a boil. Reduce the heat and simmer, uncovered, for 20 minutes. Serve over the spaghetti and sprinkle with cheese. Serve with a salad and a semi-dry red wine.

CHEESE TORTELLINI
WITH THREE-BELL PEPPER SAUCE

This dish can also be served cold as a flavorful pasta salad.

MAKES 4 SERVINGS

2¹/₂ cups frozen cheese tortellini
2 tablespoons olive oil
2 or 3 garlic cloves, minced
¹/₂ onion, finely chopped
2 or 3 tomatoes, seeded and
    finely chopped
¹/₂ cup diced red bell pepper
¹/₂ cup diced green bell pepper
¹/₂ cup diced yellow bell pepper
1 (8-ounce) can tomato sauce
1 teaspoon basil, crushed
1 teaspoon oregano, crushed
1 teaspoon thyme, crushed
1 teaspoon marjoram, crushed
¹/₄ teaspoon red pepper flakes
Salt and black pepper to taste
2 tablespoons olive oil
Grated Parmesan cheese to taste

Cook the tortellini using the package directions; drain and keep warm. Heat 2 tablespoons olive oil in a large skillet over medium-high heat. Add the garlic and onion and sauté until the onion is translucent. Add the tomatoes, bell peppers, tomato sauce, basil, oregano, thyme, marjoram, red pepper flakes, salt, and black pepper and mix well. Simmer over medium-low heat for 10 to 15 minutes, stirring occasionally. Adjust the seasonings to taste. Stir in the tortellini, 2 tablespoons olive oil, and Parmesan cheese and toss gently.

FRIED VERMICELLI IN TOMATO SAUCE

Quick & Easy

MAKES 5 SERVINGS

1 tablespoon vegetable oil
16 ounces vermicelli, crushed
1/2 (14-ounce) can crushed
   tomatoes

1 (8-ounce) can tomato sauce
2 cups water
1/2 teaspoon ground cumin
Salt to taste

Heat the oil in a large skillet and add the vermicelli. Sauté until light brown. Add the crushed tomatoes, tomato sauce, water, cumin, and salt. Simmer, uncovered, for 15 minutes or to the desired consistency.

PASTA CARBONARA

MAKES 6 SERVINGS

8 slices bacon
1 large onion, chopped
2 garlic cloves, minced
1 teaspoon red pepper flakes
3/4 cup grated Parmesan
   cheese
3 eggs, or equivalent amount
   of pasteurized egg
   substitute

3/4 cup half-and-half
1 tablespoon parsley flakes, or
   2 tablespoons minced fresh
   parsley
12 ounces linguini, cooked
   and drained
Additional grated Parmesan
   cheese

Cook the bacon in a large skillet until crisp; remove and drain on paper towels, reserving 3 tablespoons drippings in the skillet. Sauté the onion, garlic, and red pepper flakes in the drippings for 5 minutes or until the onion is translucent. Turn off the heat. Whisk the cheese and eggs in a medium bowl until frothy. Whisk in the half-and-half until blended. Stir in the parsley. Add the linguini to the onion mixture and cook over medium heat until hot, stirring constantly. Reduce the heat to very low or remove from the heat and stir in the egg mixture, tossing quickly to thicken the egg mixture and coat the pasta. Stir in the bacon and serve immediately with Parmesan cheese. Serve with a green salad and hot Italian bread.

NOTE: *This is a classic Italian dish that is a little tricky to make. Be sure that the egg mixture is added to hot pasta that is on low heat, or no heat at all, so that you don't scramble the eggs rather than coating the pasta. Well worth a few attempts to get it right. For the weight-conscious, chicken broth may be substituted for the half-and-half.*

CALAMARI AND PASTA WITH SUGAR SNAP PEAS AND CARROTS

MAKES 8 SERVINGS

16 ounces fettuccini or linguini
2 tablespoons butter
2 tablespoons olive oil
8 garlic cloves, minced
3 cups thinly sliced carrots, or 1 large red
    or green bell pepper, chopped
4 cups sugar snap peas or mushrooms
2/3 cup thinly sliced green onions
1 cup dry white wine
2 tablespoons snipped fresh dill weed,
    or 2 teaspoons dried dill weed
2 teaspoons chicken or vegetable
    bouillon granules
2 teaspoons red pepper flakes
2/3 cup water
2 pounds fresh or frozen calamari, thawed
1/4 cup cornstarch
6 tablespoons water
1/2 cup grated Romano cheese
Cracked black pepper

Cook the pasta using the package directions; drain. Toss with the butter in a large bowl and keep warm. Heat the olive oil over medium-high heat in a large skillet or wok. Add the garlic and stir-fry for 15 seconds. Add the carrots and stir-fry for 4 minutes. Add the snap peas and green onions and stir-fry for 2 to 3 minutes or until tender-crisp. Remove the vegetables to a bowl and keep warm. Allow the skillet to cool.

Add the wine, dill weed, bouillon granules, red pepper flakes, and 2/3 cup water to the skillet and bring to a boil. Add the calamari. Reduce the heat and simmer, uncovered, for 2 to 3 minutes or until the calamari is opaque and slightly firm, stirring occasionally.

Combine the cornstarch and 6 tablespoons water in a small bowl, stirring until dissolved. Stir into the skillet and cook until thickened and bubbly, stirring constantly. Return the vegetables to the skillet and add the pasta, tossing to coat. Heat through. Sprinkle with the cheese and pepper before serving.

CHICKEN AND PASTA IN CURRIED MUSHROOM SAUCE

MAKES 4 SERVINGS

12 ounces tagliarini or other
   thin pasta
2 tablespoons butter
2 small chicken breasts or
   turkey breast slices,
   cut into cubes
Salt and pepper to taste
1 tablespoon chopped fresh
   rosemary leaves (optional)
Dry white wine

8 ounces small brown
   mushrooms, sliced
1 cup heavy cream
1/2 cup veal sweetbreads,
   cut into cubes (optional)
1 teaspoon curry powder,
   or to taste
6 ounces Parmesan cheese,
   grated

Cook the pasta in boiling salted water until al dente; drain and place in a large bowl with a small amount of the cooking water. Melt the butter in a large skillet. Add the chicken, salt, and pepper and sauté over low heat until very brown. Add the rosemary and a splash of wine. Cook until the wine evaporates. Add the mushrooms and cook until tender. Stir in the cream, sweetbreads, and curry powder and bring to a gentle boil. Reduce the heat to low and simmer until heated through, stirring constantly. Stir in the pasta and cheese and toss to coat. Stir in a small amount of cream if the mixture is too thick. Serve immediately.

NOTE: *Do not drain the pasta completely, or the dish will be too dry.*

MIGHTY FINE RICE

MAKES 8 SERVINGS

1 (8-ounce) package saffron
   rice, or 1 cup uncooked
   white rice and a pinch of
   saffron
1/4 cup (1/2 stick) butter
2 onions, sliced

1/4 cup (1/2 stick) butter
1 pound mushrooms, sliced
3 dashes of ground nutmeg
Salt and pepper to taste
1 cup heavy cream

Cook the rice using the package directions. Melt 1/4 cup butter in a large skillet. Add the onions and sauté over low heat for 30 minutes, stirring occasionally. Remove the onions from the skillet. Melt 1/4 cup butter in the skillet. Add the mushrooms and sauté for 10 minutes. Return the onions to the skillet and season with the nutmeg, salt, and pepper. Add the cream and bring to a gentle boil, stirring constantly. Reduce the heat and stir in the rice. Heat through.

RICE WITH PINE NUTS

1/2 cup olive oil
1 cup chopped onion
1 cup pine nuts
1/4 teaspoon hot red pepper
   sauce

3/4 teaspoon paprika
5 cups hot cooked rice
Salt and pepper to taste
Chopped parsley
6 pimentos, chopped

Heat the olive oil in a large skillet. Add the onion, pine nuts, hot red pepper sauce, and paprika and sauté for 8 minutes. Add to the rice in a large bowl and toss, using 2 forks. Season with salt and pepper. Spoon into a serving dish and garnish with parsley and pimentos.

WILD RICE CASSEROLE WITH SAUSAGE AND MACADAMIA NUTS

MAKES 6 TO 8 SERVINGS

2 (6-ounce) packages mixed
   long grain and wild rice
1 teaspoon salt
Freshly ground pepper
Pinch of oregano
Pinch of thyme
Pinch of marjoram
1 1/2 pounds mild Italian
   sausage links, thinly sliced

1 pound mushrooms, sliced
3 or 4 green onions, sliced
1/4 cup all-purpose flour
1 cup heavy cream
2 1/2 cups chicken broth
Chopped macadamia nuts

Cook the rice using the package directions. Add the salt, pepper, oregano, thyme, and marjoram to the cooked rice. Preheat the oven to 350 degrees. Sauté the sausage in a large skillet until well browned. Remove from the skillet to paper towels, reserving the drippings in the skillet. Add the mushrooms and green onions to the skillet and sauté until tender. Spoon into a bowl. Stir together the flour and cream until blended and add to the skillet. Stir in the broth and bring to a boil. Cook over medium-high heat until thickened, stirring constantly. Stir in the sausage, mushroom mixture, and rice and mix well. Spoon into a large baking dish and top with macadamia nuts. Bake, covered, for 30 minutes or until hot.

Cowboy Joe Tailgate Party

When the Wyoming Cowboy football team plays at home, people from all corners of the state congregate for food, fun, and camaraderie. They come to partake of outstanding Western-style tailgating fare and to see Cowboy Joe, the team's Shetland pony mascot, celebrate Cowboy scores with a trot in the end zone.

The Menu

SAN ANTONIO GUACAMOLE WITH SOY CHIPS

TERIYAKI-GLAZED CHICKEN WINGS

BAMPY'S BAKED BEANS*

GINGERED COLESLAW WITH LIME DRESSING*

COWBOY JOE'S HOOFPRINTS*

PULL-OFF-THE-BONE BARBECUED BEEF BRISKET
AND HAMBURGER BUNS*

COWBOY CAKE

PINWHEEL DATE COOKIES

*pictured recipes

Vegetables & Side Dishes

ASPARAGUS CHINOIS

MAKES 6 SERVINGS

1¹/₂ pounds asparagus spears
1 tablespoon sesame oil
1 tablespoon vegetable oil
4 teaspoons Worcestershire sauce
Sesame seeds, toasted
Freshly ground pepper

Slice the asparagus diagonally into 1¹/₂-inch pieces. Heat the sesame oil, vegetable oil, and Worcestershire sauce in a wok or large skillet and add the asparagus. Stir-fry just until tender. Spoon into a serving dish and sprinkle with sesame seeds and pepper.

NO-FAIL HOLLANDAISE SAUCE

To prepare No-Fail Hollandaise Sauce that is different than all of 'em because it's quick, combine 2 eggs, 1 stick of butter, 2 tablespoons lemon juice, and ¹/₂ teaspoon salt in a bowl and blend until smooth. Add ¹/₂ cup of hot water gradually, stirring constantly. Pour the mixture into the top of a double boiler and cook over hot water, stirring constantly until the mixture is of a custard consistency. Serve hot or cold over vegetables. It is a perfect accompaniment to freshly steamed asparagus.

It really doesn't take long to prepare this, and there's a switch here from all other Hollandaise recipes, and that is—if it begins to separate, drop in ice shavings and keep stirring, and it will return to a custard consistency. Have a chilled little glass of pinot grigio on hand to cut through the calories and the creaminess of this dazzling sauce.

BAMPY'S BAKED BEANS

MAKES 16 TO 20 SERVINGS

4 cups mixed dried beans
2 tablespoons salt
1 1/2 quarts water
2 or 3 smoked ham hocks
1 cup packed brown sugar
1 cup dark molasses
1/4 cup Catalina salad dressing
1/4 cup light corn syrup
1 pound cooked ham, cubed
1 (15-ounce) can tomatoes, chopped
1 onion, chopped
1/4 cup ketchup
1 tablespoon chili powder
2 teaspoons lemon juice
1 teaspoon salt
1/2 teaspoon pepper
1 teaspoon liquid smoke (optional)
1/2 pound diced cooked bacon (optional)

Sort and rinse the beans and combine with water to cover in a 4- to 6-quart stockpot. Add 2 tablespoons salt and soak for 8 to 10 hours. Drain the water from the beans and add 1 1/2 quarts fresh water and the ham hocks. Bring to a boil. Reduce the heat and simmer, covered, for 2 to 3 hours, stirring occasionally. Preheat the oven to 350 degrees. Remove the ham hocks and cut the meat off the bones into bite-size pieces. Pour the beans and liquid into a large roasting pan and add the ham. Stir in the brown sugar, molasses, salad dressing, corn syrup, cubed ham, tomatoes, onion, ketchup, chili powder, lemon juice, 1 teaspoon salt, pepper, and liquid smoke. Top with the bacon. Bake for 2 to 3 hours or until the beans are tender.

According to a recent article in the *UWYO* magazine, branding, a Wyoming ranching tradition, "has become a rite of spring for the UW Cowboy wrestlers." Every spring, the wrestlers help brand and inoculate almost one thousand calves for local ranchers. This arrangement benefits the wrestlers by giving them some off-season training, and the ranchers benefit by getting the job done more quickly. Following the work, the wrestlers are treated to a hearty meal, which might include baked beans, just as Bampy's Baked Beans were served several generations ago to ranch hands on branding day.

FRESH GREEN BEANS IN HERB BUTTER

MAKES 4 SERVINGS

1/4 cup (1/2 stick) butter
3/4 cup minced onion
1/3 cup minced celery
2 garlic cloves
1/4 cup chopped fresh parsley
2 teaspoons chopped fresh
    basil, or 1/4 teaspoon dried
    basil, crushed

1 teaspoon chopped fresh
    rosemary leaves, or
    1/4 teaspoon dried
    rosemary, crushed
1/2 to 3/4 teaspoon salt
Freshly ground pepper
1 pound fresh green beans,
    steamed

Melt the butter in a medium saucepan and add the onion, celery, and garlic. Sauté for 5 to 7 minutes or until tender. Add the parsley, basil, rosemary, salt, and pepper and cook for 5 minutes longer. Pour over the hot green beans and toss to coat.

GREEN BEANS, FETA CHEESE, AND PECANS

MAKES 4 TO 6 SERVINGS

1 1/2 pounds fresh green
    beans, trimmed and cut
    into 1-inch pieces
1 cup coarsely chopped
    pecans, toasted
1 cup diced red onion
1 cup crumbled feta cheese

3/4 cup olive oil
1 tablespoon dill weed
1/4 cup white wine vinegar
1/2 teaspoon minced garlic
1/4 teaspoon salt
1/4 teaspoon freshly ground
    pepper

Cook the green beans in boiling water in a large saucepan for 4 minutes; drain and immediately immerse in cold water to stop the cooking process. Drain and pat dry. Place the beans in a serving dish and sprinkle with the pecans, onion, and cheese. Whisk together the olive oil, dill weed, vinegar, garlic, salt, and pepper in a small bowl until blended. Pour over the beans and toss just before serving.

Cabbage with Toasted Pine Nuts and Bacon

1/2 cup sugar
1/2 cup salt
1 large head cabbage,
   coarsely chopped
2 cups water

4 to 6 slices bacon,
   crisp-cooked and diced
1/4 cup (1/2 stick) butter,
   melted
1/4 cup pine nuts, toasted

Combine the sugar, salt, and enough cold water to cover the cabbage in a large nonmetallic bowl, stirring until the sugar is dissolved. Add the cabbage and let stand, covered, in the refrigerator for 3 hours or longer; drain. Bring 2 cups water to a boil in a large saucepan and add the cabbage. Cook for 5 to 8 minutes or just until tender; drain. Stir in the bacon, butter, and pine nuts and remove to a serving bowl.

Creamy Cheese Corn

Quick & Easy

Great for a crowd or a potluck. You can easily double this recipe.

Makes 8 to 10 servings

2 (15-ounce) cans whole kernel corn, drained
1 (15-ounce) can cream-style corn
8 ounces cream cheese, cut into cubes

Place the whole kernel corn, cream-style corn, and cream cheese in a slow cooker and stir until combined. Cook on High for 2 to 3 hours or until the cheese is melted and the mixture is hot, stirring occasionally.

FRESH CORN PUDDING

MAKES 4 SERVINGS

2 egg whites
2 egg yolks
2 cups fresh corn kernels
2 tablespoons all-purpose
    flour

2 tablespoon sugar
$^1/_2$ teaspoon salt
$^1/_8$ teaspoon pepper
1 cup 2% milk
1 tablespoon butter

Preheat the oven to 350 degrees. Beat the egg whites in a small bowl until stiff peaks form. Whisk the egg yolks in a mixing bowl until frothy. Whisk in the corn, flour, sugar, salt, and pepper until combined. Add the milk and mix well. Fold in the beaten egg whites. Pour into a buttered 1-quart casserole and dot with the butter. Bake, uncovered, for 45 to 50 minutes or until the center is set.

GRILLED MEDITERRANEAN EGGPLANT

MAKES 4 TO 6 SERVINGS

1 red bell pepper, halved
1 eggplant, cut into 3/8-inch-thick slices
Olive oil
1 tomato, sliced
1 cup crumbled feta cheese
1 (4-ounce) jar marinated artichoke hearts, chopped
1/2 cup sliced black olives
2 tablespoons chopped fresh basil
Salt and pepper to taste

Preheat the grill and coat the grill rack with nonstick cooking spray, if desired. Grill the bell pepper halves, skin side down, over medium heat just until the skin begins to darken. Remove from the grill and cool slightly. Chop the cooled bell pepper. Brush both sides of the eggplant slices with olive oil and grill for a few minutes per side or just until tender. With the eggplant slices still on the grill, top each slice with a tomato slice and sprinkle with the cheese. Top with the artichokes, roasted pepper, olives, and basil. Season with salt and pepper and heat just until warmed through.

EGGPLANT AU GRATIN

*Serve this eggplant au gratin over spaghetti
for a great meatless entrée.*

MAKES 5 TO 6 SERVINGS

1 (1¹/2-pound) eggplant, peeled
¹/3 cup butter
1 medium or 2 small onions, thinly sliced
3 tomatoes, diced, or 20 cherry tomatoes, halved
1 cup (4 ounces) shredded Cheddar cheese
¹/2 cup fine dry bread crumbs
Salt and pepper to taste
2 tablespoons butter, cut into pieces

Preheat the oven to 375 degrees. Cut the eggplant into ¹/2-inch-thick slices and cut each slice into cubes. Melt ¹/3 cup butter in a large skillet and add the eggplant. Sauté until golden brown, stirring frequently. Spoon half the eggplant into a buttered 1¹/2-quart baking dish. Layer with half the onion, half the tomatoes, half the cheese, and half the bread crumbs. Season with salt and pepper. Repeat the layers with the remaining eggplant, onion, tomatoes, cheese, bread crumbs, salt, and pepper. Dot with 2 tablespoons butter. Bake for 35 minutes or until the eggplant is tender.

NAPOLEON MUSHROOMS

*This is a nice dish served with beef tenderloin and delicious enough
to go with a simple hamburger.*

MAKES 6 SERVINGS

3 tablespoons butter
2 pounds mushrooms, sliced
2 teaspoons herbes de Provence
1 teaspoon garlic salt
1 teaspoon white pepper
3 tablespoons Cognac or brandy (preferably Courvoisier)
3 tablespoons heavy cream

Melt the butter in a large skillet. Add the mushrooms, herbes de Provence, garlic salt, and white pepper and sauté until tender. Add the Cognac and cook for 1 minute longer. Stir in the cream and cook until the liquid has evaporated, stirring constantly.

NOTE: *This dish warms well in the microwave.*

PORTOBELLO TOWERS WITH MASHED POTATOES, PROSCIUTTO, AND GRUYÈRE

MAKES 8 SERVINGS

2 1/2 pounds russet potatoes, peeled and diced
Salt and pepper to taste
8 small portobello mushroom caps
3 to 4 tablespoons olive oil
1/2 cup sliced shallots
1/2 cup sliced leeks (white and pale green part only)
1 cup heavy cream
1/4 cup (1/2 stick) butter
8 garlic cloves, diced
3 tablespoons chopped mixed fresh herbs (marjoram, tarragon, basil, rosemary)
4 teaspoons butter, softened
1 1/2 cups (6 ounces) shredded Gruyère cheese
4 ounces minced prosciutto
Whole chives

Cook the potatoes in boiling salted water in a large saucepan for 30 minutes or until very tender; drain. Let cool for 10 minutes. Season with salt and pepper and mash. Preheat the broiler. Brush the mushroom caps with 1 to 2 tablespoons of the olive oil and season with salt and pepper. Arrange on a broiler pan and broil on both sides for about 5 minutes or until tender. Heat the remaining 2 tablespoons olive oil in a small heavy skillet. Add the shallots and leeks and cook for 3 minutes or just until the leeks begin to brown. Stir into the potatoes. Add the cream, butter, garlic, and fresh herbs to the potatoes and mix well. Place the mushroom caps, top side down, on the broiler pan and top each with 1/2 teaspoon butter. Mound the mashed potato mixture equally onto the mushroom caps. Sprinkle generously with the cheese and the prosciutto. Broil until the cheese melts, the prosciutto is brown, and the potatoes are hot. Garnish with whole chives sticking out of the potatoes. Serve immediately.

Omit the prosciutto to make a wonderful vegetarian dish. You can add prepared stems of asparagus on top of the mushrooms, but be sure that you can press the potatoes around and under the asparagus. Heap the rest of the potato mixture on top to make the tower.

PORTOBELLOS IN PUFF PASTRY

MAKES 2 SERVINGS

2 large portobello mushroom
  caps
2 teaspoons olive oil
1 (10-ounce) package frozen
  chopped spinach, thawed
  and squeezed dry
4 ounces low-fat cream
  cheese, softened
4 ounces feta cheese,
  crumbled

1/4 cup chopped onion
2 tablespoons slivered
  almonds
1 teaspoon minced garlic
2 sheets frozen puff pastry,
  thawed, at room
  temperature
2 tablespoons milk

Preheat the oven to 400 degrees. Brush the insides of the mushroom caps with the olive oil. Combine the spinach, cream cheese, feta cheese, onion, almonds, and garlic in a bowl and mix well. Divide the spinach mixture equally between the mushroom caps. Invert each mushroom cap onto a pastry sheet and wrap the pastry around the mushroom, pressing the edges together to seal. Place, seam side down, on a baking sheet. Brush with the milk and cut small slits in the top of the pastry. Bake for 20 minutes or until brown.

CARAMELIZED ONIONS AND RICE

MAKES 8 TO 10 SERVINGS

1/4 cup (1/2 stick) butter
7 1/2 cups chopped or sliced
  Walla Walla onions
2 cups water
1/2 cup uncooked rice

3/4 cup (6 ounces) shredded
  Swiss, Cheddar, or
  Monterey Jack cheese
2/3 cup half-and-half

Preheat the oven to 300 degrees. Melt the butter in a large skillet. Add the onions and sauté for 15 minutes or until the onions are tender and caramelized. Bring the water to a boil in a small saucepan. Add the rice and cook for 5 minutes; drain. Stir into the caramelized onions. Add the cheese and half-and-half and mix well. Spoon the mixture into a buttered 1 1/2-quart baking dish. Bake, covered, for 1 hour.

NOTE: *If Walla Walla onions are not available, another brand of sweet onions can be substituted. If you can't find sweet onions, substitute yellow onions.*

CHEDDAR CHEESE ONION BAKE

MAKES 6 TO 8 SERVINGS

6 onions, thinly sliced into rings
1/4 cup (1/2 stick) butter
1/4 cup all-purpose flour
1/2 teaspoon salt
2 cups milk
2 cups (8 ounces) shredded Cheddar cheese

Preheat the oven to 350 degrees. Cook the onions in boiling water in a saucepan until tender; drain. Spoon into a buttered 2-quart baking dish. Melt the butter in a saucepan and stir in the flour and salt. Add the milk gradually and cook until thickened and bubbly, stirring constantly. Pour the sauce over the onions and sprinkle with the cheese. Bake, uncovered, for 30 minutes or until the top is light brown.

NOTE: *To serve as a hot dip with crusty bread or crackers, chop the onions instead of slicing them.*

COWBOY ONION RINGS

MAKES 8 SERVINGS

1 egg
1 cup milk
1 tablespoon lemon juice
2 tablespoons vegetable oil
2 cups all-purpose flour
1/2 teaspoon baking soda
1 teaspoon salt
2 sweet onions, cut into 1/2-inch slices and
    separated into rings
4 cups panko (Japanese bread crumbs)
Vegetable oil for deep-frying

Whisk together the egg, milk, lemon juice, and 2 tablespoons oil in a large bowl. Stir together the flour, baking soda, and salt and whisk into the egg mixture until blended. The batter will be thick. Dip the onion rings into the batter, then into the panko, coating generously. Heat oil in a heavy saucepan to 350 degrees. Fry the onion rings, a few at a time, until golden brown. Serve warm.

WYOMING POTATOES

Quick & Easy

MAKES 8 SERVINGS

1 (24- to 26-ounce) package
   frozen shredded hash
   brown potatoes, thawed
3/4 cup finely chopped onion
1 (10-ounce) can cream of
   chicken soup

1 cup sour cream
1/2 cup (1 stick) butter, melted
Salt and pepper to taste
1 cup cornflakes, crushed
1/4 cup (1/2 stick) butter,
   melted

Preheat the oven to 350 degrees. Combine the potatoes, onion, soup, sour cream, and 1/2 cup melted butter in a large bowl and mix well. Season with salt and pepper. Spread into a 9×13-inch or other shallow baking dish. Top with the cornflakes and drizzle with 1/4 cup butter. Bake, uncovered, for 45 minutes.

NOTE: *Nine frozen shredded hash brown patties, thawed, can be used instead of the bag of hash browns.*

SAVORY SAUTÉED SWEET POTATOES

MAKES 8 TO 12 SERVINGS

6 tablespoons butter
5 large sweet potatoes, peeled
   and shredded
1 tablespoon sugar
1 teaspoon salt

1/2 teaspoon white pepper
1/4 teaspoon freshly ground
   nutmeg
Fresh sage leaves

Melt the butter in a large skillet. Add the sweet potatoes and sauté for 5 minutes or until tender. Stir in the sugar, salt, white pepper, and nutmeg. Adjust the seasonings to taste. Serve immediately or chill, covered, until ready to serve. Reheat in the microwave or in a 350-degree oven for 10 minutes. Garnish with sage.

NOTE: *A food processor can be used to shred the sweet potatoes. For a festive way to serve this dish, press the hot sweet potatoes into individual ramekins or small plastic cups and unmold onto the serving plates.*

SWEET POTATO PIE

MAKES 8 TO 10 SERVINGS

1 (15-ounce) can juice-pack pineapple chunks
1/2 cup (1 stick) butter
1 cup packed brown sugar
3 tablespoons all-purpose flour
1 1/4 teaspoons ground cinnamon
1/2 teaspoon ground nutmeg
1/4 teaspoon ground allspice
1/3 cup maple syrup
2 tablespoons orange juice
3 (29-ounce) cans sweet potatoes, drained
1 (10-inch) unbaked deep-dish pie shell (optional)
1/2 cup pecan pieces
Large marshmallows

Preheat the oven to 350 degrees. Drain the pineapple, reserving the juice. Melt the butter in a medium saucepan over medium heat. Add the brown sugar and cook until smooth and blended, stirring constantly. Stir in the flour, cinnamon, nutmeg, and allspice and mix well. Add the reserved juice, maple syrup, and orange juice and mix well. Cook over medium heat for 10 minutes, stirring occasionally. Remove from the heat. Arrange the sweet potatoes in a 3-quart baking dish or in the pie shell and pour the syrup mixture evenly over the top. Top with the pecans, pineapple chunks, and marshmallows. Bake for 20 minutes or until the mixture is heated through and the top is brown.

NOTE: *If using a piecrust, there may be extra filling, so do not overfill.*

PECAN STREUSEL TOPPING

MAKES ABOUT
2 1/2 CUPS

1/2 cup all-purpose flour
1/2 cup packed brown
  sugar
1/4 cup (1/2 stick) cold
  butter or margarine,
  cut into pieces
1 cup chopped pecans

Combine the flour and brown sugar in a bowl and cut in the butter until crumbly. Stir in the pecans.

SWEET POTATO SOUFFLÉ

MAKES 12 SERVINGS

3 eggs
3 cups mashed cooked
  sweet potatoes
1/2 cup sweetened
  condensed milk

1 cup sugar
1/4 cup (1/2 stick) butter or
  margarine, melted
1 tablespoon vanilla extract
Pecan Streusel Topping

Preheat the oven to 325 degrees. Whisk the eggs in a large bowl until frothy. Whisk in the sweet potatoes, sweetened condensed milk, sugar, melted butter, and vanilla until blended. Pour into a buttered baking dish. Sprinkle with the Pecan Streusel Topping. Bake for 45 to 60 minutes or until the top is brown and bubbly.

BUTTERNUT SQUASH CASSEROLE

MAKES 10 TO 12 SERVINGS

1 large butternut squash
3/4 cup sugar
1 teaspoon ground ginger
Pinch of salt
1 teaspoon coconut flavoring

3 extra-large eggs, beaten
6 tablespoons butter, melted
1 cup milk
Shredded coconut or crushed
  butter crackers (optional)

Preheat the oven to 350 degrees. Pierce the butternut squash with a fork and bake for 1 hour or until fork-tender. Cut the squash in half and scoop out and discard the seeds. Scoop out the flesh into a large bowl and mash. Reduce the oven temperature to 325 degrees. Add the sugar, ginger, salt, and coconut flavoring to the squash and mix well. Stir in the eggs. Add the butter and milk and mix well. Pour into a buttered 2 1/2- to 3-quart baking dish. Bake for 1 hour or until hot and bubbly. Garnish with shredded coconut or cracker crumbs, if desired.

NOTE: *Two 11-ounce packages of frozen butternut squash, thawed, can be substituted for the mashed fresh squash.*

ROASTED VEGETABLES

MAKES 8 SERVINGS

8 red potatoes, quartered
8 small sweet onions
2 tablespoons olive oil
Salt and pepper to taste
4 zucchini, cut into
   1/2-inch slices

2 red bell peppers, quartered
16 ounces baby carrots
1 tablespoon thyme
1 lemon, thinly sliced
2 tablespoons olive oil

Preheat the oven to 425 degrees. Toss the potatoes and onions
in 2 tablespoons olive oil in a large roasting pan or baking dish.
Season with salt and pepper. Roast, uncovered, for 15 to 20 minutes.
Add the zucchini, bell peppers, carrots, thyme, and lemon slices and
mix well. Drizzle with 2 tablespoons olive oil and return to the oven.
Roast, uncovered, for 45 minutes, tossing occasionally.

POLENTA TOPPED WITH VEGETABLES AND GOAT CHEESE

MAKES 6 SERVINGS

2/3 cup walnuts
1 tablespoon olive oil
1/4 cup chopped red onion
3/4 cup sliced fresh
   mushrooms
3/4 cup chopped broccoli
2 tablespoons chopped
   fresh sage

3/4 cup vegetable broth or
   chicken broth
1 (16-ounce) package polenta,
   cut into 12 slices
2 tablespoons olive oil
3/4 cup crumbled goat cheese
Red pepper flakes

Preheat the oven to 350 degrees. Toast the walnuts in a skillet over medium heat until fragrant; remove from the skillet. Heat 1 tablespoon olive oil in the skillet. Add the onion, mushrooms, broccoli, and sage and sauté over medium-high heat until the onions are translucent. Add the broth and cook, covered, for 1 minute. Bring to a boil and simmer, uncovered, until reduced by 1/2. Keep warm. Brush the polenta slices with 2 tablespoons olive oil and arrange on a nonstick baking sheet. Bake for 15 minutes; then broil, 4 inches from the heat, until golden brown. To serve, place 2 polenta slices on individual plates and top with the vegetable mixture, goat cheese, walnuts, and red pepper flakes.

FRESH ZUCCHINI AND CARROT BAKE

MAKES 8 SERVINGS

2 tablespoons butter
4 to 5 cups chopped zucchini
2 tablespoons chopped onion
1 cup shredded carrots
1 (10-ounce) can cream of
   chicken soup

1 cup sour cream
1 (8-ounce) package herb-
   seasoned stuffing mix
1/2 cup (1 stick) butter, melted

Preheat the oven to 350 degrees. Melt 2 tablespoons butter in a large skillet. Add the zucchini and onion and sauté until tender. Add the carrots, soup, and sour cream and mix well. Combine the stuffing mix and 1/2 cup butter in a bowl. Spoon half the stuffing into a 9×13-inch baking dish and pour the zucchini mixture evenly over the top. Top with the remaining stuffing. Bake for 30 minutes.

MAPLE CHILI-GLAZED APPLES

This is a nice do-ahead dish that reheats well—an excellent accompaniment to roast pork, ham, or sausages.

6 Granny Smith apples, each cut into 8 wedges
1/4 cup (1/2 stick) butter, melted
1/3 cup maple syrup
1 tablespoon chili powder
1 tablespoon lemon juice

Preheat the oven to 375 degrees. Toss together the apples, butter, maple syrup, chili powder, and lemon juice in a large bowl. Spoon into a foil-lined shallow baking pan coated with nonstick cooking spray. Bake, uncovered, for 30 to 40 minutes, basting with pan juices every 10 minutes.

SWEET AND SAVORY FRUIT COMPOTE

This is easy, wonderful, and can accompany any meat or fish.

MAKES 10 SERVINGS

1 (20-ounce) can sliced peaches, drained
1 (20-ounce) can pears, drained and sliced
1 (20-ounce) can pineapple chunks, drained
2 (15-ounce) cans apricot halves, drained
1/4 cup (1/2 stick) butter, melted
2/3 cup packed light brown sugar
2 teaspoons ground cinnamon
1/4 teaspoon ground ginger
1/4 teaspoon ground nutmeg
1/8 teaspoon curry powder
Pitted maraschino cherries, drained and chopped

Preheat the oven to 350 degrees. Combine all the fruit in a 9×13-inch baking dish. Combine the butter, brown sugar, cinnamon, ginger, nutmeg, and curry powder in a small bowl and mix well. Spoon over the fruit and mix well. Top with the maraschino cherries. Bake for 2 hours, stirring occasionally. Serve warm or chilled.

NOTE: *Any leftovers keep at least a week in the refrigerator to accompany another meal. Kids love this dish!*

Art Exhibition Opening: Champagne and Desserts to Celebrate!

The University of Wyoming Art Museum is located in the dramatic Centennial Complex, whose centerpiece is a cone-shaped "archival" mountain representing the slow but certain geological upheaval that defines the Wyoming landscape. A place of intellectual and social rendezvous, the museum offers exhibition openings throughout the year, calling people together to celebrate art.

The Menu

DOUBLE CHOCOLATE IRISH SPICE CAKE*

MALTED MILK CHOCOLATE CHIP COOKIES*

KAHLUA FUDGE*

CHOCOLATE CHIP CHEESECAKE*

LACE COOKIES*

OLD-FASHIONED GINGER CAKE DOUGHNUT HOLES*

CHAMPAGNE

CAPPUCCINO

*pictured recipes

Desserts

SARDI'S CASSATA ROYALE BOMBE

MAKES 20 SERVINGS

1 (2-layer) package white cake mix
1 teaspoon grated orange zest
1/2 cup orange juice
4 cups ricotta cheese
1/4 to 1/2 cup confectioners' sugar, or to taste
1/3 to 1/2 cup raspberries, halved, or
  1/2 to 2/3 cup mixed candied fruit
4 ounces sweet chocolate, grated
2/3 cup kirsch, brandy, or framboise
4 cups whipping cream, whipped
1/4 cup confectioners' sugar
1 (1-ounce) square chocolate, at room temperature
1/2 cup maraschino cherries, drained and halved
1/3 cup pistachio nuts

Prepare the cake mix using the package directions, adding the orange zest and using the orange juice to replace part of the water. Spoon into a greased tube pan and bake for 45 to 50 minutes. Cool in the pan for 10 minutes. Invert onto a wire rack to cool completely.

Combine the ricotta cheese, 1/4 to 1/2 cup confectioners' sugar, the raspberries, 4 ounces chocolate, and kirsch in a large bowl and mix gently. Fold in half the whipped cream. Cut the cake into 1/2-inch slices. Line the bottom of a well-buttered 4-quart glass bowl with cake slices. Spread some of the ricotta mixture over the cake. Continue layering the cake and ricotta mixture alternately until the bowl is filled, ending with cake slices. Chill, covered, for 6 to 12 hours.

Fold 1/4 cup confectioners' sugar into the remaining whipped cream. Cut curls from the chocolate square using a swivel-blade vegetable peeler. Place on waxed paper and store in the refrigerator. To serve, loosen the side of the bombe with a spatula and unmold onto a serving plate. Frost with the sweetened whipped cream and garnish with the chocolate curls, cherries, and pistachios.

NOTE: *The unfrosted bombe may be made ahead and frozen, tightly wrapped.*

HOT BREAD PUDDING WITH WHISKEY SAUCE

MAKES 12 TO 15 SERVINGS

1 cup raisins
1/2 cup whiskey, warmed
3 eggs
4 cups milk
2 cups granulated sugar
3 tablespoons butter, melted
2 tablespoons vanilla extract
1 loaf stale French bread, cut into 1-inch pieces
1 cup flaked coconut (optional)
2 cups chopped pecans
1/2 cup (1 stick) butter
1 cup confectioners' sugar
1 egg yolk, beaten

Preheat the oven to 375 degrees. Combine the raisins and the whiskey in a small bowl and let stand for 10 minutes; drain, reserving the whiskey. Beat the eggs in a large mixing bowl until light and frothy. Add the milk, granulated sugar, 3 tablespoons melted butter, and vanilla and beat until the sugar is dissolved. Add the bread, coconut, and pecans and stir until the bread is moistened. Pour into a buttered 9×13-inch baking dish. Bake for 45 to 50 minutes.

Melt 1/2 cup butter with the confectioners' sugar in a small saucepan over medium heat, stirring constantly until blended. Whisk in the egg yolk and cook over medium-low heat for 5 minutes or until thickened and bubbly, stirring constantly. Remove from the heat and whisk in the reserved whiskey until smooth. The sauce will thicken as it cools. Serve the sauce over the warm bread pudding.

FLAMED CHERRY CREPES

1 pound frozen pitted tart red cherries,
  thawed
2 tablespoons sugar
2 tablespoons cornstarch
1/4 cup brandy
Crepes
Vanilla ice cream or whipped cream

Drain the cherries and reserve the liquid. Add water to the reserved cherry liquid to equal 1 cup. Stir together the sugar and cornstarch in a small saucepan. Add the cherry liquid and stir until blended. Bring to a boil and cook until the mixture thickens, stirring constantly. Stir in the cherries. Heat the brandy in a small saucepan. Do not boil. Remove the cherry mixture from the heat. Pour the brandy over the cherry mixture and ignite with a long match. Fill the crepes with the warm cherry sauce and serve with ice cream or garnish with whipped cream.

NOTE: *Pre-made crepes can be found in the produce section of most supermarkets.*

CREPES

MAKES 4 TO 6 SERVINGS

2 eggs, beaten
1 1/2 cups milk
1 cup all-purpose flour
1 tablespoon vegetable oil
2 tablespoons sugar

Beat the eggs, milk, flour, oil, and sugar in a bowl until blended. Heat a lightly greased 6-inch skillet over medium heat. Remove from the heat. Pour 2 tablespoons of the batter into the heated skillet, tilting the skillet until the batter is spread over the bottom. Return the skillet to the heat and cook until the crepe is brown on 1 side. Place the crepe on a paper towel. Repeat the procedure with the remaining batter, greasing the skillet occasionally.

APPLE CHEESECAKE
CHIMICHANGAS

MAKES 5 TO 6 SERVINGS

8 ounces cream cheese, softened
$1/4$ cup sugar
2 tablespoons all-purpose flour
$3/4$ cup cooked chopped apple
$1/2$ teaspoon vanilla extract
10 ($6^1/2$-inch) flour tortillas or egg roll wrappers, warmed
Vegetable oil for deep-frying
$1/4$ cup sugar
1 tablespoon ground cinnamon
Vanilla ice cream
Caramel ice cream topping

Beat the cream cheese in a mixing bowl until fluffy. Add $1/4$ cup sugar and the flour and beat well. Stir in the apple and vanilla. Place 2 to 3 tablespoons of the cream cheese mixture in the center of each tortilla. Fold 2 sides of the tortilla over the filling, overlapping slightly; tuck in the ends. Chill for 1 hour.

Preheat the oven to 350 degrees. Heat at least 3 inches of oil to 375 degrees in a large heavy pan. Place the chimichangas, 1 or 2 at a time, top sides down, in the hot oil and cook until golden brown. Turn over and cook the bottom sides until golden brown. Remove to paper towels to drain. Arrange on a baking sheet. Bake for 20 to 25 minutes. Combine $1/4$ cup sugar and the cinnamon and sprinkle over the chimichangas. Serve warm with a scoop of vanilla ice cream and a drizzle of caramel topping.

NOTE: *Canned apples are available in some stores, and you may substitute them for the fresh apples, but do not use canned apple pie filling. It has too much gooey starch.*

CHOCOLATE CHEESECAKE

MAKES 12 TO 16 SERVINGS

1¹/₃ cups finely crushed creme-filled chocolate
    sandwich cookies (about 20 cookies)
2 tablespoons sugar
¹/₄ teaspoon ground cinnamon
¹/₄ cup (¹/₂ stick) butter, melted
16 ounces cream cheese, softened
2 eggs
¹/₂ cup sugar
2 cups sour cream
2 tablespoons butter, melted
2 cups (12 ounces) semisweet chocolate chips,
    melted and slightly cooled
Whipped cream

Preheat the oven to 325 degrees. Combine the cookie crumbs,
2 tablespoons sugar, the cinnamon, and ¹/₄ cup melted butter in a
bowl and mix well. Press onto the bottom of a 9-inch springform pan.
Beat the cream cheese in a large mixing bowl until fluffy. Beat in the
eggs and ¹/₂ cup sugar until smooth and blended. Add the sour cream
and mix well. Stir in 2 tablespoons melted butter and the chocolate
chips and mix well. Pour over the crust. Bake for 45 minutes or until
set. Remove to a wire rack to cool. Chill for 6 hours. Place on a serving
plate and remove the side of the pan. Top each serving with a dollop
of whipped cream.

CHOCOLATE CHIP CHEESECAKE

This cheesecake is for people who like very rich desserts.

MAKES 12 SERVINGS

1¹/4 cups vanilla wafer crumbs
¹/4 cup chopped walnuts
3 tablespoons confectioners' sugar
2 tablespoons margarine, melted
1 cup (6 ounces) semisweet chocolate chips, melted
16 ounces cream cheese, softened
2 eggs
³/4 cup granulated sugar
2 tablespoons all-purpose flour
1 teaspoon vanilla extract
1 teaspoon lemon juice
1 cup miniature semisweet chocolate chips

Preheat the oven to 325 degrees. Combine the vanilla wafer crumbs, walnuts, confectioners' sugar, and melted margarine in a bowl and mix well. Stir in the melted chocolate. Press onto the bottom and up the side of a 9-inch springform pan. Beat the cream cheese in a large mixing bowl until fluffy. Beat in the eggs, sugar, flour, vanilla, and lemon juice until smooth. Fold in the miniature chocolate chips and pour over the crust. Bake for 1 hour or until the top is golden brown. Turn off the heat and leave the cheesecake in the oven for 1 hour. Remove to a wire rack to cool completely. Chill until serving time. Place on a serving plate and remove the side of the pan.

NOTE: *To avoid cracks in the cheesecake, do not overbeat the ingredients.*

NEW YORK-STYLE CHEESECAKE

MAKES 10 TO 12 SERVINGS

2 cups graham cracker crumbs
1/2 cup sugar
1 teaspoon ground cinnamon
1/2 cup (1 stick) butter, softened
1 cup chopped pecans
24 ounces Neufchâtel cheese, softened
1 cup sugar
1 teaspoon vanilla extract
1 teaspoon almond extract
3 eggs
2 cups sour cream
1/4 cup sugar
1 teaspoon vanilla extract

Preheat the oven to 350 degrees. Combine the graham cracker crumbs, 1/2 cup sugar, and 1 teaspoon cinnamon in a bowl. Add the butter and mix well. Stir in the pecans. Press onto the bottom and 2 inches up the side of a 10-inch springform pan. Bake for 7 minutes; cool. Beat the cheese in a large mixing bowl for 3 minutes or until fluffy. Add the sugar, 1 teaspoon vanilla, and the almond extract and beat for 2 minutes. Beat in the eggs 1 at a time. Add 1 cup of the sour cream and beat for 2 minutes. Pour over the crust, spreading evenly. Bake for 1 hour. Combine the remaining 1 cup sour cream, 1/4 cup sugar, and 1 teaspoon vanilla in a small bowl and mix well; chill.

Remove the cheesecake from the oven and spread the topping evenly over the top. Return to the oven and bake for 10 minutes longer. Turn off the heat and leave the cheesecake in the oven for 1 hour with the oven door ajar. Remove to a wire rack to cool completely. Chill for 8 to 10 hours. Place on a serving plate and remove the side of the pan. Serve with fresh raspberries or strawberries, if desired.

PINEAPPLE CHEESECAKE

*This cheesecake was a favorite of former Governor Ed Herschler
when he resided in the Wyoming governor's residence in the 1970s.*

MAKES 12 TO 16 SERVINGS

1 1/2 cups graham cracker crumbs
3 tablespoons sugar
1/4 teaspoon ground cinnamon
1/4 cup (1/2 stick) butter or margarine, melted
1 (16-ounce) carton creamed cottage cheese
4 eggs
24 ounces cream cheese, softened
1 cup sugar
2 tablespoons all-purpose flour
1/4 teaspoon salt
1 1/4 teaspoons vanilla extract
1/2 teaspoon almond extract
2 (8-ounce) cans crushed pineapple, drained
2 cups sour cream
3 tablespoons sugar
1 teaspoon vanilla extract

Preheat the oven to 350 degrees. Combine the graham cracker
crumbs, 3 tablespoons sugar, the cinnamon, and melted butter in a
bowl and mix well. Press onto the bottom and 1 1/2 inches up the side
of a 10-inch springform pan. Bake for 10 minutes; cool. Combine the
cottage cheese and the eggs in a blender and blend until smooth. Beat
the cream cheese, 1 cup sugar, the flour, salt, 1 1/4 teaspoons vanilla,
and almond extract in a large mixing bowl until fluffy. Add the
cottage cheese mixture and mix well. Fold in the pineapple and pour
over the crust. Bake for 1 1/2 hours. Turn off the heat and leave the
cheesecake in the oven for 1 hour with the oven door ajar. Combine
the sour cream, 3 tablespoons sugar, and 1 teaspoon vanilla in a bowl
and mix well. Remove the cheesecake to a wire rack and spread with
the topping. Cool completely, then chill for 8 to 10 hours.

GREEK CUSTARD IN PHYLLO

If you have never worked with phyllo dough, this is a great recipe with which to start.

MAKES 30 SERVINGS

6 cups milk
2 cups sugar
1 1/4 cups Cream of Wheat
1 tablespoon butter
1 teaspoon vanilla extract
6 eggs, beaten
16 sheets frozen phyllo pastry, thawed
   (about 1/2 of a 1-pound package)
1/4 cup (1/2 stick) butter, melted
3/4 cup water
Juice of 2 lemons
1 1/2 cups sugar

Preheat the oven to 350 degrees. Scald the milk in a large saucepan. Add 2 cups sugar and stir until dissolved. Add the Cream of Wheat gradually, stirring constantly to prevent lumps. Cook over medium-high heat until thickened to a pudding consistency. Remove from the heat and immediately add 1 tablespoon butter and the vanilla; cool. Add the eggs gradually to the custard mixture, stirring constantly.

Coat the bottom of a 9×13-inch baking dish with nonstick cooking spray. Place 2 phyllo sheets in the baking dish and brush with some of the melted butter. Top with 6 phyllo sheets, brushing with the butter between every 2 sheets. Pour the custard mixture over the phyllo and spread. Top with 8 phyllo sheets, brushing with the butter between every 2 sheets.

Bake for 30 to 40 minutes or until the top is light brown. Combine the water, lemon juice, and 1 1/2 cups sugar in a small saucepan and bring to a boil, stirring to dissolve the sugar. Boil for 5 minutes. Remove the custard from the oven and pour the hot syrup over the top. Let stand for 10 minutes before serving. Serve hot or chilled.

Molten Chocolate Cake

MAKES 8 SERVINGS

1 cup all-purpose flour
3/4 cup granulated sugar
1 1/2 tablespoons baking cocoa
2 teaspoons baking powder
1/4 teaspoon salt
1/2 cup milk
2 tablespoons melted butter
1 teaspoon vanilla extract
1/2 cup chopped nuts (optional)
1/2 cup granulated sugar
1/2 cup packed brown sugar
1/4 cup baking cocoa
1 cup hot water
Whipped cream or ice cream

Preheat the oven to 350 degrees. Stir together the flour, 3/4 cup granulated sugar, 1 1/2 tablespoons cocoa, the baking powder, and salt in a medium bowl. Add the milk, butter, vanilla, and nuts and mix well. Pour into a buttered 9×9-inch baking dish or 8 individual ramekins. Combine 1/2 cup granulated sugar, the brown sugar, and 1/4 cup cocoa and sprinkle over the batter. Pour the hot water over the top. (Use 2 tablespoons water for each ramekin.) Bake until the top of the cake layer is set, 35 to 40 minutes for the baking dish, 25 to 30 minutes for the ramekins. Serve warm with whipped cream or ice cream.

NOTE: *For high altitudes, decrease the baking powder to 1 teaspoon.*

FINEST CHOCOLATE GÂTEAU

*This was the official dessert served at the
Wyoming governor's residence from 1986 to 1994,
during Governor Mike Sullivan's term.*

MAKES 8 SERVINGS

1/4 cup raisins
1/4 cup scotch, bourbon, or coffee
4 1/2 tablespoons cake flour
2/3 cup ground almonds
Pinch of salt
7 ounces good-quality bittersweet chocolate
3 tablespoons water
1/2 cup (1 stick) unsalted butter, at room temperature
3 egg whites, at room temperature
3 egg yolks
2/3 cup sugar
Chocolate Butter Frosting

Steep the raisins in the scotch in a small bowl for 15 minutes. Stir together the cake flour, ground almonds, and salt. Melt the chocolate with the water in a double boiler over hot water, then stir in the butter until smooth. Beat the egg whites in a large bowl until soft, moist peaks form. Beat the egg yolks and sugar in a large bowl until thick and pale yellow. Stir the chocolate into the egg yolks. Add the flour mixture and raisins with liquid, stirring constantly. Stir 1/3 of the egg whites into the chocolate mixture. Fold the chocolate mixture into the remaining egg whites. Pour the batter into a waxed paper-lined and buttered 9-inch cake pan or a springform pan. Bake for 20 to 25 minutes or until the cake has pulled away from the side of the pan and the top is cracked. Remove to a wire rack and cool for 30 minutes. Run a knife blade around the edge of the pan and invert the cake onto the rack. Remove the waxed paper or the side of the springform pan and spread with the Chocolate Butter Frosting.

CHOCOLATE BUTTER FROSTING

MAKES ABOUT 1/2 CUP

3 ounces good-quality bittersweet chocolate
3 tablespoons confectioners' sugar
3 tablespoons unsalted butter

Melt the chocolate in the top of a double boiler over hot water. Whisk in the confectioners' sugar and butter until smooth and satiny.

GRAND MARNIER CHOCOLATE TORTE

MAKES 8 SERVINGS

16 ounces semisweet
   chocolate chips
1 tablespoon water
1 tablespoon all-purpose flour
1 tablespoon sugar
1/2 cup (1 stick) butter,
   softened

1 tablespoon Grand Marnier
   liqueur
4 egg whites, at room
   temperature
4 egg yolks
Unsweetened whipped cream

Preheat the oven to 425 degrees. Microwave the chocolate chips
with the water in a large microwave-safe bowl on High for 3 to
4 minutes or until melted, stirring after each minute. Stir in the flour,
sugar, butter, and liqueur and mix well. Beat the egg whites in a small
bowl until stiff peaks form. Beat the egg yolks in a small bowl until
thick and pale yellow. Add to the chocolate mixture gradually, stirring
constantly. Fold the egg whites into the chocolate mixture. Pour into
an 8-inch springform or torte pan. Bake for 15 to 20 minutes. Remove
to a wire rack to cool. Chill, covered, in the refrigerator before serving.
Serve with unsweetened whipped cream.

OLD-FASHIONED GINGER CAKE DOUGHNUT HOLES

These doughnut holes are best when served immediately.

2 cups all-purpose flour
1 tablespoon baking powder
1 1/2 teaspoons ground ginger
1/2 teaspoon salt
1/3 cup finely chopped crystallized ginger
4 eggs
1/2 cup sugar
1/4 cup heavy cream
1/2 teaspoon vanilla extract
1 tablespoon butter, melted
Vegetable oil for deep-frying
3/4 cup sugar
1 teaspoon ground ginger

Stir together the flour, baking powder, 1 1/2 teaspoons ground ginger, and salt in a large bowl. Stir in the crystallized ginger. Whisk the eggs until frothy in a medium bowl. Whisk in the sugar, cream, vanilla, and melted butter until blended. Add the egg mixture to the dry ingredients, stirring to form a slightly sticky dough. Turn the dough onto a lightly floured surface and roll out to 3/4-inch thickness. Cut with a 1 1/2-inch round cookie cutter and place on a parchment paper-lined baking sheet. Reroll the scraps to use all the dough. Heat at least 3 inches of oil to 350 degrees in a large heavy pan. Stir together 3/4 cup sugar and 1 teaspoon ground ginger in a shallow dish. Place the doughnut holes, 3 or 4 at a time, in the hot oil, using a slotted spoon. Cook for 2 minutes per side or until golden brown. Remove to a paper towel-lined baking sheet. Roll the warm doughnut holes in the sugar-ginger mixture, coating completely. Serve warm.

NOTE: *For high altitudes, decrease the baking powder to 1 1/2 teaspoons. The dough may be made 1 day ahead. Store, covered, in the refrigerator.*

ORANGE FLAN

MAKES 6 TO 8 SERVINGS

2/3 cup sugar
4 cups milk
1 tablespoon grated
  orange zest

1 cup sugar
1 teaspoon vanilla extract
4 eggs, lightly beaten

Preheat the oven to 350 degrees. Heat 2/3 cup sugar in a small saucepan until melted and caramelized to a rich brown color, moving the pan constantly to prevent burning. Immediately pour the caramel onto the bottom of a 9-inch pie plate or 6 to 8 individual ramekins or custard cups. Bring the milk to a gentle boil in a large saucepan. Add the orange zest and 1 cup sugar, stirring to dissolve the sugar. Cook for 5 minutes, stirring occasionally. Remove from the heat and add the vanilla; cool. Add the eggs and mix well. Pour the custard over the caramel. Place the pie plate or ramekins in a larger shallow baking pan and add 1 inch of cold water to the larger pan. Bake for 35 to 40 minutes or until the custard is set and the top is light brown; cool. Chill for 4 hours. Unmold onto a rimmed plate and serve.

PUMPKIN SPICE MOUSSE

Quick & Easy

So simple, so delicious—a perfect ending to a Thanksgiving feast

MAKES 4 TO 6 SERVINGS

3 ounces fat-free cream cheese, softened
1 (15-ounce) can pumpkin
1 teaspoon pumpkin pie spice
1 (8-ounce) container fat-free frozen
   whipped topping, thawed
2/3 cup Splenda sugar substitute
Ground nutmeg
Gingersnaps

Combine the cream cheese, pumpkin, and pumpkin pie spice in a mixing bowl and beat until blended. Fold in 1 to 1 1/2 cups whipped topping and the sugar substitute. Spoon into a serving bowl or individual dishes. Chill before serving. Garnish each serving with a dollop of the remaining whipped topping and sprinkle with nutmeg. Serve the gingersnaps on the side.

SPICED RUM MOUSSE WITH FRESH BERRIES

MAKES 6 SERVINGS

1/2 cup sugar
1 envelope unflavored gelatin
1/2 cup water
1 cup heavy cream
1 cup sour cream
1 teaspoon vanilla extract
3 tablespoons spiced rum or brandy
Fresh berries

Combine the sugar and gelatin in a saucepan. Add the water and bring to a boil, stirring constantly. Remove from the heat and stir in the cream. Combine the sour cream, vanilla, and rum in a large mixing bowl and beat well. Add the gelatin mixture and beat well. Chill until slightly thickened. Beat until smooth and fluffy. Spoon into individual serving dishes and chill until set. Top with fresh berries.

FRUIT PIZZA

MAKES 12 SERVINGS

1 1/2 cups all-purpose flour
1/4 cup plus 2 tablespoons
   confectioners' sugar
3/4 cup (1 1/2 sticks) butter,
   softened
3 tablespoons water
3 ounces cream cheese,
   softened
1/3 cup granulated sugar

1 teaspoon vanilla extract
1 cup whipping cream,
   whipped
1 cup strawberries, halved
Blueberries, kiwifruit slices,
   apricot halves, peach slices
1/4 to 1/2 cup apple jelly,
   melted and cooled

Preheat the oven to 400 degrees. Combine the flour, confectioners' sugar, butter, and water in a small bowl and stir with a fork until crumbly. Press onto the bottom of a 12-inch pizza pan. Bake for 10 to 15 minutes or until light brown; cool. Combine the cream cheese, granulated sugar, and vanilla in a mixing bowl and beat until smooth. Add the whipped cream and beat on low until the mixture forms soft peaks. Spread the cream mixture over the crust to within 1/4 inch of the edge. Arrange the strawberries and other fruit in a decorative pattern over the filling. Spoon the apple jelly over the fruit and chill.

RASPBERRY ROUSSE

MAKES 8 TO 12 SERVINGS

1 (12-ounce) package frozen
   sweetened raspberries,
   thawed
1 cup water
1/4 cup lemon juice
1 cup sugar
8 ounces cream cheese,
   softened

1/2 cup sugar
2 cups whipping cream, well
   chilled
48 ladyfingers
Fresh raspberries, mint sprigs,
   lemon peel twists

Purée the raspberries in a blender and pour into a fine mesh strainer set over a medium bowl. Press the puréed berries through the strainer using the back of a spoon; reserve the pulp and discard the seeds. Combine the water, lemon juice, and 1 cup sugar in a small saucepan and bring to a boil, stirring to dissolve the sugar. Remove from the heat and let stand until cool. Beat the cream cheese with 1/2 cup sugar in a large mixing bowl until fluffy. Whip the cream in a mixing bowl until soft peaks form. Fold half the whipped cream into the raspberry purée. Fold the remaining whipped cream into the cream cheese mixture. Line a 11/2-quart shallow mold, bowl, or springform pan with plastic wrap. Line the bottom and side of the mold with the ladyfingers, rounded sides out. Spoon half the raspberry mixture into the mold, spreading evenly. Spread half the cream cheese mixture over the raspberry layer. Dip the remaining ladyfingers into the lemon syrup and place a layer on the cream cheese mixture. Repeat the layers with the remaining raspberry mixture, cream cheese mixture, and ladyfingers. Chill, covered, for 8 to 10 hours. Invert onto a serving plate and remove the plastic wrap. Garnish with raspberries, mint, and lemon twists.

RICE PUDDING

MAKES 4 SERVINGS

2 eggs
2¹/₄ cups milk
²/₃ cup sugar
1¹/₂ cups cooked rice
¹/₂ cup golden raisins
1¹/₂ teaspoons vanilla extract
Dash of ground nutmeg

Preheat the oven to 350 degrees. Whisk the eggs in a medium bowl until frothy. Whisk in the milk and sugar. Add the rice, raisins, and vanilla and mix well. Pour into a buttered 2-quart baking dish and sprinkle with the nutmeg. Place the baking dish in a larger shallow baking pan and add 1 inch of hot water to the larger pan. Bake for 1 hour. Remove the pudding dish from the oven and stir, lifting the pudding from the bottom of the dish. Return the dish to the water bath and bake for 10 minutes longer. Serve warm or chilled.

STRAWBERRIES WITH GRAND MARNIER AND SAMBUCA CREAM

If the black pepper is omitted from this German recipe, purists claim that the dessert is ruined!

MAKES 4 TO 6 SERVINGS

1 quart strawberries, quartered
¹/₄ cup sugar
¹/₂ cup plus 1 tablespoon half-and-half
2 tablespoons Grand Marnier, or to taste
2 tablespoons sambuca, or to taste
¹/₂ gallon vanilla ice cream
Freshly ground black pepper

Combine the strawberries, sugar, and half-and-half in a large bowl and stir gently. Stir in the liqueurs. Scoop the ice cream into individual serving dishes. Top with the strawberry mixture. Grind 2 complete turns of the pepper grinder over each serving.

STRAWBERRY SHERBET JELLY ROLL

MAKES 8 SERVINGS

24 edible violets or pansies
5 egg yolks
1/3 cup granulated sugar
1 tablespoon plus 1 teaspoon
  vegetable oil
1 teaspoon vanilla extract
5 egg whites, at room
  temperature

2/3 cup granulated sugar
3/4 cup cake flour
11/4 teaspoons baking powder
1/4 teaspoon salt
2 tablespoons confectioners'
  sugar
Strawberry sherbet, softened

Preheat the oven to 350 degrees. Grease the bottom of a jelly roll pan and line with waxed paper. Grease and flour the waxed paper and the sides of the pan. Arrange the flowers, stems up, in the pan. Beat the egg yolks in a large mixing bowl at high speed for 5 minutes or until thick and pale yellow. Add 1/3 cup sugar gradually, beating well. Stir in the oil and vanilla. Beat the egg whites in a mixing bowl at high speed until foamy. Add 2/3 cup sugar, 1 tablespoon at a time, beating for 2 to 4 minutes or until stiff peaks form and the sugar is dissolved. Gently fold the egg whites into the egg yolk mixture. Stir together the flour, baking powder, and salt and fold into the egg yolk mixture. Spread the batter in the prepared pan. Bake for 12 to 14 minutes or until the top springs back when lightly touched. Sift the confectioners' sugar into a 10×15-inch rectangle on a clean cloth towel. Loosen the cake from the sides of the pan and invert onto the sugared towel. Remove the waxed paper and turn the cake over, flower side down. Roll the cake and towel together, starting at the narrow end. Place on a wire rack, seam side down, to cool. Unroll the cake and remove the towel. Spread a thin layer of the sherbet over the cake and reroll. Wrap in plastic wrap and freeze. Slice to serve.

NOTE: *Other fillings, such as the Lemon Cream Cheese Filling (below), lemon curd, raspberry sherbet, strawberry preserves, or chocolate, may be used.*

LEMON CREAM CHEESE FILLING

MAKES ABOUT 11/3 CUPS

8 ounces cream cheese, softened
2 tablespoons butter or margarine, softened
1/4 cup plus 2 tablespoons lemon curd

Beat the cream cheese and butter in a mixing bowl on medium speed until smooth and creamy. Stir in the lemon curd and mix well. Chill. Spread on the cake roll and reroll; chill.

If you enjoy trying something different, you might want to consider including edible flowers in some of your recipes. The Chinese, Greeks, and Romans used edible flowers in their culinary creations thousands of years ago. Many cooks today use edible flowers as a garnish or a salad ingredient. When purchasing edible flowers, you should buy them from a supermarket or a florist, and make sure they have not been sprayed with pesticides. Popular edible flowers include daisies, nasturtiums, geraniums, lavender, marigolds, pansies, roses, and violets. It is best to eat edible flowers in small quantities.

CRANBERRY MARSH ICE

MAKES 12 SERVINGS

1 envelope unflavored gelatin
1 cup cold water
1 (12-ounce) bag cranberries, sorted and rinsed
1³/4 cups water
2 cups sugar
¹/4 cup lemon juice
Dash of salt

Soften the gelatin in 1 cup cold water in a small bowl. Combine the cranberries, 1³/4 cups water, the sugar, and lemon juice in a large saucepan and bring to a boil. Cook over medium heat for 5 minutes or until the cranberries pop. Pour into a mesh strainer set over a medium bowl and press the cranberries through the strainer using the back of a spoon. Reserve the pulp and liquid and discard the skins. Add the gelatin mixture and salt to the cranberry purée and mix well. Spoon the mixture into a freezer-safe container and freeze, covered, for 8 to 10 hours or until solid. Put the frozen mixture into a blender or food processor and blend until slushy. Refreeze. Serve frozen.

Some find it hard to keep straight the differences between all the wonderful frozen desserts that are available. Here's the scoop: ice cream is made with cream and whole milk; sherbet and gelato are made with milk and fruit juice; sorbet, ices, and granitas are made with water and fruit juice.

CITRUS ICE CREAM

MAKES 1 QUART

2 cups heavy cream
2 cups milk
2 cups sugar
Juice of 3 lemons or 3 limes
Grated zest of 1 orange
Juice of 1 orange
Dash of salt

Combine the cream, milk, sugar, lemon juice, orange zest, orange juice, and salt in a large bowl, stirring until the sugar is dissolved. Transfer the mixture to an ice cream freezer and freeze using the manufacturer's directions.

NOTE: *1 quart half-and-half may be substituted for the cream and milk.*

ICE CREAM WITH A COWBOY KICK

Quick & Easy

MAKES 15 SERVINGS

8 ice cream sandwich bars
1/2 cup Kahlúa
1/2 cup toffee bits
1 (8-ounce) container frozen whipped topping, thawed
Chocolate ice cream syrup
1/2 cup chopped walnuts, pecans, or
   salted peanuts (optional)

Place the ice cream sandwich bars in a 9×13-inch pan, cutting to fit. Drizzle with the Kahlúa and sprinkle with the toffee bits. Spread the whipped topping over the bars, covering completely. Drizzle the chocolate syrup in a decorative design over the topping and sprinkle with the nuts. Freeze until ready to serve.

NOTE: *This can be made up to 24 hours ahead of time.*

FRANGO MINT CAKE

1/2 cup (1 stick) margarine, softened
1 cup granulated sugar
4 eggs
1 teaspoon vanilla extract
1 (16-ounce) can chocolate syrup
1 cup all-purpose flour
Mint Icing
Chocolate Icing

Preheat the oven to 350 degrees. Cream the margarine and sugar together in a large mixing bowl until light and fluffy. Add the eggs, vanilla, and chocolate syrup and beat until smooth. Add the flour and mix well. Pour into a greased and floured 9×13-inch baking pan. Bake for 35 to 40 minutes; cool. Spread the Mint Icing over the top of the cooled cake and chill. Spread the Chocolate Icing over the cooled Mint Icing and chill before serving.

NOTE: *For high altitudes, add 2 tablespoons flour.*

MINT ICING

2 cups confectioners' sugar
1/2 cup (1 stick) margarine, softened
2 tablespoons milk
1 teaspoon peppermint extract
Few drops of green food coloring (optional)

Combine the confectioners' sugar, 1/2 cup margarine, milk, peppermint extract, and food coloring and mix well.

CHOCOLATE ICING

1 cup (6 ounces) semisweet chocolate chips
6 tablespoons margarine

Melt the chocolate chips and margarine in a small saucepan, stirring until smooth and satiny. Remove from the heat and let stand until cool.

14-KARAT CAKE

MAKES 12 SERVINGS

1¹/2 cups vegetable oil
4 eggs
2 cups sugar
2¹/2 cups all-purpose flour
1¹/2 teaspoons baking powder
1 teaspoon ground cinnamon
1 teaspoon ground cloves
1 teaspoon ground nutmeg
2 cups finely shredded carrots
1 cup chopped pecans (optional)
Cream Cheese Frosting

Preheat the oven to 350 degrees. Combine the oil, eggs, and sugar in a large mixing bowl and beat until blended. Combine the flour, baking powder, cinnamon, cloves, and nutmeg in a bowl. Add to the egg mixture and stir just until moistened. Stir in the carrots and pecans and mix well. Pour into a greased bundt pan. Bake for 1 hour or until a knife inserted in the center comes out clean. Cool in the pan for 10 minutes. Invert the cake onto a wire rack and cool completely. Frost with Cream Cheese Frosting.

CREAM CHEESE FROSTING

MAKES ABOUT 1¹/2 CUPS

3 ounces cream cheese, softened
1¹/4 cups confectioners' sugar
1 tablespoon light corn syrup
1 tablespoon milk
1/2 teaspoon vanilla extract

Beat the cream cheese in a small mixing bowl until fluffy. Beat in the confectioners' sugar, corn syrup, milk, and vanilla until smooth.

I f you want to avoid the mess that results from greasing a baking pan with your fingers, try this: simply put a plastic food-storage bag over your hand before greasing the pan, and then use the same plastic bag to press the dough into the pan. Voilà— one less mess in the kitchen!

CHOCOLATE ZUCCHINI CAKE

1/2 cup (1 stick) butter or margarine, softened
1/2 cup vegetable oil
1 3/4 cups sugar
1 teaspoon vanilla extract
1/2 cup buttermilk
2 1/2 cups all-purpose flour
1/4 cup baking cocoa
1 teaspoon ground cinnamon
1/2 teaspoon ground cloves
1/2 teaspoon salt
1/2 teaspoon baking powder
1/2 teaspoon baking soda
2 cups shredded peeled zucchini
3/4 cup semisweet chocolate chips

Preheat the oven to 325 degrees. Cream the butter, oil, sugar, and vanilla in a large mixing bowl until light and fluffy. Stir in the buttermilk. Combine the flour, cocoa, cinnamon, cloves, salt, baking powder, and baking soda in a bowl. Add the butter mixture and stir until combined. Stir in the zucchini and chocolate chips. Pour into a greased and floured 10-inch bundt pan. Bake for 40 minutes or until a wooden pick inserted in the center comes out clean. Cool in the pan for about 30 minutes. Invert the cake onto a wire rack and cool completely before slicing.

NOTE: *For high altitudes, decrease the baking soda to 1/2 teaspoon.*

DOUBLE CHOCOLATE IRISH SPICE CAKE

MAKES 24 SERVINGS

1 cup (2 sticks) butter, softened
2 cups sugar
4 egg yolks
1 cup unseasoned mashed cooked potatoes
1/2 cup buttermilk or sour milk
2 ounces chocolate, melted, or 1 tablespoon baking cocoa

1/2 cup raisins
1/2 cup chopped walnuts
1 teaspoon vanilla extract
2 cups all-purpose flour
2 teaspoons baking powder
1 teaspoon ground cinnamon
1 teaspoon ground cloves
1/2 teaspoon ground nutmeg
4 egg whites, stiffly beaten
Mocha Frosting

Preheat the oven to 375 degrees. Cream the butter and sugar in a large mixing bowl until light and fluffy. Beat in the egg yolks, potatoes, buttermilk, and chocolate until smooth. Add the raisins, walnuts, and vanilla and mix well. Sift together the flour, baking powder, cinnamon, cloves, and nutmeg. Add to the egg mixture and mix well. Fold in the egg whites. Divide the batter among 3 greased and floured 8-inch round cake pans. Bake for 25 to 30 minutes or until a wooden pick inserted in the center comes out clean. Cool in the pans for 10 minutes. Remove to a wire rack to cool completely. Spread the Mocha Frosting between the layers and on the top and side of the cake.

NOTE: *To make sour milk, add 1 1/2 teaspoons white or cider vinegar to 1/2 cup milk and let stand for 10 minutes.*

MOCHA FROSTING

MAKES ABOUT 2 1/2 CUPS, ENOUGH TO FILL AND FROST AN 8-INCH 3-LAYER CAKE

6 tablespoons butter
3 tablespoons baking cocoa
2 tablespoons cold coffee

1 teaspoon vanilla extract
1 1/2 cups confectioners' sugar

Melt the butter in a small saucepan. Blend in the cocoa. Add the coffee and vanilla and mix well. Add the confectioners' sugar gradually, stirring until smooth and of the desired consistency.

CHRISTMAS RUM CAKE

Quick & Easy

MAKES 16 SERVINGS

1 cup chopped pecans, walnuts, or sliced almonds
1 (2-layer) package yellow cake mix
1 (4-ounce) package vanilla instant pudding mix
1/2 cup cold water
1/2 cup vegetable oil
1/2 cup rum
4 eggs
Butter Rum Glaze
Maraschino cherries, frosting, whipped cream,
    confectioners' sugar-dusted green grapes (optional)

Preheat the oven to 325 degrees. Sprinkle the pecans over the bottom of a greased bundt pan. Combine the cake mix, pudding mix, water, oil, rum, and eggs in a large bowl and mix by hand until combined. Pour the batter over the pecans. Bake for 1 hour or until the top springs back when lightly touched. Cool in the pan for 10 minutes. Invert the cake onto a wire rack and cool completely. Place the cake on a serving plate and use a wooden pick to poke holes in the top of the cake. Pour the glaze over the cake. Decorate the cake and serving plate with maraschino cherries, a border of frosting or whipped cream, or grapes dusted with confectioners' sugar.

BUTTER RUM GLAZE

1/2 cup (1 stick) butter
1 cup sugar
1/4 cup water
1/2 cup rum

Melt the butter in a small saucepan. Stir in the sugar and water until blended. Bring to a boil and boil for 5 minutes, stirring constantly. Remove from the heat and gradually stir in the rum, mixing well. The glaze will crystallize if the rum is added too quickly.

COWBOY CAKE

This cake is always popular with the ranch hands at branding time.

MAKES 12 TO 15 SERVINGS

1 cup chopped dates
1 teaspoon baking soda
1 cup plus 3 tablespoons hot
   water
1 cup (2 sticks) butter, softened
1 cup granulated sugar
2 eggs
2 cups all-purpose flour

1 tablespoon baking cocoa
1/2 teaspoon salt
1 tablespoon vanilla extract
1 cup (6 ounces) semisweet
   chocolate chips
1/2 cup chopped pecans
Confectioners' sugar
Additional chocolate chips

Preheat the oven to 350 degrees. Combine the dates and baking soda in a small bowl with the hot water and let stand for a few minutes. Cream the butter and sugar in a large mixing bowl until light and fluffy. Add the date mixture, eggs, flour, cocoa, salt, and vanilla and beat well. Stir in 1/2 cup of the chocolate chips. Pour into a greased and floured 9×13-inch cake pan. Sprinkle with the remaining 1/2 cup chocolate chips and the pecans. Bake for 30 to 40 minutes. Do not overbake. Cool on a wire rack. Garnish the cake with confectioners' sugar and chocolate chips before it has completely cooled.

NOTE: *For high altitudes, add 1/2 cup flour.*

HARVEY WALLBANGER CAKE

Quick & Easy

MAKES 16 SERVINGS

1 (2-layer) package yellow cake mix
1 (4-ounce) package vanilla instant pudding mix
1 cup vegetable oil
4 eggs
1/4 cup vodka
1/4 cup Galliano
3/4 cup orange juice
Vanilla Glaze

Preheat the oven to 350 degrees. Combine the cake mix, pudding mix, oil, eggs, vodka, liqueur, and orange juice in a large mixing bowl and beat for 4 minutes. Pour into a greased and floured 12-cup bundt pan. Bake for 45 minutes. Cool in the pan for 10 minutes. Invert the cake onto a wire rack to cool completely. Place on a serving plate and pour the warm Vanilla Glaze over the cake.

VANILLA GLAZE

MAKES ABOUT 2 CUPS

1/2 cup (1 stick) butter
1 cup sugar
1/2 cup buttermilk, or 1/2 cup milk plus 1 teaspoon vinegar
1 tablespoon light corn syrup
1/2 teaspoon baking soda
11/2 teaspoons vanilla extract

Combine the butter, sugar, buttermilk, corn syrup, baking soda, and vanilla in a large saucepan and bring to a boil over medium-high heat. The mixture will foam up. Boil for 2 minutes, skimming off the foam and stirring constantly until the foaming stops. Serve warm over cake, ice cream, or steamed puddings. The sauce will darken to a caramel color when reheated.

OATMEAL CAKE WITH COCONUT PECAN FROSTING

MAKES 12 TO 15 SERVINGS

1 1/2 cups packed brown sugar
1 1/2 cups granulated sugar
3/4 cup (1 1/2 sticks) margarine, softened
3 eggs
2 1/4 cups boiling water
1 1/2 cups oats
2 1/4 cups all-purpose flour
1 1/2 teaspoons baking soda
1/2 teaspoon ground cinnamon
Coconut Pecan Frosting

Preheat the oven to 350 degrees. Cream the brown sugar, granulated sugar, and margarine in a large mixing bowl until light and fluffy. Beat in the eggs. Combine the boiling water and the oats and stir into the egg mixture. Combine the flour, baking soda, and cinnamon in a bowl. Add to the batter and mix well. Pour into a greased 9×13-inch baking pan. Bake for 35 to 45 minutes or until a knife inserted in the center comes out clean. Cool on a wire rack. Spread the Coconut Pecan Frosting on top of the cooled cake.

COCONUT PECAN FROSTING

MAKES ABOUT 3 CUPS

6 tablespoons margarine
1 cup packed brown sugar
5 tablespoons milk
1 cup chopped pecans
1 cup flaked or shredded coconut

Combine the margarine, brown sugar, and milk in a saucepan and bring to a boil over medium heat, stirring to dissolve the sugar. Boil for 1 minute. Remove from the heat and stir in the pecans and coconut.

APPLE PIE IN A BAG WITH RUM-CRANBERRY ICE CREAM

4 cups sliced peeled Granny Smith apples
1/2 cup sugar
2 tablespoons all-purpose flour
1 teaspoon ground nutmeg
2 tablespoons lemon juice
1 unbaked (9-inch) pie shell
1/2 cup sugar
1/2 cup all-purpose flour
1/2 cup (1 stick) cold butter or margarine, cut into pieces
2 teaspoons ground cinnamon

Preheat the oven to 425 degrees. Combine the apples, 1/2 cup sugar, 2 tablespoons flour, the nutmeg, and lemon juice in a large bowl and mix well. Spoon into the pie shell. Combine 1/2 cup sugar and 1/2 cup flour in a bowl and cut in the butter until crumbly. Sprinkle over the apples. Sprinkle with the cinnamon. Place the pie in a clean brown paper bag and staple the bag closed. Place the bag on a baking sheet to prevent burning. Bake for 1 hour. Remove from the bag to a wire rack and cool slightly before slicing. Serve with Rum-Cranberry Ice Cream.

RUM-CRANBERRY ICE CREAM

MAKES 1 QUART

1 quart French vanilla ice cream
1/4 cup rum
2/3 cup dried cranberries

Soften the ice cream slightly and spoon into a large bowl, reserving the carton. Stir in the rum and cranberries. Spoon the ice cream back into the carton and freeze for 2 hours or longer.

UPSIDE-DOWN APPLE-PECAN BOURBON PIE

MAKES 8 TO 10 SERVINGS

2/3 cup raisins
2 tablespoons bourbon
1/4 cup (1/2 stick) butter,
   softened
3/4 cup pecan halves
2/3 cup packed brown sugar
Pie Pastry
4 cups sliced peeled apples

1/2 cup sugar
2 tablespoons lemon juice
1 tablespoon all-purpose flour
1/2 teaspoon ground
   cinnamon
1/2 teaspoon ground nutmeg
1/4 teaspoon salt
Whipped cream

Combine the raisins and bourbon in a small bowl and let stand for several hours. Preheat the oven to 450 degrees. Spread the butter evenly over the bottom of a 9-inch glass pie plate. Place the pecan halves, rounded side down, in the butter. Pat the brown sugar evenly over the pecans. Roll out 1 Pie Pastry dough ball to a 10-inch round on a lightly floured surface. Place in the pie plate over the pecans. Drain the raisins and combine with the apples, sugar, lemon juice, flour, cinnamon, nutmeg, and salt in a large bowl and mix well. Spoon into the pie plate. Roll out the remaining dough ball to a 10-inch round and place over the apples; seal and crimp the edges. Prick the top crust with a fork. Bake for 10 minutes. Reduce the oven temperature to 350 degrees and bake for 40 minutes longer. Cool on a wire rack for 5 minutes or until the filling stops bubbling. Place a rimmed serving plate over the warm pie and invert carefully onto the plate. Garnish with whipped cream and serve.

PIE PASTRY

MAKES ENOUGH FOR A 2-CRUST 9-INCH PIE

3 cups all-purpose flour
1 teaspoon salt
2/3 cup shortening, chilled

2 egg yolks
1/2 cup plus 2 tablespoons
   ice water

Sift the flour and salt together in a large bowl. Cut in the shortening until crumbly. Whisk the egg yolks in a bowl until blended. Whisk in the water. Add the egg mixture gradually to the flour, stirring to form a dough. Divide the dough in half and shape each half into a ball.

RED CHERRY LATTICE-TOP PIE

This pie was a state winner in a national pie baking contest.

MAKES 8 SERVINGS

3 cups frozen pitted tart red
    cherries, thawed
1 cup sugar
1/4 cup all-purpose flour
1 tablespoon cornstarch
1/4 teaspoon salt

2 tablespoons butter
1/2 teaspoon red food coloring
    (optional)
1/4 teaspoon almond extract
Blue Ribbon Pie Pastry

Preheat the oven to 375 degrees. Drain the cherries, reserving the liquid. Add water to the reserved liquid to equal 3/4 cup. Stir together the sugar, flour, cornstarch, and salt in a saucepan. Add the cherry liquid and stir until blended. Bring to a boil. Boil vigorously for 5 minutes, stirring occasionally. Add the butter and remove from the heat. Stir in the food coloring, almond extract, and the cherries. Let stand until cool. Roll out 1 Blue Ribbon Pie Pastry dough ball on a lightly floured surface to a 10-inch round, 1/2 to 1/8 inch thick, and place in a 9-inch pie plate. Roll out the remaining dough ball to 1/8-inch thickness and cut into 1/2-inch-wide strips. Pour the cherry filling into the pastry-lined pie plate and weave the dough strips to form a lattice over the top. Crimp the edges, sealing the lattice strips to the bottom crust. Bake for 35 minutes. Cover the crust with foil during the last few minutes of baking if needed to prevent overbrowning. Cool on a wire rack.

BLUE RIBBON PIE PASTRY

MAKES ENOUGH FOR A
2-CRUST 9-INCH PIE

2 cups sifted all-purpose
    flour
1 teaspoon salt
1 tablespoon sugar
3/4 cup lard
5 tablespoons ice water

Combine the flour, salt, and sugar in a large bowl. Cut in 1/2 cup of the lard with a pastry blender until the mixture is the consistency of cornmeal. Cut in the remaining 1/4 cup lard, blending until the pieces are the size of peas. Sprinkle 1 tablespoon of the water over part of the mixture and toss gently with a fork until moistened. Push the moistened dough to the side and repeat, adding the water, 1 tablespoon at a time, until all of the dough is moistened. Divide the dough in half and shape each into a ball.

RHUBARB SOUR CREAM PIE

MAKES 8 SERVINGS

2 eggs
1 cup sour cream
3 tablespoons tapioca
1 cup sugar
2 cups chopped rhubarb
1 (8-ounce) can crushed pineapple
1 unbaked (10-inch) pie shell

Preheat the oven to 375 degrees. Whisk the eggs in a large bowl until frothy. Whisk in the sour cream, tapioca, and sugar until combined. Add the rhubarb and pineapple and mix well. Pour into the pie shell. Bake for 15 minutes. Reduce the oven temperature to 325 degrees and bake for 30 minutes longer. Cool on a wire rack.

THREE BARS-AND-A-BOX BROWNIES

Quick & Easy

These oh-so-simple brownies are always the hit of any party!

MAKES 15 SERVINGS

1 (22- to 24-ounce) package fudge brownie mix
3 (6-ounce) chocolate candy bars with
    almonds and toffee bits

Preheat the oven to 350 degrees. Prepare the brownie mix using the package directions for cake-like brownies or substitute 1/2 cup applesauce for 1/2 cup of the oil for a lower-fat version. Spread half the brownie batter in a 9×13-inch baking pan coated with nonstick cooking spray. Top with the chocolate bars. Spread with the remaining batter. Bake using the package directions.

NOTE: *For the holiday season, sprinkle crushed peppermint candy on the bottom brownie layer before adding the chocolate bars. Proceed as above.*

BUCKAROO BROWNIES

2 cups all-purpose flour
2 cups sugar
1/2 cup (1 stick) butter
1/2 cup shortening
1 cup strong brewed coffee or water
1/4 cup baking cocoa
1/2 cup buttermilk
2 eggs
1 teaspoon baking soda
1 teaspoon vanilla extract
Butter Frosting

Preheat the oven to 400 degrees. Stir together the flour and sugar in a large mixing bowl. Combine the butter, shortening, coffee, and cocoa in a heavy saucepan and bring to a boil, stirring constantly. Pour the mixture over the flour and sugar. Add the buttermilk, eggs, baking soda, and vanilla and mix well. Pour into a generously buttered 10×15-inch baking pan, spreading evenly. Bake for 20 minutes or until the brownies test done in the center. Remove from the oven and pour the warm Butter Frosting over the top, spreading evenly. Cool on a wire rack. Cut into bars.

NOTE: *If you don't have buttermilk on hand, substitute 2 teaspoons vinegar or lemon juice mixed into 1/2 cup milk, or use powdered buttermilk.*

BUTTER FROSTING

MAKES ABOUT 3 CUPS

1/2 cup (1 stick) butter
2 teaspoons baking cocoa
1/4 cup milk
3 1/2 cups confectioners' sugar
1 teaspoon vanilla extract

Combine the butter, cocoa, and milk in a saucepan and bring to a boil, stirring constantly. Add the confectioners' sugar and vanilla and stir until smooth and satiny. Use the frosting while warm.

HAWAIIAN BARS

MAKES 12 SERVINGS

1/3 cup butter or margarine, melted
1 1/2 cups graham cracker crumbs
2 tablespoons granulated sugar
1/3 cup baking cocoa
1 egg
1 cup shredded coconut
1/2 cup finely chopped macadamia nuts
1 teaspoon vanilla extract

6 tablespoons butter or margarine, softened
3 cups confectioners' sugar
3/4 teaspoon vanilla extract
4 1/2 tablespoons milk
1 ounce unsweetened chocolate
1/4 cup (1/2 stick) butter or margarine
1/2 cup coarsely chopped macadamia nuts

Preheat the oven to 350 degrees. Combine 1/3 cup butter and the next 7 ingredients in a bowl and mix well. Press onto the bottom of a buttered 7×11-inch baking pan. Bake for 10 minutes. Cool completely. Combine 6 tablespoons butter, the confectioners' sugar, 3/4 teaspoon vanilla, and the milk in a bowl and beat until light and fluffy. Spread evenly over the crust; chill. Melt the chocolate and 1/4 cup butter together in a small saucepan, stirring until smooth and satiny. Drizzle over the filling, tilting the baking pan to evenly spread the chocolate over the filling. Sprinkle with the coarsely chopped nuts. Cut into bars and chill until the chocolate hardens.

CARAMEL DREAM BARS

MAKES 24 BARS

64 caramels, unwrapped
1/2 cup plus 2 tablespoons heavy cream
2 cups all-purpose flour
1 1/2 cups packed brown sugar
2 cups oats
1 teaspoon baking soda

1 1/2 cups (3 sticks) margarine, melted
1 cup (6 ounces) semisweet chocolate chips
1 cup chopped walnuts or pecans

Preheat the oven to 350 degrees. Microwave the caramels and cream in a large microwave-safe bowl for 3 to 4 minutes or until melted, stirring after each minute. Cool slightly. Mix the next 5 ingredients in a bowl. Press half the oat mixture onto the bottom of a 9×13-inch baking pan. Bake for 10 minutes. Cool slightly. Sprinkle the chocolate chips and walnuts over the crust. Pour the caramel mixture over the top. Sprinkle with the remaining oat mixture, pressing down lightly. Bake for 20 to 25 minutes or until brown. Cool on a wire rack and cut into bars.

LEMON PISTACHIO BARS

2 cups sifted all-purpose flour
1/2 cup confectioners' sugar
1 cup (2 sticks) butter or
    margarine, cut into pieces
1 cup granulated sugar
3 tablespoons all-purpose
    flour
1/2 teaspoon baking powder

4 eggs
1 cup flaked coconut
Grated zest of 1 lemon, or
    2 teaspoons dried lemon zest
1/3 cup fresh lemon juice
Decorative Icing or
    confectioners' sugar
Pistachio nuts

Preheat the oven to 350 degrees. Sift 2 cups flour and 1/2 cup confectioners' sugar together in a large bowl. Cut in the butter until crumbly. Press the mixture onto the bottom of a 9×13-inch baking pan. Bake for 25 minutes or until light brown. Combine the granulated sugar, 3 tablespoons flour, and the baking powder in a bowl. Beat the eggs in a large mixing bowl. Beat in the flour mixture until combined. Stir in the coconut, lemon zest, and lemon juice and pour over the crust. Bake for 20 to 25 minutes. Cool on a wire rack. Pipe Decorative Icing into lines on the top or sprinkle with confectioners' sugar. Sprinkle with pistachios and cut into bars.

NOTE: *For high altitudes, add 1/4 cup flour to the filling.*

DECORATIVE ICING

1/2 cup confectioners' sugar
1 teaspoon butter, melted
1 tablespoon fresh lemon juice

Combine the confectioners' sugar, butter, and lemon juice in a small bowl and mix until smooth. Spoon into a pastry bag.

WYOMING PUMPKIN BARS

This is the first time this recipe has been shared outside the family.
It is always a hit at parties.

MAKES 48 BARS

2 cups sugar
1 cup vegetable oil
1³/4 cups canned pumpkin
4 eggs
2 cups all-purpose flour
2¹/2 teaspoons ground cinnamon
2 teaspoons baking powder
1 teaspoon baking soda
¹/2 teaspoon salt
¹/4 teaspoon ground nutmeg
Cream Cheese Butter Frosting

Preheat the oven to 350 degrees. Combine the sugar, oil, pumpkin, and eggs in a large mixing bowl and beat until blended. Stir together the flour, cinnamon, baking powder, baking soda, salt and nutmeg. Add to the pumpkin mixture and beat for 1 minute. Pour into a greased 10×15-inch baking pan. Bake for 25 minutes. Do not overbake. Cool on a wire rack. Frost with Cream Cheese Butter Frosting and cut into bars.

CREAM CHEESE BUTTER FROSTING

MAKES ABOUT 2¹/2 CUPS

3 ounces cream cheese, softened
6 tablespoons butter or margarine, softened
1 tablespoon cream
1³/4 cups confectioners' sugar

Combine the cream cheese, butter, cream, and confectioners' sugar in a mixing bowl and beat until smooth.

PEANUT BUTTER FINGERS

MAKES 30 SERVINGS

1/2 cup margarine, melted
1/2 cup granulated sugar
1/2 cup packed brown sugar
1 egg
1/3 cup peanut butter
1/2 teaspoon baking soda
1/2 teaspoon vanilla extract
1/4 teaspoon salt
1 cup all-purpose flour
1 cup oats
3/4 cup semisweet chocolate chips
Peanut Butter Icing

Preheat the oven to 350 degrees. Cream the margarine, granulated sugar, and brown sugar in a large mixing bowl until light and fluffy. Add the egg, peanut butter, baking soda, vanilla, and salt and mix well. Stir in the flour and oats. Spread into a greased 9×13-inch baking pan. Bake for 15 to 20 minutes. Remove from the oven to a wire rack and sprinkle with the chocolate chips. Let stand for 5 minutes. Spread the melted chips over the top. Drizzle the Peanut Butter Icing over the chocolate. Cool and cut into bars.

PEANUT BUTTER ICING

MAKES ABOUT 1 1/2 CUPS

1 cup confectioners' sugar
1/2 cup peanut butter
6 to 8 tablespoons milk

Combine the confectioners' sugar and peanut butter in a bowl, stirring until blended. Add the milk gradually, stirring until smooth and of the desired consistency.

YUM-YUM BARS

1/2 cup butter or margarine, softened
1 cup granulated sugar
2 egg yolks

1 1/2 cups all-purpose flour
2 egg whites
1 cup packed brown sugar
1 cup chopped pecans

Preheat the oven to 275 degrees. Cream the butter and granulated sugar in a large mixing bowl until light and fluffy. Beat in the egg yolks. Add the flour gradually, beating well after each addition. Spoon into an ungreased 8×12-inch or 7×11-inch baking pan and press the dough onto the bottom of the pan. Beat the egg whites in a medium bowl until stiff peaks form. Fold in the brown sugar and pecans and spread over the dough. Bake for 30 to 35 minutes, checking frequently to prevent overbrowning. Cool on a wire rack for 5 minutes. Cut into bars while still warm.

NOTE: *Use a very sharp knife, dipped in water between each cut, to cut the warm bars.*

CORNFLAKE COOKIES

These always turn out perfectly.

MAKES 2 DOZEN

1/2 cup butter, softened
1/2 cup shortening
1 cup granulated sugar
1 cup packed brown sugar
2 eggs
2 cups all-purpose flour
2 tablespoons wheat germ
1 teaspoon baking powder

1 teaspoon baking soda
Dash of salt
2 cups oats
2 cups cornflakes
1 cup chopped nuts
2 cups (12 ounces) semisweet chocolate chips

Preheat the oven to 325 degrees. Cream the butter, shortening, granulated sugar, brown sugar, and eggs in a large mixing bowl until light and fluffy. Stir together the flour, wheat germ, baking powder, baking soda, and salt. Beat into the sugar mixture. Add the oats, cornflakes, nuts, and chocolate chips and beat well. Drop by tablespoonfuls onto an ungreased cookie sheet. Bake for 10 to 12 minutes. Cool on a wire rack.

GINGERBREAD BOYS AND GIRLS

It is fun to take these cookies to school holiday parties,
or they make great Christmas tree decorations.

MAKES 3 TO 4 DOZEN COOKIES

1 cup molasses
1 tablespoon baking soda
3/4 cup hot water
1 cup shortening, melted
1 cup sugar
1 egg, beaten
1 tablespoon ground ginger

5 cups (about)
   all-purpose flour
1 1/2 teaspoons salt
1 teaspoon ground
   cinnamon
Dash of ground cloves
Raisins, quartered

Combine the molasses and baking soda in a large mixing bowl
and let stand for 10 minutes. The mixture will foam. Beat the molasses
mixture until smooth. Gradually add the hot water and shortening and
mix well. Beat in the sugar. Beat in the egg. Sift together the ginger, flour,
salt, cinnamon, and cloves in a bowl. Add to the molasses mixture
gradually, beating well after each addition and scraping the side of the
bowl frequently. Add additional flour, a spoonful at a time, if needed
to make a stiff dough. Chill the dough, covered, for 4 to 10 hours.

Preheat the oven to 350 degrees. Roll out the dough on a lightly
floured surface to the desired thickness. (The dough will nearly double
in size when baked.) Cut with floured gingerbread boy and girl cookie
cutters and place, 2 inches apart, on a lightly greased cookie sheet.
Make eyes, nose, and buttons on each cookie using the raisin pieces.
Bake for 8 to 10 minutes or until the edges are light brown. Do not
overbake. Cool on the cookie sheet for 1 minute. Remove to a wire
rack to cool completely. Decorate with frosting, if desired.

ITALIAN CHOCOLATE-SPICE COOKIES

MAKES 7 DOZEN COOKIES

1/4 cup butter, softened
1/4 cup margarine, softened
11/4 cups granulated sugar
2 eggs
1/2 cup milk, at room temperature
4 cups all-purpose flour
1/4 cup baking cocoa
21/2 teaspoons baking powder
1/2 teaspoon baking soda
1 teaspoon ground cinnamon
1 teaspoon ground cloves
1 teaspoon ground nutmeg
3/4 cup chopped walnuts
2 cups confectioners' sugar
2 tablespoons (about) milk

Preheat the oven to 350 degrees. Cream the butter, margarine, and granulated sugar in a large mixing bowl until light and fluffy. Beat in the eggs and 1/2 cup milk until smooth. Sift together the flour, cocoa, baking powder, baking soda, cinnamon, cloves, and nutmeg in a bowl. Add to the egg mixture gradually, beating well after each addition. Mix by hand until the dough is firm and pulls away from the side of the bowl. Add the walnuts and mix well.

Shape into 1-inch balls. Flatten slightly and place on a greased cookie sheet. Bake for 10 to 12 minutes. The cookies should still be a little soft in the center. Cool on the cookie sheet for 1 minute. Remove to a wire rack to cool completely. Combine the confectioners' sugar and 1 tablespoon of the milk in a small bowl, stirring until smooth. Add additional milk to reach the desired consistency. Spread on the cooled cookies.

NOTE: *For high altitudes, decrease the baking powder to 11/2 teaspoons; decrease the baking soda to 1/4 teaspoon.*

Many of the recipes in this cookbook originated far from Wyoming, in such places as Italy, Nepal, Spain, Norway, France, and Ireland, where it was a "family" affair for everyone to get together in the kitchen to bake cookies or chop the ingredients for a big pot of soup. The original recipes may not have been written down, but over the years, in an effort to keep traditions and memories alive, children or grandchildren have tried to replicate them for new family members and others, so they too can enjoy the good food and wonderful times.

MALTED MILK CHOCOLATE CHIP COOKIES

MAKES 1½ DOZEN COOKIES

1 cup butter-flavor shortening
1¼ cups packed brown sugar
¾ cup malted milk powder
1 tablespoon vanilla extract
1 egg
2 cups all-purpose flour
1½ teaspoons baking soda
½ teaspoon salt
1½ cups milk chocolate chips
½ cup toffee bits
½ cup chopped pecans

Preheat the oven to 375 degrees. Combine the shortening, brown sugar, malted milk powder, and vanilla in a large mixing bowl and beat for 2 minutes or until fluffy. Beat in the egg. Sift together the flour, baking soda, and salt. Add to the egg mixture gradually, beating well after each addition. Stir in the chocolate chips, toffee bits, and pecans. Shape into 2-inch balls and place on an ungreased cookie sheet. Bake for 10 to 12 minutes. Cool on the cookie sheet for 2 minutes. Remove to a wire rack to cool completely.

NOTE: *For high altitudes, decrease the baking soda to 1 teaspoon.*

LACE COOKIES

MAKES ABOUT 5½ DOZEN COOKIES

1 cup (2 sticks) butter, softened
3 cups packed brown sugar
2 eggs, beaten

1 tablespoon vanilla extract
2 cups quick-cooking oats
1 cup chopped pecans

Preheat the oven to 350 degrees. Cream the butter and brown sugar in a large mixing bowl just until blended. Stir in the eggs and vanilla. Add the oats and pecans and mix well. Drop by teaspoonfuls, 3 inches apart, onto a parchment paper-lined cookie sheet. Bake for 7 to 10 minutes. Cool on the cookie sheet before removing.

PEANUT BUTTER DROP
COOKIES WITH HONEY

MAKES 3 DOZEN COOKIES

5 tablespoons shortening
1/2 cup sugar
1/2 cup honey
2/3 cup peanut butter

2 small eggs, beaten
1 1/3 cups all-purpose flour
1/4 teaspoon baking powder
1/2 teaspoon salt

Preheat the oven to 350 degrees. Cream the shortening and sugar in a mixing bowl until light and fluffy. Beat in the honey and peanut butter. Stir in the eggs. Sift together the flour, baking powder, and salt. Add to the honey mixture and mix well. Drop by teaspoonfuls onto a greased cookie sheet. Bake for 12 minutes. Cool on the cookie sheet for 1 to 2 minutes. Remove to a wire rack to cool completely.

This recipe was submitted in memory of an individual who worked as an apiculturist for thirty-seven years on the University of Wyoming campus doing research for the United States Department of Agriculture on the diseases of honeybees.

PINWHEEL DATE COOKIES

MAKES 5 TO 6 DOZEN COOKIES

3 cups finely chopped dates
1 cup water
1 cup granulated sugar
1 cup ground walnuts
1 cup (2 sticks) butter, or 1/2
    cup each butter and
    margarine

1 1/4 cups packed brown sugar
1/3 cup granulated sugar
3 eggs
4 cups all-purpose flour
1 teaspoon salt
1/2 teaspoon baking soda

Combine the dates, water, and 1 cup granulated sugar in a large saucepan. Cook over low heat until the mixture has thickened and the sugar is dissolved, stirring occasionally. Remove from the heat and stir in the walnuts. Cool completely. Cream the butter, brown sugar, and 1/3 cup granulated sugar in a mixing bowl until light and fluffy. Beat in the eggs 1 at a time. Stir together the flour, salt, and baking soda. Add to the egg mixture, stirring just until combined. Divide the dough in half. Roll out half the dough, between waxed paper, to a large rectangle, about 10×14 inches, 1/4-inch thick. Spread with half the date filling. Starting on a long side, roll up the dough and filling. Moisten the edges of the dough and press to seal. Wrap in waxed paper or plastic wrap and chill for 8 to 10 hours. Repeat the procedure with the remaining dough and filling. Preheat the oven to 375 degrees. Cut the rolls into 1/2-inch slices and place on a greased cookie sheet. Bake for 10 to 12 minutes or until golden brown.

Scottish Shortbread

This shortbread is especially tasty when warm.

Makes 12 servings

1 cup (2 sticks) butter, softened
1/2 cup sugar, sifted
2 cups all-purpose flour, sifted
1/4 teaspoon salt

Preheat the oven to 325 degrees. Cream the butter and sugar in a mixing bowl until light and fluffy. Add the flour and salt and mix well. Divide the dough in half. Press each half into a 9-inch pie plate. Bake for 25 to 30 minutes. Cut into wedges while hot. Serve warm.

NOTE: *The dough can be made ahead and stored, wrapped in plastic wrap, in the refrigerator until ready to use. Bake 1/2 hour before serving.*

Winter Tumbleweeds

Quick & Easy

Makes 5 dozen cookies

1 (12-ounce) can salted peanuts
1 (9-ounce) can shoestring potatoes
2 cups (12 ounces) butterscotch chips
1/4 cup peanut butter

Combine the peanuts and shoestring potatoes in a large bowl. Microwave the butterscotch chips and peanut butter on Medium-High for 2 minutes or until melted, stirring after 1 minute. Add to the peanut mixture and mix well to coat evenly. Drop by rounded teaspoonfuls onto nonstick baking sheets. Chill for 5 minutes or until set. Store in airtight containers.

NOTE: *If you do not have nonstick baking sheets, line the baking sheets with waxed paper or parchment paper.*

CREOLE KISSES WITH MAPLE CREAM FROSTING

MAKES ABOUT 3 DOZEN COOKIES

3 egg whites, at room temperature
1/2 cup granulated sugar
3/4 cup packed brown sugar
1 teaspoon vanilla extract
1 teaspoon vinegar
1/2 cup chopped nuts (optional)
Maple Cream Frosting

Preheat the oven to 300 degrees. Beat the egg whites in a medium mixing bowl until stiff peaks form. Add the granulated sugar gradually, beating constantly. Beat in the brown sugar gradually. Beat in the vanilla and vinegar. Fold in the nuts. Drop by teaspoonfuls, 2 inches apart, onto 2 parchment paper-lined baking sheets. Place the baking sheets on the center oven rack and bake for 45 minutes. Do not overbake or the cookies will be brittle. Cool on a wire rack and frost with the Maple Cream Frosting. Store in an uncovered container.

NOTE: *This recipe is from* Baking at High Altitude, *Bulletin 427—University of Wyoming Cooperative Extension Service, 2003.*

MAPLE CREAM FROSTING

MAKES ABOUT 1/2 CUP

2 tablespoons butter, softened
6 tablespoons confectioners' sugar
1/4 teaspoon maple flavoring
1/4 teaspoon vanilla extract

Cream the butter and confectioners' sugar in a small bowl until fluffy. Blend in the maple flavoring and vanilla.

Kahlúa Fudge

Makes 16 (2-inch) pieces

1¹/₃ cups sugar
1 (7-ounce) jar marshmallow creme
²/₃ cup evaporated milk
¹/₄ cup (¹/₂ stick) butter
¹/₄ cup Kahlúa
¹/₄ teaspoon salt
2 cups (12 ounces) good-quality semisweet chocolate pieces
1 cup (6 ounces) good-quality milk chocolate pieces
1 teaspoon vanilla extract
²/₃ cup chopped pecans or other nuts

Combine the sugar, marshmallow creme, evaporated milk, butter, Kahlúa, and salt in a 2-quart saucepan and bring to a boil. Boil rapidly for 5 minutes, stirring constantly. Remove from the heat and add the chocolates, stirring until completely melted. Add the vanilla and stir until the mixture is no longer shiny. Stir in the pecans and pour into a foil-lined 8×8-inch baking pan. Chill until firm. Cut into squares and serve.

NOTE: *Stir for the entire 5 minutes after the mixture comes to a boil. Completely melt the chocolate. Use only good-quality ingredients. If you skimp, you'll know it when you taste it. The recipe can be doubled.*

Black Tie & Boots
Steering Committee

CHAIRMAN
Lisa Lewis Dubois

VICE CHAIRMEN
Brenda Bland, *Development Coordinator,*
UW Art Museum

Rhoda Schantz, *Associate Professor,*
Department of Family and Consumer Sciences
and Director, Didactic Program in Dietetics

PRODUCTION/RECIPE CHAIRMAN
Shannon Jaeger, *Coordinator,*
University Public Relations

MARKETING CHAIRMAN
Jay Fromkin, *Director, University Public Relations*

MARKETING CO-CHAIRMEN
Lynda Rinker, *Assistant Manager, UW Bookstore*
Shaun Ziegler, *Manager, UW Licensing Office*

ART DIRECTOR
Paula Wilson-Caziér, *Art Director,*
University Public Relations

FOOD PHOTOGRAPHER
Ted Brummond, *UW Photo Service*

FOOD STYLISTS
John Hendry Reid Jr., *Executive Chef, UW Catering*
Becky Brown, *Sous Chef, UW Catering*
Paula Wilson-Caziér, *Art Director,*
University Public Relations

RECIPE TESTING CHAIRMAN
Rhoda Schantz, *Associate Professor,*
Department of Family and Consumer Sciences

SECTION HEAD COORDINATOR
Brenda Bland, *Development Coordinator,*
UW Art Museum

NON-RECIPE TEXT COORDINATORS
Nancy Nichols, *Manager, Visual Communications,*
University Public Relations
Shannon Jaeger, *Coordinator,*
University Public Relations

ADMINISTRATIVE ASSISTANTS
Adrienne Weisz, *Office Associate,*
University Public Relations
Andrea Shablo, *Office Associate,*
University Public Relations

SECTION HEADS
Dolores Hart, *Appetizers & Beverages*
Jane Greaser, *Appetizers & Beverages*
Beth Hallingbye, *Appetizers & Beverages*
Leslie Roth, *Breads & Brunches*
Kandi Furphy, *Salads & Dressings*
Amy Thurow, *Soups & Stews*
Linda Kotby, *Meats*
Joan Mader, *Meats*
Amy Jenkins, *Poultry*
Jacque Buchanan, *Fish & Seafood*
Lynda Rinker, *Pasta & Rice*
Deborah Turchetta, *Vegetables & Side Dishes*
Becky Lewis, *Desserts*
Pennie Espeland, *Quick & Easy*
Kim McClain, *Menu Testing and*
Last-Minute Testing Chair

Recipe Contributors

We of the Black Tie & Boots Steering Committee wish to thank the hundreds of contributors who submitted recipes from their families, their friends, and their own personal favorites. Without their recipes, this cookbook would not have been possible.

Carolyn Abernethy
Rollin Abernethy
Carol Adams
Cindy Adams
Judy Adams
Michelle Adams
Sandy Adams
Ruth Anderson
Sharon Ando
Esther Andrau
David Anton
Ruth Arnold
Darci Arsene
Arsene Family
Kim Artery
Donna Bagby
R. E. "Dick" Bailey
Sally Baker
Miriam Pietala Balog
Tim Banks
Marion Barcus
Carol Hull Barnett
Richard Barratt
Janet Bass
Henry Bauer
Jenna Beahm
Cheri Bellamy
Bellamy Family
Carolyn Bennett
Margo Bennett
Marian Berger
Annie Bergman
Kate Bieber
Becky Blalock

Brenda Bland
Shana Blankenship
Trent Blankenship*
Erma Bohrer
Nan Boileau
Janet Winninger Bolz
Margaret Boyd
June Boyle
Cindy Brady
Tom Brady
Leellen Brigman
Becky Brown
Judson Brown
Margaret Brown
Bev Brust
Jacque Buchanan
Kelly Winninger Byerley
Vicki Carlisle
Dana Russell Carlsen
Joan Carr
Shirley Cheramy
Maxine Chisholm
Rod Chisholm
Lew Christensen
Jennifer Clark
Patti Hageman Cobb
Patricia Colberg
Carol Collier
Donna Connor
Janet Constantinides
Kathi Cook
Robyne Cote
Shane Cote
Carolyn Barnett Creger

Dorothy Crout
Barbara Cubin*
Kathie Cuomo
Susan Cuthbertson
Marcia Dale
Marie Redd Dalgarno
Ann Davidson
Tom Davidson
Ibby Davis
James Davis
Lisa De Bruin
Rod De Bruin
Diane DeLany
Fred DeVore
Joni Dietz
Jillane Bailey Disbrow
Donna Beth Downer
Judy Dray
Dennis Dreher
Dana Lynn Dreinhofer
Lisa Lewis Dubois
Melody Duncan
Valina Eckley
Cathy Ellis
Frank "Pinky" Ellis
Jackie Ellis
Cindy Ker Elrod
Judy Emmons
Chuck Engebretsen
Mary Engebretsen
Michelle Erdman
Pennie Espeland
Carol Fagan
Debbie Fanning

Asterisk indicates elected state and federal officials.

Recipe Contributors

Maggie Farrell
Jo Ferguson
Jacqueline Ferrall
Fayetta Fields
Nan Thorne Fogel
Elaine Force
Dave Foreman
Melanie Francis
Cindy Frederick
Lois Freeman
Nancy Freudenthal
Gloria Friesen
Jay Fromkin
Brian Fulton
Kandi Furphy
Sandra Gabriel
Mary Lou Gale
Frank Galey
Mary Gallatin
Mary Ellbogen Garland
Pravina Gondalia
Patricia Goodson
Betsy Grainger
Jane Greaser
Jane Grzybowski
Mary Thorson Gullikson
Mona Gupton
Nancy Guthrie
Gina Guy
Marion Hageman
Ardeth Hahn
Marlisa Hall
Beth Hallingbye
Jacqueline Hamilton
Duncan Harris
Janice Harris
Helga Haub
Vicki Borgialli Hayman
Larry Hazlett

Lynn Heeren
Susan "Sue" Heide
Will Herbold
Phyllis Herdendorf
Joscelyn Herzberg
Gloria Hicks
Yvette Hileman
Robin Hill
Rebecca Hilliker
Marion Hitchcock
Dominic Hodgen
Sandy Hoffman
Mary Hopkins
Connie Winninger Hunt
Donald Hunton
Maggie Jackson
David Jaeger
Shannon Jaeger
Gary Jefferis
Jan Jefferis
Jerry Johnson
Lynda Dees Kammer
Anita Karl
Janet Friedl Kavinoky
Jamie Kearley
Marcia Kelley
Shirley Kembel
Bim Kendall
Dawn Kent
Harriett Kepler
Lydia Kercher
Channing Kimball
Marion Kimball
Erin Kinney
Judith Knight
Kim Krueger
Laural Krueger
Rosanne Latimer
Charlotte Pulscher Laycock

Linda Nielsen Lebeda
Marcia Lee
Becky Lewis
Mary Alice Lewis
Cheri Lipiec
Carey Pearson Loch
Lynn Lockhart
Cynthia Lummis*
Lorraine Lupton
Kimm Malody
Stewart Manville
Linda Homar Martin
Hank Mayland
Tina McCarty
Kim McClain
Patricia McClurg
Gerald McDermott
Sue McDonald
Sharyl McGrew
Sue McLean
Linda Smith McMurtrie
Jan Lehan Meeboer
Larry Meeboer
Esther Mary Mellizo
Barbara Mendicino
Lib Menger
Diana Meyer
Gayle Miech
Carolyn Miller
Susan Moldenhauer
Joan Moler
Bob Moore
Sonya Moore
Cherish Morrell
Katharine Morton
Pamela Moses
Genna Mulkey
Michell Nacey
Dan Nelson

Recipe Contributors

Osea Nelson
Abbey Nicklas
Jim Nielson
Maureen O'Leary
Milton Ontiveroz
Virginia Palik
Candace Paradis
Lisa Skiles Parady
Suzanne Pelican
Grace Peterson
Donna Petsch
Judith Pettigrew
Bonnie Phillips
Vicki Pollock
Tammy Powell
Cathy Quenelle
Heather Rader
Mack Rawhouser
Sandra Reher
John Hendry Reid Jr.
Judy Richards
Kristen Doolittle Rieman
Beth Robertson
Marian Rochelle
Nikki Rogers
Rod Rogers
Don Roth
Eileen Routson
Jack Routson
Nancy Rowse
Lynne Ruggles
Anne Sager
Patti Salvagio
Susan McMurry Samuelson
Jan Sarmiere
Greg Schaefer
Lori Schaefer
Rhoda Schantz
Linda Scheider

Jennifer Schultes
Erik Seastedt
Courtney Seegmiller
Ann Seidman
Claire Sikora
Becky Simmons
Shelley Simonton
Alan Simpson*
Ann Simpson
Donna Sitton
Owen Sitton
Jacquie Smith
Rosalie Smith
Tom Smith
Faye Snyder
Larry Spears
Lyle Spence
Shelley Spence
Ruthe Rollins Spencer
Debbe Spicer
Tom Spicer
Christine Winninger Sprague
Clarice Strannigan
Dianna Strannigan
Marta Stroock
Susan Stroud
Abby Sullivan
Jane Sullivan
Winifred Sullivan
Pat Scott Sutton
Carol Swaim
Charlotte Swanson
Craig Thomas*
Susan Thomas
Donna Thompson
Tanya Thompson
Rob Thurman
Peg Tobin
Ann Tollefson

Dick Torgerud
Jeff Truchot
Deborah Turchetta
Lili Turnell
Elizabeth Ann Devitt Turner
Grace Ullrich
Rusty Vannoy
Dianne Van Pelt
Audrey Varnado
Kim Viner
Susan Vittitow
J. Fred Volk
Robin Volk
Bobbi Wade
John Richard Waggener
Kristi Wallin
Misty Walsh
Carole Ward
Angela Weber
Adrienne Weisz
James Welke
Ruth Welke
Linda Wells
Jeff White
Gladys Wilding
Connie Wilkie
Carl Williams
Molly Williams
Stephen Earl Williams
Belenda Willson
JoNel Wilmot
Chuck Winninger
JoAnn Winninger
Cynthia Wintermote
Jane Wold
Mary Wolf
Janet Woods
Denise Yennie
Anne Young

In Memory/Honor Of

We would also like to acknowledge the special people in whose memory or honor many of our contributors submitted recipes.

Terry Anderson
Catherine Atkinson
Jean Barratt
Doug Bartlett
Elaine Bauer
Mary Bell
Clara Prahl Bendt
Dolores Bolander
Carter Bruns
Hattie Campbell
Florence Francis Caziér-Montaigne
Annisa Chesnut
Margaret Chesnut
Sandra Christensen
Doris Cleary
Jesse Coates
Manda Collier
Ruth Copeland
Lucia Girardi Cuomo
Isabell Dees
Rose DeGise
Lizzie Wilson Devitt
Julia Doolittle
Mary Rose Dorn
Mildred Emmons
Mildred Evans
Brenda Farrell
Gwen Fitzpatrick
Tim Fitzpatrick
Frances Mifflin "Frickie" Galey
Rosemary Menger Gilmore
Sally Gligorea
Garrett Gowan

Leila Green
Lucille Schopf Guy
Louise Hatch
Henry Hathaway
Dawn Herbold
John Hitchcock
Shirley Seaman Hladky
Esther Hoffman
Sally Homar
Johnny Hopkins
Ruth Jackson
Phyllis Jaeger
Katy Ker
Byra Kite
Bob Knight
Joan Ligocki
Charlene Taylor Little
Ethel MacKenzie
Shirlee Malody
Catherine Daly Martinez
Iswar Maskey
Lulie Sewall McDougall
Hilda Menger
Glen Morse
Wayne Morse
David Murray
Laura Larsen Nelson
Ragnhild Groven Olson
Inez "Chata" Ontiveroz
Pat Opler
Emily Long Owen
Mrs. W. E. Pearson
Rosemary Peduzzi

Betty Jane Pelican
Perry Peyton
Gretchen Poulson
Gordon Powers
John Prahl
Jane Dees Richardson
Merlin Eyre Rollins
Donald Rounds
Amelia Homar Sabec
Mary Schuman
Sarah Rogers Seaman
Halyna Seredyuk
Edgar Shopmyer
Carolyn Sinsinig
Owen Sitton
Susan Snoddy
Beatrice Thomson Steik
Amy Stinson
Ilka Stoffer
Clarice Strannigan
Burky Stroud
Frances Tafoya
Jeff Thompson
Inga Thorson
Willa Thring
Peg Tobin
Robert Waggener
Ruth Webb
Howard Willson
Helene "Witty" Wittmer
Ken Wolf
Ada Zaccaria

Recipe Testers

The Black Tie & Boots Steering Committee also wishes to extend its warmest thanks to the following people who tested recipes for this cookbook. Their generous gifts of time, talent, and dollars helped in the selection and perfection of the recipes we have included.

Carolyn Abernethy
Judy Adams
Michelle Adams
Gail Adamson
Paula Alan
Betsy Anderson
Hans Anklam
Roberta Atty
Donna Bagby
Lew Bagby
Barbara Balthaser
Doris Bane
Barbara Barnes
Deb Barnes
Jane Bartee
Doris Bayne
Wendy Berelson
Thad Blair
Becky Blalock
Brenda Bland
Rhonda Bonett
Betsy Bress
Mary Brinkman
Becky Brown
Joyce Brown
Jacque Buchanan
Tom Buchanan
Jessica Buckles
Karen Case
Ruth Casta
Patty Campbell
Virginia Chai
A. Scott Corcoran
Susan Day
Roberta Deti

Tracy Dooley
Lisa Lewis Dubois
Cathy Duncil
Sally Edgar
Jamie Egolf
Pennie Espeland
Debra Evertson
Paul Fanning
Barb Farley
Leeann Friedrichs
Susan Fuller
Kandi Furphy
Jane Greaser
Sharon Greenlee
Franz-Peter Griesmaier
Marlena Gross
Ali Grossman
Nancy Haffer
Beth Hallingbye
Jacqueline Hamilton
Ruth Hanks
Alison Harkin
Loretta Harris
Paula Harris
Phill Harris
Sue Harris
Dolores Hart
Sean Hart
Marilyn Hixon
Mary Hixon
Sandra Honken
Julie Howard
Connie Hoyer
Alison Hrakin
Kathy Hunt

Sandy Inniss
Gregg Jackson
Maggie Jackson
Vanessa Jacquot
Margaret Jaeger
Shannon Jaeger
Amy Jenkins
Barbara Jenkins
Don Jenkins
Chris Jensen
Jeanne Jerden
Katie Johnson
Bill Jones
Susan Jones
Dolly Kerr
Susie Kidwiler
Maryanne Kirkpatrick
Audrey Kleinsasser
Judy Knight
Linda Kotby
Meg Kransberger
Kathy Krell
Kim Krueger
Sharon Kyhl
Cindy LaBonde
Dottie Landis
Jamie Legerski
Rikki Leslie
Becky Lewis
Cindy Lewis
Lorrie Lewis
Leslie Loos
Richelle Luca
Joan Mader
Kimm Malody

Recipe Testers

Kathy Manker	Laurie Peel	Mary Spitler
Lois Marquardt	Kathy Perkins	Jim Steidtmann
Janice Marshall	Barb Powell	Deb Stern
Randi Martensen	Norma Powell	Rivers Stilwell
Kim Mayo	Vickie Quisenberry	Bonnie Swiatek
Dauna McBride	Melissa Radcliffe	Linda Thayer
Kim McClain	Mack Rawhouser	Julie Bateman Thomas
Colleen McKinnon	Ruth Rawhouser	Donna Thompson
Eileen Milam	Christine Recht	Amy Thurow
Bonnie Miller	Jill Rettinger	Peggy Tomky
Susan Moldenhauer	Jane Reverand	Deborah Turchetta
Anne Moore	Lynda Rinker	Tom Turchetta
Bob Moore	Jamie Robb	Alice Varbell
Susan Moore	Sally Rogers	Kim Viner
Kari Morgan	Deb Rote	Marla Voos
Maggi Murdock	Deb Roth	Eleanor Waggener
Nick Murdock	Leslie Roth	Chris Wald
Gary Negich	Rhoda Schantz	Sylvia Wears
Marci Newell	T. Schlegel	Judy Weatherwax
Jean Nichols	Cheryl Schroeder	Ruth Weverstad
Jeanine Niemoller	Kacee Schutterle	Phyllis Whitmire
Karen Nijland	Corrine Seebart	Tom Wiersman
Lisa Norris	Ann Seidman	Connie Wilbert
Debi Ockers	Shanen Shaw	Janet Wilkey
Sarahmae Ockers	Linda Sheets	Sharon Wilkinson
Lois Olson	Leslie Shores	Wanda Willems
Cheryl O'Malley	Pam Shuster	Renee Williams
Shanen Onken-Shaw	Margaret Skinner	Dana Wilson
Joyce Osterhoudt	Cheryl Snow	Genee Witte
Debra Owens	Trudy Snyder	Debbie Wyckoff
Mark Pantier	Ronnie Socha	Jeff Wyckoff
Marti Pantier	Lani Sorensen	Cindy Yeoman

And a special thanks to Professor Schantz and her students, who gave countless
hours to the testing and revising of our recipes. Thank you, UW students:

Julie Krugman   Haiying Lin   Amy Little
Yolonda McDowell   Samantha Moelter

Photo Shoot Thanks

Finally, we wish to extend our sincerest thanks to the following community individuals and businesses, family members, and friends who generously lent us their treasures and time for our photo shoots.

Artisans' Gallery	Annie Burman
Back of the Wagon Antiques	Rosanne Chapp
BBJ Linens	Lisa Lewis Dubois
Bernie's Mexican Restaurant	Becky Green
Distinctive Details	Dolores Hart
El Conquistador	Andy Hysong
Laramie Plains Museum	Twila Hysong
Longhorn Saddle Shop	Shannon Jaeger
Mountain Woods Furniture	Amy Jenkins
Rinker Salvage	Tamara Lehner
The Grand Bazaar	Becky Lewis
The Reata Collection	Mary Mountain
Touch of Country	John Hendry Reid Jr.
University of Wyoming Art Museum	Lynda Rinker
University of Wyoming Art Museum Store	Jeanetta Schmidt
University of Wyoming Bookstore	Andrea Shablo
University of Wyoming Catering	Connie Trowbridge
University of Wyoming President's Office	Dan Trowbridge
University Public Relations	Deborah Turchetta
Sandy Adams	Adrienne Weisz
Erik Anderson	Andrée Wilson
Clint Beavers	Paula Wilson-Caziér
Jack Beavers	Matt Winninger
Brenda Bland	Natalie Winninger
Becky Brown	Lillian Wise

It is our sincere hope that we have not inadvertently omitted any testers, contributors, or other individuals who helped to make this cookbook possible.

Index